Genes, Trade, and Regulation

Genes, Trade, and Regulation

THE SEEDS OF CONFLICT IN FOOD BIOTECHNOLOGY

Thomas Bernauer

PRINCETON UNIVERSITY PRESS

PRINCETON AND OXFORD

Copyright © 2003 by Princeton University Press
Published by Princeton University Press, 41 William Street,
Princeton, New Jersey 08540
In the United Kingdom: Princeton University Press,
3 Market Place, Woodstock, Oxfordshire OX20 1SY

Library of Congress Cataloging-in-Publication Data
Bernauer, Thomas.
   Genes, trade, and regulation : the seeds of conflict in food biotechnology / by
Thomas Bernauer.
      p. cm.
   Includes bibliographic references and index.
   ISBN 0-691-11348-3 (alk. paper)
      1. Food industry and trade—Government policy—United States. 2. Biotech-
nology industries—Government policy—United States. 3. Genetic engineering
industry—Government policy—United States. 4. Agricultural biotechnology—
Government policy—United States. 5. Food industry and trade—Technological
innovations—United States. 6. Food—Labeling—Government policy—United
States. I. Title.

   HD9006.B45 2003
   338.4'7664—dc21   2003051735

British Library Cataloguing-in-Publication Data is available

This book has been composed in Sabon

Printed on acid-free paper ∞

www.pupress.princeton.edu

Printed in the United States of America

10 9 8 7 6 5 4 3 2 1

Contents

Preface   vii

CHAPTER ONE
Introduction and Summary   1

CHAPTER TWO
Challenges   22

CHAPTER THREE
Polarization   44

CHAPTER FOUR
Interest Group Politics   66

CHAPTER FIVE
Regulatory Federalism   102

CHAPTER SIX
International Trade Conflict   118

CHAPTER SEVEN
Coping with Diversity   168

Notes   185

References   213

Index   225

Preface

THE SHEER mass of publications on agricultural (or "green") biotechnology must be truly intimidating to anyone attempting to add one more piece to that literature. Why on earth should a political scientist like this author, whose knowledge of the technology per se barely extends beyond high-school level biology, venture into this area?

The first, and perhaps most trivial, reason is that technological innovation is hardly driven by the natural sciences and engineering alone. Whether new technologies succeed, both in research and development (R&D) terms and in consumer markets, depends also on how societies respond to technological opportunities. In other words, success (or failure) of technological innovation hinges not only on what natural scientists or engineers achieve in their labs, but also on consumer perceptions, campaigns by non-governmental organizations (NGOs), the political behavior of firms, government regulation, and the like. These phenomena are key subjects of inquiry in political science.

The second reason for this book project emanated from my personal working environment. I operate in a small social science department within a large technical university (the Swiss Federal Institute of Technology in Zurich). This allows for frequent interaction with world class natural scientists and engineers. In 1998, Swiss voters rejected by two-thirds majority an initiative that, had it been accepted, would have prohibited many forms of biotech R&D as well as commercial applications of that technology in Switzerland. All of a sudden, many of my colleagues from the "hard" sciences discovered that there were social scientists at their university who might have something useful to say about issues they were concerned about. This was the good news. The bad news was that many of them—at least initially—appeared to be caught in a social science time warp dominated by an early 1970s version of theories of technology diffusion.

Proponents of these theories assumed that a given technology was useful. They regarded social scientists as producers of knowledge on the societal environment in which that technology was to be placed. Such knowledge was supposed to help in increasing acceptance and speed up diffusion. Technological changes and societal changes were thus regarded as separate spheres. A corollary of this view was the assumption that, whenever there was low public support for a particular technology, knowledge deficits among consumers or technology users were primarily responsible. Social scientists were, therefore, seen as social engineers whose task it was to distinguish early from late technology adopters, identify gatekeepers in this regard, and facilitate technology diffusion by developing communication and marketing strategies that work well with particular societal groups.[1] Not surprisingly then, consumer survey data was just about the most useful output my colleagues could see in whatever social science work happened to draw their attention.

In the meantime, many of my colleagues have fortunately developed a more sophisticated understanding of when, why and how technological innovation succeeds or fails in practice. They have come to realize that technological innovation is not a one-way street, but is shaped by permanent interaction between technology producers and society. They are also aware that social scientists' principal task is to gauge and explain societal forces that promote or slow down particular forms of innovation, but not to educate or even manipulate stakeholders.

And yet, even a brief look at the content of the many internet-based discussion fora on biotech issues (e.g., www.agbioworld.org; www.isaaa.org) will provide sufficient illustration of a still dominant view that social science work should focus on educating "scientifically illiterate idiots opposed to a wonderful new technology that could make the world a better place."

I have written this book hoping that a novel look at the political, economic, and societal challenges to agricultural biotechnology may facilitate a more facts-oriented discussion among proponents and critics of the technology, and ultimately also a sensible balance between public safety concerns and private economic freedom in this area. Thus I adopt the posture of a fence-walker in a policy-area that is populated largely by analysts who fall hard on the pro- or anti-biotech side of the fence. I largely evade the question of whether agricultural biotechnology is "good" or "bad." Such sweeping valuations appear as assumptions in large parts of the social science literature on the issue and negatively affect that work's credibility. As far as possible, I let empirical facts and associated explanations speak for themselves. I view agricultural biotechnology as a potentially useful but controversial new technology whose fate is open. Ultimately, it is not up to natural or social scientists or engineers to determine what is good or bad for society. In pluralist democracies, such decisions will be made by consumers, investors, biotech firms, technology users (e.g., farmers), food processors and retailers, voters (citizens), and government authorities.

In the course of writing this book I have benefited from the knowledge of so many people that I can mention only a few. I am particularly grateful to Ladina Caduff, Philipp Aerni, Jim Foster, and four anonymous reviewers of Princeton University Press for highly useful comments on various versions of the book proposal and the manuscript. I am also grateful to Erika Meins for our collaborative work, on which I draw in chapter 4. Through collaboration with Jim Foster and Ken Oye in a project on environmental, health and safety policies I learned a lot about issues of regulation, trade, and industrial competition. Richard Baggaley, Thomas Schmalberger, and David Vogel were crucial in the effort to find a title for the book.

I would also like to thank the following persons (in alphabetical order) for supporting my book project in all sorts of ways: Kym Anderson, Awudu Abdulai, Ross Barnard, Roger Baud, Lars-Erik Cederman, Sylvia Dorn, Willy de Greef, Arthur Einsele, Thomas Epprecht, Rudolf Frei-Bischof, Bruno Frey, Tom Hoban, Joanne Kauffmann, Vally Koubi, Eric Millstone, Ronald Mitchell, Thomas Plümper, Susanna Priest, Peter Rieder, Dieter Ruloff, Thomas Sattler, Renate Schubert, Bruce Silverglade, Thomas Streiff, Vit Styrsky, David Victor, and Sabine Wiedmann.

Thomas Bernauer

Genes, Trade, and Regulation

CHAPTER ONE

Introduction and Summary

AGRICULTURAL (or "green") biotechnology, the most cutting-edge contemporary technology in food production, faces an uncertain future. Will it follow the example of nuclear energy, which turned out to be one of the most unpopular and uneconomical innovations in history? Or will it revolutionize food production around the world? Are prevailing public and private sector strategies for coping with the most important political, economic, and societal challenges to agri-biotechnology effective in terms of creating a long-term global market for the technology? What policies could be adopted to shape the evolution of the technology in ways that benefit humanity and the environment?

In this book I argue that global *regulatory polarization* and *trade conflicts* have exacerbated already existing domestic controversies over agricultural biotechnology and have thrown the latter into a deep crisis.

Regulatory polarization has emerged as European Union (EU) countries have imposed severe regulatory constraints on agri-biotechnology, whereas the United States has opened its market to most agri-biotech applications. Other countries have either aligned with one or the other of the world's two largest economies, or they have been struggling to find some middle ground.

The analysis in this book shows that regulatory polarization has been driven by differences across countries in public opinion, interest group politics, and institutional structures. It also shows that regulatory polarization has created strong tensions in the world trading system. International conflicts over regulatory differences, which tend to act as non-tariff barriers to trade, have been intensifying since the first genetically engineered (GE) crops appeared on international markets in 1996.

The largest part of the book concentrates on: describing *how* regulatory polarization has emerged (chapter 3); explaining *why* it has emerged (chapters 4 and 5); and assessing the likelihood of escalation of international trade tensions over regulatory differences (chapter 6).

In light of this analysis I conclude that prevailing public and private sector policies do not add up to an effective strategy for mitigating or overcoming regulatory polarization, diffusing trade tensions, and creating a long-term global market for the technology. The dominant public sector policies include: establishing ever more complex and stringent regulations that are increasingly divorced from scientific evidence and insufficiently backed by robust institutional structures for implementation (this is largely the European Union's strategy for increasing public acceptance of green biotechnology); threats of escalating trade disputes over differing regulations to force open foreign markets for the technology (a strategy favored by parts of the US government, the US biotech industry, and US farmers). The dominant private sector policies include: educating consumers about the benefits and (low) risks of the technology; highlighting consumer benefits of future GE products; ad hoc efforts to accommodate consumer demand for non-GE products through market-driven product differentiation (crop segregation and labeling); lobbying the US government to force open foreign markets via trade disputes.

Continuing regulatory polarization and trade conflict darken agri-biotechnology's prospects for three reasons.

First, regulatory polarization locks in or even increases fragmentation of international agricultural markets, and it implies reduced market access for agri-biotechnology and its products. It thus reduces scale economies and returns on investment into the technology. And it discourages further private sector investment in a new sector that could otherwise grow into a market worth several hundred billion dollars. Because of uncertainties about market access for GE products, it also exerts a chilling effect on adoption of the technology by farmers around the world.

Second, as I will show in chapter 6, trade conflicts over differing agri-biotech regulations are very difficult to solve, particularly within the World Trade Organization (WTO). Thus, they threaten to tax international institutions and impact negatively on efforts to liberalize global trade in agricultural goods and services. They exacerbate problems of global market fragmentation and uncertainties about market access caused by regulatory polarization. And they amplify already existing domestic controversies over the technology. All this, again, impacts negatively on investment, research and development, and adoption of the technology.

Third, regulatory polarization and trade conflict slow down public sector support for agri-biotechnology. This concerns in particular support by richer nations for developing countries where the technology might be needed most for increasing agricultural productivity. EU countries, Japan, and other agri-biotech adverse states have been highly reluctant to include biotechnology in their development assistance programs. So have non-governmental organizations (NGOs). Moreover, many developing countries have refused help of this nature for fear of losing agricultural export opportunities in biotech adverse markets. This situation creates a "legitimacy trap." Agri-biotech proponents have made "feeding the poor" one of their key selling points. Continuing emphasis of this legitimating argument, but failure to deliver on this account, could undermine the legitimacy of the technology in both rich and poor countries.

The book ends with suggestions for policy reforms that could help to avoid the seemingly unavoidable trajectory that leads from regulatory polarization to trade conflict to stagnation or decline of agri-biotechnology (chapter 7). These suggestions focus on establishing strong regulatory authorities backed by robust liability laws, market-driven product differentiation based on mandatory labeling of GE products, and support for developing countries.

The genie is out of the bottle. Food biotechnology and its applications are with us, and the technology is developing rapidly. Based on current knowledge about the benefits and risks of agri-biotechnology, neither blanket bans nor libertarian solutions appear warranted. As with many other new technologies, complex trade-offs between public safety concerns and private economic freedom have to be found. Whether one supports or opposes food biotechnology, the starting point for politically stable and economically and ecologically sensible trade-offs must be a sophisticated understanding of where we stand, how we got here, where we are likely to go, and what the pressures towards particular futures are. If this book can help both supporters and critics of agri-biotechnology in this process I will have achieved more than I could hope for.

Finally, I have tried to present conceptual (or theoretical) arguments and the associated evidence in a way that makes the book accessible to non-social scientists and non-experts in biotech issues. I am confident, however, that social scientists and biotech experts will also find much theoretical and empirical food for thought.

TECHNOLOGICAL REVOLUTION

Breathtaking innovation in biotechnology has brought humankind to the doorstep of a third "green revolution" within less than a century. The first green revolution, which began in the 1930s, was initiated by three developments: large-scale application of Gregor Mendel's work, carried out in the 19th century, on inheritance in plant breeding; discovery of inexpensive methods for the production of nitrogen fertilizer; and development of high yield hybrid corn. Rapid yield increases throughout the 1970s in corn and other temperate-climate crops were, in addition, obtained through increasingly effective fertilizers, pesticides, crop species, machinery, and farm management. The average farmer in modern agriculture is thus able to feed up to 30 non-farmers.

The second green revolution, which took place in the 1960s and 1970s, carried the same technologies to the developing world and crops grown in the tropics (notably, rice).

The third green revolution, which is still at an early stage, was born in the 1970s[1] and commercialized in the 1990s. It has been led by agricultural biotechnology.[2] According to the proponents of this technology, it will result in another massive increase in productivity, with a predicted feeding ability far beyond 1:30. It is also expected to provide qualitative improvements in the food supply (e.g., healthier food).

CONTROVERSY

The advent of agricultural biotechnology sparked a worldwide public controversy of breadth and intensity unseen since the peak of the anti-nuclear energy movement in the 1970s and 1980s. The controversy over green biotechnology forms part of wider ranging societal controversies over various applications of biotechnology, notably, cloning and other biotech-related reproductive technologies, stem-cell research, xenotransplantation, transgenic animals, and genetic testing. Debates over such biotech applications also tie in with more general issues, such as world trade and globalization, intellectual property rights and the patenting of life forms, the future of agriculture, poverty and hunger, and the role of science in society.[3] All of these issues involve clashes between natural science paradigms and political measures designed to cope with uncertainty and ethics. They also involve disputes over how to balance economic competitiveness and politically legitimate and viable regulatory systems for new technologies.

Most analysts regard 1996–97 as the watershed years in the controversy over green biotechnology. In those years, the first agri-biotech mass commodities appeared on international markets: Roundup Ready soybeans and Bt corn. At the same time, the first successful cloning of an animal (Dolly, a sheep) from an adult cell took place at the Roslin Institute in Scotland. Ever since, regulatory authorities around the world have been struggling with the issue. Media coverage has exploded. NGO campaigns and consumer revolts have become part of the political landscape of many countries. International trade tensions over differences across countries in agri-biotech regulation have built up. And the concept of the modern life sciences firm that integrates agrochemicals, crop sciences, pharmaceuticals, and health and food products has experienced a profound crisis.[4]

The proponents of the technology claim that it will, in the medium to long term, help in reducing hunger, public health problems, and environmental stress. It will, in their view, result in cheaper and better food and it is necessary to prevent massive food shortages and environmental degradation as the world's population approaches 9–10 billion in 2050. Consumer benefits are said to include food with less organic contaminants and microorganisms, less pesticide residues, more vitamin A and other vitamins, higher iron and protein content, less cholesterol, longer shelf-life, and better keeping quality. Future products are expected to contain more micronutrients, less toxins, edible vaccines, and less allergens. Environmental benefits are said to include increased yields, which reduces the need to convert forests and habitat into farmland, reduced use of insecticides, herbicides, and nitrogen fertilizers, improved water quality and biodiversity, and soil conservation. Benefits to farmers purportedly include higher and more stable yields, more cost efficient and convenient pest control, reduced fertilizer cost, and higher profits.[5]

The critics of agricultural biotechnology maintain that the medium- to long-term health and environmental risks of GE (or transgenic) organisms are poorly understood, and that the technology promotes excessive corporate power through patenting of the food chain. They also invoke a range of ethical concerns, arguing, for example, that the technology involves "tampering with nature."

STAKES

Whether consumer health, the environment, and the hungry will, in the long term, benefit or suffer from agricultural biotechnology remains open and contested. If the proponents' predictions materialized at some point in the future, humanity and the environment would benefit enormously. However, the public health, environmental, and commercial risks could also be considerable. Some readers may recall the prediction by Admiral Lewis Strauss, the head of the US Atomic Energy Commission, who claimed in the 1950s that nuclear power would eventually be too cheap to meter.[6] Nuclear power turned out to be one of the most uneconomical and unpopular technological innovations in human history. It has not collapsed entirely. But it has never reached the adoption rate and market share that its proponents originally predicted.

Will green biotechnology suffer the same fate? We will probably know in 10–20 years from now. In the meantime, a better understanding of the political, economic, and societal determinants of the future of green biotechnology can help stakeholders to make well-informed predictions. It can contribute to more accurate assessments of public and private sector strategies for coping with challenges to agri-biotechnology. And it can be helpful in devising policy solutions that promote applications of agri-biotechnology that benefit both rich and poor inhabitants of our planet in ecological, human health, and economic terms.

For proponents and opponents of green biotechnology, the public health, environmental, and ethical stakes are obviously large. So are the more narrow economic stakes for biotech firms, farmers, food processors, and retailers.

As of 2002, the world market for transgenic crops and GE food products and ingredients was estimated at around 17 billion USD. It consisted largely of insect-resistant corn and cotton and herbicide-tolerant soybeans. By 2006, this market, in which soybeans and cotton will still hold the lion's share, is predicted to reach over 20 billion USD. The potential market for "white biotechnology", i.e., the use of GE plants for the production of vaccines, renewable sources of energy (e.g. ethanol), biodegradable plastics, and other goods could be much larger, possibly up to 100–500 billion USD per year by 2020.[7] The area planted to GE crops stood at over 58 million hectares (145 million acres) in 2002 and is likely to grow further.[8] Investment in agri-biotech research and development is difficult to estimate, but runs into billions of USD per year. Input suppliers (agri-biotech firms), GE crop farmers, as well as food processors and retailers that support agri-biotechnology have a lot to lose if the tide turns against this technology. Finally, billions of dollars in exports of GE crops or processed foods that contain GE organisms are also at stake.

CHALLENGES ON THE DEMAND AND SUPPLY SIDE

In chapter 2 I claim that, despite ongoing scientific innovation and persistent emphasis by the technology's proponents of large upcoming benefits, agricultural biotechnology is facing a profound crisis. To support this claim I discuss the most relevant demand (i.e., consumer) and supply (i.e., producer) issues[9] in agri-biotechnology. This analysis provides the starting point for describing and explaining regulatory responses and international trade tensions that exacerbate the current crisis. Chapter 2 also equips readers less familiar with agri-biotech issues with some background knowledge that will facilitate reading of subsequent chapters.

On the demand side, consumers have so far not benefited significantly from GE crops and it is still open whether they will, on average, do so in future. Nelson et al. (1999), for example, have calculated that full adoption of GE corn and GE soy around the world would (compared to no adoption anywhere) result in no more than a 4.9 percent price reduction (and less than a 2 percent increase in output) for corn and a 1.7 percent price reduction (and 0.5 percent increase in output) for soybeans. Other agri-biotech applications may produce more impressive results in terms of more and cheaper food, but we simply do not know at this stage. Moreover, because virtually all agri-biotech applications currently on the market focus on agronomic (or input) traits, GE products have not benefited consumers in terms of superior product quality (e.g., healthier food). Again, future products may provide such benefits. But whether and when such products will appear on mass consumer markets is still guesswork. These problems on the demand side (small consumer benefits) have been exacerbated by public controversies over health, environmental, and economic effects of the technology, as well as opposition on ethical grounds.

On the supply side, according to proponents of agri-biotechnology, increasing GE crop acreage testifies to the success of the technology. The same holds for the growing number of countries that engage in research and development in this area.[10] In chapter 2 I conclude that such arguments mask fundamental problems on the supply side of agri-biotechnology. Technology adoption is limited primarily to the United States, Argentina, and Canada. The farm-level benefits of the technology remain disputed. At this stage, the available evidence shows that some farmers have indeed benefited from GE crops. But it does not support the more general claim by the proponents that the average farmer growing GE crops between 1996 and 2002 has benefited substantially, particularly when one considers not only narrow agronomic benefits (e.g., yields) but also farm profits.[11] Future GE crops may result in much higher yields, lower pest-control costs, and higher profits for farmers. So far, this remains no more than an optimistic scenario based on some encouraging evidence from field trials with a wide range of GE crops. Thus far, farm-level adoption of GE crops seems to have been driven by factors other than profitability, for example, marketing strategies of biotech firms, structures of grain-handling systems, and convenience effects in farm management. Whether current adoption rates can be sustained is questionable, particularly if problems on the demand side also persist.

Regulatory polarization and international trade tensions over differences in regulation across countries have added considerably to these problems. Regulatory differences are described in chapter 3 and explained in chapters 4 and 5. International trade implications are examined in chapter 6.

REGULATORY POLARIZATION

In the mid-1980s, the biotechnology policies of West European countries, the United States, and other countries were similar. At the end of the 1980s, they began to diverge. Since 1990, the European Union and its member states have moved towards ever more stringent approval and labeling standards, with strong emphasis on the *precautionary principle*.[12] As a consequence, very few agricultural biotech applications have been approved for commercialization in the European Union, commercial planting of GE crops is almost non-existent in EU countries, and the number of field trials is far lower than in the United States. The number of labeled GE foods on the EU market has approached zero as food processors and retailers have chosen to avoid them rather than label GE foods. The EU market for GE food products has shrunk to GE enzymes, food ingredients and animal feed not subject to mandatory labeling.

In stark contrast, US policy-makers have embraced agricultural biotechnology. They have taken the position that agri-biotechnology is simply a new and innovative food and feed production technology that does not per se make produced food and feed less safe than their conventional counterparts. The US Food and Drug Administration (FDA), the Department of Agriculture (USDA), and the Environmental Protection Agency (EPA) have, through relatively informal notification procedures and with very little governmental pre-market risk assessments, approved most industry requests for field testing and commercialization of GE products. Producers may voluntarily label GE foods but are not obliged to do so. More than 50 GE crop varieties are on the US market. Many more GE varieties have been authorized for field testing. GE crop acreage increased dramatically between 1996 and 2002. And GE ingredients can be found in thousands of processed food products.

These differences between the European Union and the United States are at the heart of a trend I call regulatory polarization: an increasing gap is developing between agri-biotech promoting and agri-biotech restricting countries, both in terms of approval and labeling regulation and at the market level. The hard core of the pro-agri-biotech world clusters around the United States and includes in particular Argentina and Canada. The agri-biotech restricting part of the world clusters around the European Union and also includes a range of non-EU states, such as Norway, Switzerland, and many Central and Eastern European countries.

Many other nations (e.g., Australia, Brazil, China, India, Japan, Mexico, Russia, and South Africa) have moved towards stricter approval procedures. And many of these countries (e.g., Australia, China, Japan, South Korea, Russia) have adopted mandatory labeling requirements for GE food. While these regulations differ very much in terms of their stringency, on average they position these countries somewhere in between the European Union and the United States.

Developing countries in particular have been struggling to make sense of scientific and political controversies about risks and benefits of the technology. Disputes in 2002 over US food aid to sub-Saharan Africa that included GE crops are only the tip of the iceberg: for many developing countries establishing regulatory systems that are effective, cost efficient, affordable, and do not antagonize the United States or the European Union amounts to squaring a circle.

These "tectonic shifts" in the world's landscape of agri-biotech regulation have thus far not generated much pressure for reform of US approval and labeling standards (nor those of Argentina and Canada). But they have influenced markets. Most analysts note a chilling effect on GE corn and GE soybean cultivation in the United States and other GE crop producing countries. The exception, GE cotton, is a non-food product. Regulatory polarization has contributed substantially to delaying commercialization of new GE crops, most notably, GE wheat and rice. Moreover, it has all but promoted public funding of agri-biotech R&D in developing countries where the technology might be most beneficial. The increasing regulatory divide is also affecting global agricultural trade.

EXPLAINING REGULATORY POLARIZATION

Conventional wisdom tends to account for differences between countries in agri-biotech regulation with arguments about differences in "regulatory culture." The following text exemplifies this type of explanation in somewhat poetic form:

The Risk of Nations
In the US products are safe until proven risky
In France products are risky until proven safe
In the UK products are risky even when proven safe
In India products are safe even when proven risky
In Switzerland products are risky especially after they have been proven safe
In Kenya products are safe especially after they have been proven risky
In Canada products are neither safe nor risky
In Brazil products are both safe and risky
In Ethiopia products are risky even if they have not been developed

Source: anonymous contributor to www.agbioworld.org.

Arguments such as the above probably contain a grain of truth, but are dangerously close to stereotypes. Most social science work has thus combined arguments about national regulatory styles (or culture) with empirical research on institutional structures, the media, consumer perceptions, and NGO and industry behavior.[13] The explanation of regulatory polarization offered in chapters 4 and 5 builds on this work, but casts it into a more systematic and parsimonious framework. It also takes into account driving forces not or inadequately examined in previous research. And it shows that some of the most popular explanations of transatlantic differences in agri-biotech regulation (notably, technophobia and protectionist interests as driving forces of stricter EU regulations) are wrong.

I explain differences in regulatory outcomes across jurisdictions in terms of consumer perceptions, activity of NGOs, interests and behavior of biotech firms, farmers, processors and retailers, and institutional characteristics of the political systems concerned. The analysis illuminates market processes as well as domestic and international political processes. It focuses on the European Union and the United States because these two political units exhibit the most striking variation in regulatory outcomes, and because EU and US behavior in this policy area has a strong effect on what other countries do.

The explanation combines two theoretical perspectives. The first views regulation as the result of a struggle for political and market influence among different interest groups within the European Union and the United States; that is, among input suppliers (agri-biotech firms), farmers, processors and retailers, and consumer and environmental groups. This explanation sheds light on why these groups have different preferences, and on when and why particular interests prevail in the policy-making process. The second perspective explores the effect of interactions among different jurisdictions (EU countries, US states) in federalist political systems (the European Union, the United States).

While the former explanation focuses on societal influences that operate from the individual or firm level upward (bottom up perspective), the latter concentrates on the effects of system-wide political structures and institutions (top down perspective). In the European Union, both processes have worked in ways that have driven agri-biotech regulation towards greater stringency. In the United States, they have worked in ways that have sustained agri-biotech promoting regulation.

Interest Group Perspective

Conventional politico-economic theories of regulation claim that environmental and consumer groups, because of their large and heterogeneous membership, experience greater problems than producers (industry) in mobilizing supporters and influencing public policy. The analysis in chapter 4 shows, however, that the *collective action capacity* of environmental and consumer interests has varied substantially between the European Union and the United States. This variation can be traced back to differences in public perceptions of agricultural biotechnology, consumer trust in regulatory authorities, and institutional settings.

Due to greater public outrage, defined in terms of more negative consumer perceptions of agri-biotechnology and lower public trust in regulatory agencies, the collective action capacity of agri-biotech adverse European environmental and consumer groups has been higher than the capacity of their US counterparts. Transatlantic differences in the extent and nature of agri-biotech campaigns by NGOs reflect this variation in collective action capacity. Agri-biotech adverse groups in Europe have thus been more successful in *shaping markets* for the technology than agri-biotech adverse groups in the United States. Public outrage in combination with more institutional access due to multilevel and decentralized policy-making[14] has also enabled agri-biotech adverse interests in Europe to exert more *influence on agri-biotech policy-making*. In the United States, low public outrage and a centralized regulatory system for agri-biotechnology have acted against agri-biotech adverse interests.

The collective action capacity of pro-agri-biotech producers has also varied substantially between the European Union and the United States. In Europe, public outrage and NGO campaigns have driven a wedge between biotech firms on the one hand and food processors, retailers, and farmers on the other hand. Thus, they have reduced the collective action capacity of pro-biotech interests. Interestingly, the pro-biotech coalition in Europe has not been crippled by protectionist "piggy-backing" by some producers (notably, farmers).[15] The latter argument figures most prominently in the economic theory of regulation and in US attacks on EU agri-biotech regulation. It has been weakened because those firms most vulnerable to market pressure spearheaded by NGOs, notably, food processors and retailers, have been pushed towards support for stricter regulation. In contrast, in the United States a cohesive and well-organized pro-biotech producer coalition has prevailed due to lower public outrage and weaker campaigns by agri-biotech adverse NGOs. Differences in industrial structure (particularly, higher concentration, both in economic and organizational terms, of the retail sector in the European Union than in the United States) and associated rigidities also play a role in explaining why the pro-agri-biotech producer coalition has been much weaker in the European Union than in the United States.

Regulation in Federalist Systems

The interest group explanation does not account for differences in interests and policies of individual EU countries and US states and their implications for variation of policies at the EU and US level. Chapter 5 fills the gap. It regards EU and US agri-biotech policies as outcomes of interactions between political subunits (member states in the European Union, states in the United States) within a larger (federal) political system where these subunits can act autonomously to varying degrees. The explanation concentrates on whether political subunits within the larger political system can, by unilaterally installing stricter or laxer regulation of agricultural biotechnology, push the stringency of system-wide regulations up or down. The analysis of agri-biotech policy-making in the European Union and the United States shows that in the European Union we observe a substantial "ratcheting-up" effect, whereas "centralized laxity" has prevailed in the United States.

EU countries are bound by supranational rules that guarantee the free flow of agricultural goods within the European Union's internal market. But they maintain considerable national autonomy in closely related policy areas, such as environmental and public health regulation. For example: in many areas they have safeguarded the right to establish regulation that is stricter than minimum standards set by the European Union or that deviates from the principle of mutual recognition.[16] These conditions also apply to agri-biotechnology.

When the forces described and explained by the interest group perspective began to drive up the stringency of regulation in more risk-averse EU countries, the more agri-biotech friendly nations as well as the EU Commission faced a dilemma: how to satisfy demands, in some countries, for stricter agri-biotech regulation and, at the same time, safeguard the European Union's internal market? Variation across countries in approval and labeling standards for GE products threatened to disrupt agricultural trade in the European Union. In view of strong public support for strict agri-biotech regulation in around half of the European Union's member countries, downward harmonization to levels acceptable to pro-agri-biotech countries was impossible. Pro-agri-biotech countries in the European Union have thus regularly caved into the demands of agri-biotech adverse countries. They have done so because, in their view, the costs of market disruptions are higher than the costs of restrictive agri-biotech regulation. In this "ratcheting up" process agri-biotech adverse countries have, step by step, moved towards more stringent regulations and have dragged EU-wide regulations upward in this process. The supranational bodies of the European Union (Commission, European Court of Justice) have so far not resisted this development.

Agri-biotech regulation is more centralized in the United States than in the European Union, both in terms of political levels and institutions involved. It is largely in the hands of two independent federal agencies and one federal ministry (FDA, EPA, USDA). What might appear like a paradox in the EU case—that a fragmentation of decision-making authority produces upward harmonization and not simply paralysis—does not come into play in the United States to the extent it does in the European Union. Bottom up pressure for stricter regulation has in some cases led to diverging policy preferences among US states. However, due to institutional and legal constraints described in chapter 5, the options of US states for stricter unilateral regulation of agricultural biotechnology are much more limited than the options of individual EU countries. Even if public pressure for stricter agri-biotech regulation grew in some US states, and if these states imposed some restrictions that were upheld by the courts, a "ratcheting up" trend would emerge much more slowly in the United States than in the European Union. The most likely scenario is that some large US states introduce restrictions (e.g., mandatory labeling of GE food), and that these restrictions have negative effects on other states' agricultural exports. Farmers in the latter states, perhaps followed by their governments, would thus have an incentive to meet the higher standards in their export markets. Eventually, this "trading up"[17] effect might spread throughout the United States and motivate federal agencies to tighten regulations. But we are still far away from this scenario. In other words, as of now, relatively positive public perceptions of agri-biotechnology and weak NGO campaigns are primarily responsible for lax agri-biotech regulation in the United States. However, federal processes in the United States constitute an additional barrier against stricter regulation should bottom up pressure increase in future.

Will Regulatory Polarization Persist?

The analysis in chapters 4 and 5 shows that a combination of interest group dynamics and particular characteristics of regulatory federalism in the European Union has increased regulatory restrictions on agricultural biotechnology in the European Union. These forces are much weaker in the United States, which accounts for persistent regulatory laxity there. The analysis also suggests that both political systems will remain on their respective trajectory for the next few years.

A reversal of the European Union's policy is unlikely because of low public acceptance of GE food, low trust in regulators, pressure by NGOs, growing opposition to GE crops among farmers, strong incentives for processors and retailers to stay away or withdraw from the market for labeled GE foods, and institutional inertia in EU policy-making. The dominance of agri-biotech adverse interests in the European Union is bolstered by the characteristics of regulatory federalism in the European Union. Decision-making structures in the European Union allow agri-biotech adverse minorities to block efforts to relax existing standards. In addition, a combination of multilevel and decentralized decision-making, substantial regulatory autonomy of EU countries, and concerns about safeguarding the European Union's internal market encourage a "ratcheting up" of regulations rather than downward harmonization.

If one accepts the conclusion that the European Union will not move towards the US model of centralized laxity, will US policy move towards the EU model? The evidence presented in chapters 4 and 5 suggests it will not. Somewhat increased public concern over GE food since the late 1990s, and the StarLink controversy in particular, have produced some cracks in the pro-agri-biotech coalition. But these cracks have thus far been much too small to pose a serious threat to the cohesion of this coalition. For example, conflicts between US farmers and biotech firms in view of precarious export opportunities for GE crops have been reduced through increased government subsidies for US farmers. In addition to low interest group ("bottom up") pressure for stricter agri-biotech regulation, the characteristics of US regulatory federalism act against more restrictive agri-biotech policies. The analysis in chapter 5 shows that, even in the unlikely event that consumer pressure for tighter rules grew, heavily constrained regulatory autonomy of US states in agri-biotech matters combined with centralized decision-making at the federal level would slow down any "contagion" effect that may emanate from individual US states trying to impose more restrictive policies.

Whether regulatory polarization will persist depends not only on the domestic processes just discussed. It also depends on developments at the international level.

First, in the long run the evolution of the world's regulatory landscape for agri-biotechnology will also be shaped by the policies of countries other than the European Union and the United States. If most of these other countries moved towards the EU model, this would create pressure for stricter regulation in the United States. Pressure for a relaxation of regulation in the European Union would mount if most other countries moved towards the US model. For the time being, the world's two largest economies are clearly the principal drivers of worldwide regulatory activity. Their policy choices visibly limit the options of other countries, particularly those that are economically dependent on the European Union, the United States, or both. Switzerland, Norway, and Central and Eastern European countries have thus aligned with the European Union, Canada with the United States. Other countries, which are less dependent on EU or US markets, for example, China, Brazil, India, Japan, and Russia, have adopted regulations whose stringency lies somewhere between the EU and the US models. Agri-biotech policy in these countries is very recent and very much in flux. Both the European Union and the United States are currently battling for influence on the regulatory policies of these countries by trying to entice, coerce, or cajole them into one or the other policy. The acrimonious dispute over GE food aid deliveries to sub-Saharan Africa in 2002 exemplifies this volatile and conflictual situation.

Whether other countries will eventually move towards the EU or the US model of agri-biotech regulation remains open.

Second, whether regulatory polarization will persist depends also on how trade tensions associated with regulatory polarization are played out in regional and global trading systems. In principle, three scenarios are possible. Transatlantic (perhaps even worldwide) convergence of agri-biotech regulations could develop in two ways: through voluntary negotiations and international agreements that harmonize regulations (harmonization may occur at higher or lower levels of stringency); or through coercion exercised via international dispute settlement mechanisms (notably, those of the WTO system). Chapter 6 concentrates on these two possibilities. Alternatively, problems associated with regulatory polarization could, to some extent, be sorted out in global markets. For example, food industries could adapt to heterogeneous consumer preferences and offer an increasing range of GE and non-GE products. I will explore this option in chapters 6 and 7. This market-based approach would not reduce regulatory polarization in a direct fashion. But it could help in mitigating some of the negative consequences of polarization mentioned at the outset of this chapter.

INTERNATIONAL TRADE IMPLICATIONS

In an increasingly integrated world economy, the effects of national and regional agri-biotech regulations reach far beyond the countries adopting them. In particular, differences in biotech approval and labeling standards affect international trade flows and may result in conflict within regional and global trading systems. In chapter 6 I argue that regulatory polarization has put the world's two biggest economies, the European Union and the United States, on a collision course.

I then concentrate on cooperative and unilateral strategies for reducing regulatory polarization, with an emphasis on assessing the likelihood and consequences of a full blown dispute over agri-biotechnology in the WTO. The principal proposition in this chapter is that escalation of existing trade tensions is more likely if: (a) economic losses due to the European Union's agri-biotech restrictions are large and concentrated on politically influential economic actors in the United States; (b) non-coercive policy measures for solving the problem are ineffective; (c) the prospects for the United States to win a legal case in the WTO are good and the European Union is likely to make concessions before a WTO verdict or after a "guilty" verdict. The evidence for the first two conditions points to escalation. The evidence for the third condition is ambiguous.

The assessment of distributional consequences of regulatory polarization focuses on export revenue losses and implications for aggregate EU and US welfare. It suggests that, in aggregate welfare terms, the costs of regulatory polarization may be falling primarily on the European Union, and only to a smaller extent on the United States. Costs to the United States, however, tend to fall on a small, well-organized and funded, and politically influential group of economic actors, primarily biotech firms and export-oriented farmers. Their losses currently amount to several hundred million USD per year. But these losses could rise to several billion USD per year if the European Union tightened its regulations further and other countries followed the EU model. These economic losers of EU regulation have a powerful incentive to push the US government towards coercive measures to pry open European Union and other markets for American GE products. Studies on protectionism and trade disputes in other policy areas show that such conditions tend to promote escalation.

The analysis of non-coercive strategies for coping with growing trade tensions (notably, mutual recognition, compensation, harmonization, and unilateral regulatory or market adjustment in the United States) shows that none of these conventional policies is likely to be effective in reducing regulatory polarization and trade tensions. Mutual recognition is unacceptable to the European Union and the United States because it would undermine the legitimacy of both sides' respective policy. Compensation would founder on political legitimacy and financial grounds. All international harmonization efforts are deadlocked for the same reasons that have led to regulatory polarization. The same holds for unilateral regulatory adjustment in the United States. Unilateral market adjustment in the United States has helped in mitigating trade tensions but cannot solve the problem by itself.

The evidence on the third condition is inconclusive. On the one hand, I show that for legal and strategic/political reasons the WTO is likely to uphold the European Union's strict regulations should the United States set the WTO's dispute settlement procedure in motion. In particular, upholding is more likely if: (1) legal rules do not provide clear-cut guidance as to whether the defendant's regulations are legitimate (lawful) or not; (2) the defendant is economically powerful and is unlikely to comply with an adverse verdict; (3) the defendant is, explicitly or implicitly, supported by other influential WTO countries; (4) important negotiations on extending trade liberalization in the WTO are under way; (5) a recent and comparable case ended with substantial political backlash. The evidence on all five points suggests that we should not expect the US government to escalate the conflict because the United States would not win the legal case.

On the other hand, we know from other trade conflicts that governments sometimes escalate trade disputes in which the probability of winning the case is low. There are several reasons why governments may do so. Potential plaintiffs may conclude that winning domestic political support from crucial constituencies by escalating a trade dispute is more important than actually winning the case. Such action promises short-term gains, whereas WTO proceedings often take years and adverse outcomes occur at some point in the future. Moreover, potential plaintiffs usually do not face much domestic opposition to escalation because the costs of escalation (e.g., punitive economic measures and countermeasures, disruption of further trade talks) are often dispersed over the entire economy or a large part thereof.

By and large, the analysis in chapter 6 suggests that the likelihood of escalation of transatlantic trade tensions over agricultural biotechnology is high. Such escalation would impose an almost unmanageable task on the WTO and could disrupt efforts to liberalize world agricultural trade. It could easily develop into a cycle of punitive economic measures and countermeasures that could cost biotech firms, farmers, consumers, and taxpayers on both sides of the Atlantic billions of dollars. Moreover, as discussed in the next section, it would add further to the crisis agricultural biotechnology already finds itself in.

In other words, while voluntary harmonization, mutual recognition, compensation, and unilateral regulatory adjustment in the United States will be next to impossible in the next few years, the likelihood of coercive efforts via the WTO is growing rapidly. The assessment in chapter 6 shows, however, that escalation is a no-win and probably even counterproductive strategy. If one accepts these findings, market-based solutions, in forms to be discussed in chapter 7, may turn out to be the most effective strategy for coping with regulatory polarization and trade tensions.

In mid-May 2003, when this book went to press, the United States formally carried the dispute into the WTO by requesting consultations. Its request was supported by Argentina and Canada. WTO rules call for consultations as a first step in order to give plaintiffs and defendants a chance to solve the problem cooperatively. If a dispute cannot be settled through consultations within 60 days the plaintiff can forward the case to a dispute settlement panel. This process, including possible appeals against a panel ruling, normally takes 10–18 months, possibly longer if the WTO needs to decide on punitive measures and appeals against such measures—provided the defendant is found guilty. In other words, if neither the United States nor the European Union backs down, final WTO decisions on whether the European Union's regulations are compatible with WTO rules will probably be made in late 2004 or early 2005. The analysis in this book suggests that the dispute is likely to escalate all the way to formal WTO rulings, and that those rulings will not resolve the problem.

CRISIS

It is unlikely that regulatory polarization, escalating trade tensions, and the underlying societal controversies will lead to a collapse and disappearance of green biotechnology. But they have thrown this technology into a profound crisis. As noted by the *Economist* already in 2000,[18] "Environmentalist hate the idea, consumers don't seem to care for it, farmers are increasingly diffident, and the companies that develop it are either imploding or off-loading their GMO subsidiaries as fast as they can find anyone to buy them."

In this market and regulatory setting, research, development, and adoption of the technology will remain far behind what would otherwise be feasible and perhaps sensible from technological, economic, environmental, public health, and humanitarian viewpoints. These circumstances deter private investment in agri-biotech R&D, not only in Europe and countries with similar restrictions, but also in the United States. They have clearly increased commercial risks for biotech firms, farmers, and food processors and retailers because of greater uncertainty over export markets and fear of "spillovers" of consumer revolt and regulatory restrictions from agri-biotech adverse to agri-biotech promoting countries. Leading agri-biotech firms have invested heavily in the technology, but have become hesitant to direct more investment into this area.

Regulatory polarization, escalating trade tensions, and continuing societal controversy over agricultural biotechnology also deter public and NGO support for agri-biotech R&D in developing countries where the technology could potentially contribute most to improved living conditions. For public relations reasons and to raise political support for agri-biotechnology, some biotech firms have provided free access to patented GE crops to some developing countries. But such gifts are ad hoc and selective. Commercial incentives of input suppliers are and will remain biased towards OECD markets, where purchasing power is much higher. Intensified ties between private sector and university-based R&D, particularly in the United States but also in Europe, have reinforced that trend.

Government and NGO support is unlikely to fill the gap. In Europe and elsewhere, governments and NGOs are highly reluctant to sponsor agri-biotech R&D in developing countries, primarily because of the anticipated political backlash. Many developing countries, for their part, are reluctant to accept help in this area for several reasons. The first generation of GE crops has not provided consumer benefits (in price or quality) and current farm-level economics of existing agri-biotech applications are, on average, disputed. Moreover, many developing countries fear export revenue losses should the number and size of agri-biotech adverse markets continue to grow. In particular, financial, technical, and administrative problems in operating a reliable system of segregation, identity preservation, and labeling are likely to deter many developing countries from adopting the technology. As noted above, these conditions create a *legitimacy trap* for agri-biotechnology. While pro-biotech circles are persistently using "feeding the poor" arguments to bolster the usefulness and legitimacy of agri-biotechnology, economic, societal and regulatory constraints are hampering development and marketing of such agri-biotech applications. The industry's inability to deliver on its promises, in turn, negatively affects the legitimacy of the technology.

Policy Reforms

What could public and private sector stakeholders do to overcome the current doldrums and equip agri-biotechnology with a fair chance to prove its economic, environmental, public health, and humanitarian benefits in the long run?

In chapter 7 I start out by arguing that most alternatives to the proposed regulatory reforms, which are frequently advocated by pro-agri-biotech circles, are neither feasible from a political viewpoint (e.g., a substantial relaxation of the European Union's agri-biotech rules), nor would they create and sustain long-term consumer confidence in agricultural GE products. Notably, no convincing empirical evidence exists to support the widely held view among agri-biotech supporters that pouring millions of dollars into public relations campaigns will produce more knowledgeable consumers who are more supportive of the technology. Moreover, US efforts to pry open foreign markets via trade disputes in the WTO are very unlikely to produce the results that agri-biotech proponents are hoping for.

I propose instead that policy reforms should focus on three elements: strengthening regulatory authorities and liability laws, supporting market-driven product differentiation, and supporting developing countries.

These policy reforms would initially impose some additional costs on producers and consumers. They may, at first sight, also look particularly unattractive to those who advocate regulatory decisions based exclusively on existing scientific evidence for health and environmental risks. Indeed, scientists have thus far not been able to demonstrate that agricultural GE products currently on the market pose public health risks—there is more scientific uncertainty as to the environmental implications of agri-biotechnology. However, I will argue that, whatever the "real" risks are, the proposed reforms are the price to pay for long-term consumer confidence and sustained investment in the technology. The cost of persistent regulatory polarization, trade tensions, and turmoil in global markets for agri-biotech products—the most likely scenario in the absence of regulatory reforms along the lines suggested in chapter 7—could be much higher.

First, all jurisdictions producing and/or importing GE crops, food or feed, above all the European Union, should establish powerful, politically independent, and science-oriented regulatory authorities. I will argue that the European Union in particular finds itself in a trilemma that involves trade-offs between decentralized and multilevel regulation, food safety, and market concentration. The analysis of this trilemma shows that moving from decentralized, network-like regulation to more centralized forms of governance in food safety would be the most effective option for increasing consumer confidence.

In the absence of such reform, ever more complex and costly agri-biotech regulation that lacks a solid scientific justification is likely to produce a vicious circle involving complex regulation followed by implementation failures, further decline of public trust in food safety and regulators, even more complex regulation in response, increasing market concentration as firms try to cope with food safety problems through vertical integration and self-regulation, and so on.

The strengthening of regulatory authorities should be combined with a tightening of liability laws. Stronger regulatory authorities and stronger liability laws would go a long way towards enhancing public support for agri-biotechnology. The former in particular would also act against excessive market concentration in the food sector.

Second, public and private sector stakeholders should support market-driven product differentiation, that is, the establishment of national and international markets where GE and non-GE products can be safely and reliably traded. This necessitates that all countries cultivating GE crops and/or importing such crops or products implement strict and science-based risk assessment and approval procedures. It also necessitates efficient systems of identity preservation (IP) and labeling.

To reduce short-term disincentives among GE crop farmers, food processors, and retailers, the startup costs of IP and labeling systems could be subsidized by governments. Governments could also support market-driven product differentiation by setting tolerance levels, promoting certification and verification procedures for non-GE products, and providing detailed information on planting, yields, and prices of GE products and their conventional counterparts, thus enabling farmers to make better informed choices. To facilitate international trade in GE products, the European Union and the United States should move towards joint standards for risk assessment, approval, labeling, testing, IP, and liability that could then be implemented also in other countries.

Under conditions of market-driven product differentiation GE foods can only survive if they offer compelling consumer benefits (e.g., in terms of quality and/or price). Biotech firms, cultivators, food processors, and retailers should thus concentrate on food products that offer such benefits (unlike first generation GE crops). To improve the general legitimacy of the technology, in both rich and poor countries, genetic improvement of agronomic traits should concentrate primarily on varieties that are particularly useful also to developing countries. To facilitate the setting up and operation of differentiated markets, biotech and food firms should avoid marketing of GE products that can spread quickly throughout the food chain and/or have a high potential for cross-pollination or outcrossing.

Third, international funding and technical support will be required to set up effective regulatory systems in developing countries, including also biosafety measures for R&D. Biotech accidents in developing countries could have disastrous implications for the technology in rich and poor countries. In addition, weak regulation in developing countries could hamper those countries' agricultural export opportunities in markets subject to stricter and more effective agri-biotech rules.

Governments, biotech firms, and international scientific associations should set up and fund an independent international organization. This organization should provide financial and technical assistance for regulatory efforts in developing countries, conduct research into health and environmental issues associated with agricultural biotechnology, and fund and supervise agri-biotech R&D in developing countries in areas where private investment is not forthcoming or patents hamper technology transfers.

Even if the international community, and in particular the world's largest economies, can find a regulatory modus vivendi within the next few years we are likely to see perhaps five to ten more years of controversy and heterogeneous ad hoc responses by policy-makers around the world. If the policy reforms recommended in this book were implemented it seems more likely that the storm would eventually settle. We may then find a variety of agricultural GE products competing in the market with conventional or organic counterparts. Consumers would be more confident in the safety of the food supply and would be able to exercise informed choices based on whatever criteria they deem important. Farmers, processors, retailers, and biotech firms would experience less uncertainty on the demand side. They would be able to capture premiums with GE products deemed beneficial by consumers, and to direct longer-term investment to products and business areas where consumer demand is most promising. Residual risks to public health and the environment would be under effective government control and, should prevention fail, would be covered by robust liability laws.

CHAPTER TWO

Challenges

IN THIS CHAPTER I argue that agricultural biotechnology has run into serious problems on two fronts. On the one hand (demand side), societal controversy over health and environmental risks, solutions to food security problems in developing countries, corporate dominance of the food chain, and ethical issues have depressed consumer and political support for the technology. So has the fact that first generation GE foods have, from the perspective of consumers, been neither cheaper nor of superior quality compared to non-GE counterparts. On the other hand (supply side), uncertainties about farm-level profits and other advantages of GE crops, rising regulatory costs (which reduce profitability), and negative consumer reactions have reduced the attractiveness of GE crops from the viewpoint of farmers, food processors, and retailers.

First I describe what agricultural biotechnology is and then concentrate on the afore-mentioned challenges. To simplify the analysis, I discuss these challenges in generic terms at this point. Chapters 3–6 show that the extent and implications of these challenges have varied considerably across countries. They also show that the current crisis in agri-biotechnology has been exacerbated by regulatory polarization and the international trade tensions that such polarization has engendered. In Chapter 7, I outline policy options that could help in coping with the crisis and giving green biotechnology a fair chance to prove its benefits in the medium to long term.

WHAT IS AGRICULTURAL BIOTECHNOLOGY?

In the 19th century, an Augustinian monk from Central Europe, Gregor Mendel,[1] claimed that the traits of living organisms were inherited.[2] Only in the 1950s to 1970s, however, did scientists discover the chemical and physical properties of "genes," the key elements in the process of inheritance. They found that a molecule called DNA (deoxyribonucleic acid) contains the information that controls the synthesis of enzymes and other proteins, which in turn are responsible for the basic metabolic processes of all cells. DNA thus encodes genetic information in cells. A gene is a particular DNA sequence. The total set of genes of an organism (the genome) is organized into chromosomes within the cell nucleus. The development of a single cell into a living organism is determined by the genetic information of the cell and by the interaction of genes and gene products with environmental conditions.

Rapid scientific progress since the discovery of DNA has created unprecedented opportunities in plant and animal breeding. Traditional breeding was (and still is) based on swapping and manipulating genes by crossing plants or animals, with the aim of improving productivity, quality, or performance. While in traditional breeding thousands of genes with unknown functions are swapped in a rather haphazard fashion, genetic engineering allows for more controlled transfer of one or a few specific genes with known functions from one organism to another, and also across different species (e.g., from bacteria to corn).

Typically, one or more genes with known effects are spliced with a promoter, a regulator, and a tag. They are then inserted into an organism that includes 10,000–30,000 genes (e.g., a plant cell) by means of an agrobacterium, a so-called shotgun, or protoplast injection. Marker genetic material (a tag) and a genome are used to establish which cells have absorbed the transferred genetic material. The outcome of this transformation (called "event") depends on the components of the genetic material and the place where the novel DNA is inserted. The cell that has absorbed the inserted DNA is cultivated into a plant or animal that expresses the properties encoded in the inserted genetic material. The purpose of traditional breeding and genetic engineering is the same, namely to produce new plant or animal varieties by manipulating genetic information. Yet, genetic engineering, primarily in the form of recombinant DNA techniques, can produce new plant or animal varieties that would be impossible to produce with traditional breeding methods.

For example, Bt corn, a genetically engineered corn variety, produces toxins originally produced by a soil bacterium, *Bacillus thuringiensis* (Bt). This toxin kills some insects (notably, the European corn borer), while leaving other insects unaffected. Similarly, Bt cotton is genetically modified to control budworms and bollworms. Glyphosate-resistant soybeans include a modified growth-regulating enzyme. This enzyme is immune to glyphosate, a herbicide that inactivates the enzymes in most plants and thus kills them. Weed control with glyphosate tends to be cheaper and more convenient for farmers than weed control with other herbicides. These three transgenic crop varieties are currently the most successful commercially in terms of acreage under cultivation.[3]

CONTROVERSIES OVER AGRICULTURAL BIOTECHNOLOGY

The first genetically engineered (GE) foods were approved in the United States in the early 1990s. Commercial GE crop production on a large scale began in 1995–96 amidst great optimism among technology adopters that the new crops would result in higher yields, lower pest management costs, increased international competitiveness, and higher farm-level profits.

Most biotech firms, GE crop farmers, food processors, and retailers were caught by surprise when major controversies over the technology and its applications erupted as GE foods entered West European markets in 1996. The first and perhaps most famous case was tomato puree made from GE tomatoes. In February 1996, this product was marketed in the United Kingdom by supermarket chains Safeway and Sainsbury's. The tomatoes were modified with a shortened polygalacturonase (PG) gene to produce more pectin and less water, which reduced the need for heat treatment and concentration before canning. These production cost advantages were transferred to consumers in the form of more puree for the same price as the conventional product. The two firms did not try to hide the production technology. On the contrary, they voluntarily put a highly visible label on the product.

Initial sales were remarkable. By late 1997, Safeway's stores had sold three-quarters of a million cans. This development was abruptly halted in 1998–99 when consumer groups pressured the two supermarkets into taking the product off their shelves. By July 1999, both firms had withdrawn the product, claiming that genetically engineered tomatoes were simply an input, and that the costs of that input had become too high.

The controversy over GE food has persisted ever since and has spread from initial concerns about consumer health to include concerns over environmental risks, world food security, corporate dominance of the food supply, ethical issues, farm-level economics, and regulatory problems.

HEALTH RISKS

While proponents of the technology have claimed that it will lead to healthier food (e.g., food with more micronutrients, such as iron, zinc, and vitamin A[4]), the critics have highlighted health risks involved in consuming and producing GE food.

Initial claims by some critics that GE foods are detrimental to human health have been toned down in recent years.[5] GE foods have been on the market for around 6–7 years in some countries (particularly the United States). Yet there is virtually no scientific evidence for human health risks posed by these foods. Debate has thus moved to potential risks of future GE products, for example, transfers of allergens or carcinogens, or anti-biotic resistance problems due to the use of marker genes that make transgenic plants resistant to ampicillin.[6]

The most important disputes over the health risks of GE foods have arisen over a study on GE potatoes, published by Arpad Pusztai from the Rowett Research Institute in Aberdeen, United Kingdom;[7] over potentially aller-genic effects of StarLink corn, a corn engineered to produce a protein (Cry9C) that acts as a natural insecticide; and over the risks of contaminat-ing the food supply through biopharming (the ProdiGene problem).

In 1999, Pusztai claimed that, in his experiments, rats fed with potatoes genetically engineered to produce GNA lectin had suffered reduced organ weights and immune system damage. Subsequent research by other scien-tists did not confirm these results. But the acrimonious dispute that devel-oped among scientists over the issue (Pusztai was sacked from his job) has fueled suspicions among agri-biotech critics as to the "real" health risks of GE foods.[8]

The StarLink problem has posed the most formidable health-related challenge to GE food to date. Because of concerns over possible allergeni-city, StarLink corn was approved in May 1998 by US regulators (the US Environmental Protection Agency, EPA, in this case) only for feed and industrial use, but not for food. In September 2000, consumer groups detected traces of StarLink in foods. StarLink was subsequently found in over 300 brand products. The ensuing controversy exposed weaknesses in the US regulatory system, in particular the inability of producers to effectively prevent cross-pollination and segregate crops in the US grain-handling system. It also exposed as ineffective the EPA's 1999 request to farmers to plant non-GE buffer crops around GE crops. Recalling products, testing activity, buybacks, and other measures have cost Aven-tis (the input supplier), seed firms, farmers, processors, and retailers several hundred million USD.[9]

Interestingly, the question of whether StarLink actually has allergenic effects disappeared from this controversy. The evidence available thus far does not support the allergenicity hypothesis. But agri-biotech critics remain unimpressed by this evidence. They emphasize the inability of regulators and producers to effectively segregate GE and non-GE products and protect consumers from potentially hazardous GE foods. They wonder what would have happened if StarLink had been a GE product with carcinogenic, contraceptive, or other health-related effects. They maintain that, even if currently approved GE foods were safe, future GE applications may involve risks of transferring toxins from one organ-ism to another, of creating new toxins, or of transferring compounds that could cause unexpected allergic reactions.

Other public health concerns have centered on problems of insufficient control of agri-biotech research and development. Both proponents and critics of the technology were alarmed by reports that Australian researchers working on infertility problems of mice accidentally engineered a virus that destroys the immune system in mice. It takes little imagination to grasp the public health consequences that could flow from an escape of such organisms from a laboratory. International regulations apply exclusively to trade in GE products. There are no enforceable international standards governing public safety aspects of research and development. Safety standards around the world remain very uneven. For a variety of reasons (e.g., reputation, access to capital and labor markets), agri-biotech firms in advanced industrialized countries are unlikely to exploit this situation by moving hazardous R&D activity to jurisdictions with more lax regulations. But there are grave concerns that as some developing countries, for example, China, India, Brazil, and Cuba, push forward with biotech research and development in a poorly regulated environment, the consequences could reach far beyond these countries. A large-scale biotech accident (e.g., the spread of hazardous GE microorganisms, plants or animals) would almost certainly have disastrous effects on public support for future innovation in agri-biotechnology.

Finally, a debate over the health (and also environmental) implications of using GE plants for the production of pharmaceutical, research, and industrial chemicals emerged in 2002. Examples of such products include medicines against Fabry's and Gaucher's diseases, blood substitutes, hormones, drugs for wound repair and treatment of cystic fibrosis, vaccines against hepatitis B, malaria, and cholera, and enzymes for making plastics and detergents. In technological terms, the possibilities for producing cheaper drugs and industrial and research chemicals appear almost unlimited. However, because the GE plants used for such purposes include widely used food crops, for example, corn, canola, tobacco, soybean, tomato, and potato, critics have argued that so-called biopharming could cause contamination of the food supply and also affect animals and ecosystems more generally. As of late 2002, no pharmaceutical products from GE crops and only three research and industrial chemicals of this nature had been approved for commercial cultivation. But the controversy is likely to grow stronger as marketing of many such products gets closer, particularly because the market for such products might be far larger than the market for GE food crops.[10]

The ProdiGene case illustrates such risks. In November 2002 it was discovered that thousands of bushels of food-grade soybeans grown in Nebraska were contaminated with volunteers of a drug-producing GE corn variety that had been grown on the same field the previous year.

The US Food and Drug Administration (FDA) ordered ProdiGene Inc., the developer of the seeds, to destroy the contaminated soybeans. The US government appears to have paid a large part of the cost involved. Fortunately, the problem was discovered and resolved before the contaminated soy reached consumer markets. The US Department of Agriculture then disclosed that the same firm had been involved in a somewhat similar contamination case in Iowa a few months earlier. It also initiated a process that was expected to lead to stricter regulation of biopharming.

ENVIRONMENTAL RISKS

While scientists tend to agree that the health risks of currently marketed GE foods are very low there is much more disagreement as to the long-term environmental risks posed by GE crops.[11] Proponents of agri-biotechnology claim that without massive productivity increases today's farmland of around one billion hectares will, because of population growth, have to expand to 3.9 billion hectares by 2050 to meet world food and feed demands. Assuming that the most productive and sustainable farmland is already under cultivation and that productivity gains through conventional (non-GE) technology are limited, they fear large-scale destruction of wilderness for farming. Green biotechnology could, in their view, help in boosting agricultural productivity on existing farmland and thus contribute to protecting the environment.

The proponents also claim that the technology contributes to environmentally friendlier (more sustainable) agriculture by reducing insecticide and herbicide input and preventing soil erosion. Many studies on GE corn, soybeans, and cotton provide some support for these claims (see further below).

The critics have focused primarily on whether and how the technology might affect existing species or ecosystems.[12] The first important controversy centered on the monarch butterfly. Research results published in 1999 and 2000 suggested that pollen from Bt corn was being blown onto milkweed, killing monarch butterfly larvae feeding on this weed. A series of papers published in 2001 and 2002 questioned the earlier evidence, showing that the relevant experiments had been conduced under unrealistic conditions (e.g., force-feeding unrealistically high amounts of the toxic protein produced by Bt corn to the caterpillars).[13]

Other environmental concerns have concentrated on the possibility of outcrossing. The critics fear that outcrossing could lead to more aggressive weeds or wild relatives of common crops that are resistant to diseases or environmental stresses as insect or herbicide resistant traits are transferred to unwanted species ("genetic drift").[14] Such criticism has provided a vehicle for linking concerns over agricultural biotechnology to the global biodiversity debate.

The most important product of this link is the Cartagena Biosafety Protocol, which was adopted in 2000 as part of the 1992 UN Biodiversity Convention and will come into force in September 2003. This international agreement promotes the precautionary principle for GE crops, that is, it shifts the burden of proof with regard to health and environmental risks to the producer side. It puts into place a so-called Advance Informed Agreement mechanism to ensure that no country imports GE crops or foods/feeds against its will or without its knowledge.

The agri-biotech–biodiversity linkage again made the headlines in late 2001 and early 2002. A report by Quist and Chapela, published in the journal *Nature* in November 2001, contended that transgenic DNA had introgressed[15] into traditional Mexican corn varieties.[16] Mexico, where today's corn has developed over thousands of years, is the world's biodiversity center for corn. The issue has been particularly sensitive also because Mexico banned the cultivation of transgenic corn in 1998, and because the 1992 UN Biodiversity Convention and the associated Cartagena Protocol pronounced fundamental reservations with regard to the introduction of transgenic species into centers of biodiversity.

The acrimony of the ensuing dispute among scientists has been reminiscent of the dispute over the 1999 GE potato study by Pusztai. The scientific evidence for and against introgression remains controversial. Nonetheless, NGOs and many policy-makers in Mexico and around the world seized on the incident to demand a ban on Mexican imports of US corn (the source of introgression), and to claim that agricultural biotechnology poses a threat to biodiversity.[17] The Mexican government did not ban imports of US corn (around 60 million tons per year), but it extended the ban on domestic cultivation of GE corn. The legal implications of the transgression problem remain unclear. Under Mexican law, "genetic contamination" is a crime. Whatever the outcome of this scientific and political controversy, most scientists believe that "gene-jumping" (introgression), "super weeds," and ecological change due to GE crop cultivation (e.g., through effects of GE crops on insect populations) are possible and potentially a serious problem.[18]

FOOD FOR THE POOR

Many countries achieved a 30-fold increase in crop production between the 1930s and 1960s, primarily due to new crop varieties and improved farming technologies, such as more effective machinery, fertilizers, insecticides, and herbicides. Another five- to tenfold increase occurred in the 1970s and 1980s with integrated pest management, varietal development, and new crop species. Many agricultural analysts claim that the potential for further productivity increases through conventional technologies has reached a plateau due to constraints imposed by plant physiology, land, and water resources. They portend that a technological leap of great proportions is required to feed a rapidly growing world population without destroying the environment.

The world population will reach over seven billion by 2015. More than two-thirds of humankind will live in developing countries. Despite substantial progress in reducing hunger, around 600 million people are predicted to experience malnutrition in 2015. The projected increase of the world population to 9 billion by 2050 is bound to make things worse.[19] Additional stress on the food supply is expected to come from growing urbanization in developing countries and increasing demand for protein foods, such as meat, eggs, and milk.[20] Table 2.1 illustrates the expected stress on the world food supply.[21]

Proponents of agri-biotechnology claim that this technology can provide the necessary boost in productivity without harming the environment. They contend that it promises to substantially improve yields of inbred crops and hybrids, and to narrow yield gaps by improving tolerance to environmental stress (e.g., poor soil, arid climate) and increasing yield stability. They also claim that agri-biotechnology will result in foods with more micronutrients (e.g., iron, zinc, vitamin A).[22]

These arguments have, in fact, become key to the agri-biotech industry's current efforts to convince the public and regulators that the technology should be promoted. One frequently used example is the sweet potato, which is a staple, particularly in East Africa. This potato is easy to store and supports people through periods of drought. A new GE variety of this crop, currently being tested in Kenya, resists the sweet potato virus which often destroys a large portion of the crop. Another example is

TABLE 2.1
Projected world cereal demand

	Production in 1999 (megatons, Mt)	Production needed in 2025 (Mt)	Yield in 1999 (tons/hectare)	Yield needed in 2025 (tons/hectare)
Wheat	585	900	2.7	3.8
Rice	607	900	3.1	4.3
Corn	605	1000	4.1	5.9
All cereals	2074	3100	2.9	4.1

Sources: Borlaug (2001); www.isaaa.org.

Golden Rice, a GE rice that produces beta carotene, a precursor of vitamin A, and thus acts against blindness and some childhood diseases in developing countries. Other benefits highlighted by the biotech industry are cheaper drugs, vaccines, and research and industrial chemicals produced through genetic modification of conventional crops.[23]

The critics maintain that food security could be increased in more effective and efficient ways by addressing other causes of food shortages and malnutrition. These causes include inefficient food distribution, poor irrigation systems, deficiencies in conventional pest and farm management, lack of credit facilities, political instability and wars, population growth, and so on. The proponents counter that solving these problems might be impossible or would probably come too late to cope with increasing food shortages and malnutrition. They hold that cultivation of biotech crops is a much quicker, cheaper, and risk-free solution than efforts to address all of the complex causes of food shortages referred to by the critics. The proponents also claim that adoption of GE crops rather than improving food distribution alone would promote local production, which would benefit small farmers and reduce dependency on other countries. The critics counter that adoption of GE crops would increase the dependency of developing country farmers on large multinational firms in industrialized countries that own the technology (see also below).[24]

The controversy over Golden Rice, a GE variety of rice, highlights these differences. Vitamin A deficiency contributes to childhood diseases and blindness among children who survive on rice-dominant diets. Agribiotech proponents argue that higher beta carotene content in the rice kernel of Golden Rice, which converts into vitamin A, would save around 120 million children. Golden Rice is currently field tested in the Philippines.

The critics claim that investment in this project of more than 100 million USD was inefficient. They propose that distributing vitamin A pills and teaching people to eat unpolished rice could reduce vitamin A deficiency at much lower cost. The proponents maintain that it is unfair on the part of the critics to prevent commercialization of Golden Rice and then assess the 100 million USD investment against the one GE variety alone—the know-how gained, they propose, could quickly and at lower cost lead to other new GE varieties.[25]

PATENTING OF THE FOOD CHAIN AND INDUSTRIAL CONCENTRATION

Agri-biotech critics claim that the technology will benefit primarily Western multinational firms and equip them with unprecedented control over the world's food supply. Particularly in Europe and many parts of the developing world, the technology is widely viewed as one developed by US multinational companies, adopted by US farmers, and forced onto the world's agricultural markets by US farmers and firms with the help of the US government.[26]

Except for hybrid technology in open-pollinating crops,[27] most new (non-GE) crop varieties introduced over the past 100 years have been public goods. Most of these varieties were in fact developed in universities or other publicly funded institutions. That is, seed producers and farmers using these varieties did not have to pay "technology fees" to inventors or developers of such crop varieties. In contrast, high costs of developing GE crops, stronger patent laws,[28] and the possibility of genetic enforcement (e.g., through "terminator" techniques[29]) have strengthened the control of the private sector in crop development and cultivation.[30]

The critics argue that transfers of the technology from rich to poor countries will remain very limited because agri-biotech patents are increasingly protected not only at the national but also the international level, notably by WTO and other international agreements. They anticipate that innovation will remain restricted primarily to what markets in the affluent parts of the world demand or need, because these customers have much more purchasing power. In addition, the critics point to what they regard as predatory behavior of Western firms and researchers with regard to the developing world's genetic resources. Several recent disputes over patents seem to have confirmed the critics' viewpoint. In most of these cases Western firms or individual researchers have sought patents for new varieties, or have fought off challenges against patents they hold. Farmers, government authorities, and NGOs in developing countries have been particularly alarmed by several instances where university researchers and firms in Western countries tried to obtain patents on slightly modified versions of traditional crops, for example, Basmati and Jasmine rice. They fear that such slightly modified and patented varieties could be designed for large-scale production in industrialized countries, thus crowding out farmers in developing countries.

The proponents of agri-biotechnology have dismissed such claims by pointing to possibilities of protecting farmers' rights through agreements by the International Union for the Protection of New Varieties of Plants (UPOV). They also argue that the WTO's agreement on trade related intellectual property rights (TRIPS agreement) offers protection for indigenous crop-varieties in developing countries. Moreover, the proponents highlight benefits that the technology could produce for smaller farmers in developing countries, and to the fact that agri-biotech companies and university researchers have in many cases given developing countries free access to the technology. They frequently refer to the example of Golden Rice, which was largely funded by the Rockefeller Foundation, and the

Kenyan sweet potato case, where the technology was donated. They have also asked for more public funding of agri-biotech R&D in developing countries so as to fill the gap left by private sector R&D (which is driven largely by market demand in industrialized countries). The critics remain skeptical, arguing that such ad hoc solutions are ineffective. The most fervent opponents see such arguments as nothing more than a strategy by agri-biotech firms to use selective donations and public funding as a means to get developing country farmers "hooked" on the technology before forcing them to pay for it.

Many critics of the technology, particularly in Europe and some developing countries, also claim that it promotes industrialized agriculture and vertical integration in food production worldwide.[31] They frequently point to Monsanto's strategy in the mid-1990s of buying up many seed companies before putting its first GE products on the market, and to the "terminator" technology. They note that one of the most important first-generation GE crops, Roundup Ready soybeans, was engineered to withstand the application of a herbicide produced by the same firm (glyphosphate, trade name Roundup). The technology producer, Monsanto, has thus been able to sell both seeds and the herbicide. Many analysts regard Monsanto's marketing of GE soybeans primarily as a strategy to extend the effect of its expiring patent on the Roundup herbicide. The critics also highlight that export-oriented GE crop production in the United States has been far more industrialized and vertically integrated than production of conventional crops in other countries. Even though this may be empirically questionable, they have jumped to the conclusion that GE crop adoption will accelerate an already existing trend towards ever more industrialized farming.[32]

More generally, the technology tends to be associated with a small number of "gene giants" that control the world market. Indeed, the agri-biotech industry has experienced substantial concentration. In the 1980s small- to medium-sized firms played a very active role in innovation in this field. Many of these firms were bought up by the life sciences industry in the 1990s.[33] Input providers have also expanded their control over the seed industry. Many analysts expect that this trend will develop further "downstream" to food processors, and they point to agricultural biotechnology as the driving force.[34]

By the end of the 1990s, six firms, Novartis, Monsanto, DuPont, Zeneca, AgrEvo, and Rhône-Poulenc (the latter two merged to form Aventis), accounted for almost 100 percent of the world market for GE seeds, around 60 percent of the global crop protection market, and over 20 percent of the global seed market. Analysts have noted a slowdown in mergers in recent years and a separation of pharmaceutical and agri-biotech business in some leading firms. It appears, however, that control by large multinational firms in the agri-biotech sector has continued to grow in other ways, including through joint ventures and other forms of collaboration.[35]

High industrial concentration can also be observed on the downstream side of the food supply chain (food processors, retailers). Whereas the food processing industry is most concentrated in the United States, retailers wield more market power in the European Union. Agri-biotech critics fear that farmers could be economically squashed between an oligopoly on the input side (seeds and crop protection) and the output side (processors, retailers) if the technology was widely adopted.[36] As noted by Heffernan: "the farmer becomes a grower, providing the labour and often some capital but never owning the product as it moves through the food system and never making the major management decision."[37]

Proponents of the technology refute such arguments by pointing to studies suggesting that farmers receive a large share of the benefits of GE crops vis-à-vis seed companies, consumers, and technology inventors. They also highlight results of studies suggesting that, at least with regard to cotton, small farmers tend to benefit as much or even more from GE crops than big farmers.[38]

ETHICAL CONCERNS

Many opponents of agri-biotechnology believe that "it is not natural" and implies "tampering with nature". In their view, the technology conflicts with fundamental ethical norms, notably norms with regard to nature as well as human and animal rights. The critics point primarily to the fact that genetic engineering allows for the transfer of genetic material across different species, which is not possible in conventional breeding. They are particularly worried about the potential for genetic engineering of traits in animals or even human beings. Instances such as the transfer of genes from jelly fish to rabbits to make them glow in the dark (labeled "transgenic art" by the creators), the transfer of salmon genes into tomatoes to prevent cold storage damage, and the announcement of a group of scientists in 2001 that they would try to clone humans have all but reduced these fears. The controversies over stem-cell research and pre-implantation diagnostics in in-vitro fertilization, which emerged in the late 1990s, have served as additional catalysts for ethically motivated criticism of agricultural biotechnology.[39]

Agri-biotech proponents maintain that the technology is simply a more precise and cost-efficient method of plant and animal breeding. In their view, it serves to transfer one or a small number of genes with known effects from one organism to another. It may thus even be safer than traditional breeding, which swaps thousands of genes with unknown functions in a haphazard fashion. The proponents also argue that there is nothing immoral in transferring genes between plants, animals, or even humans. Humans, for example, share around 99 percent of their genes with chimpanzees, and around 50 percent with plants. The proponents conclude that the essence of an organism is not found in its genes.

Yet other ethical concerns derive from religious or other norms that prohibit the consumption of certain animals or animal products (e.g., swine) or meat as such. If, for example, genes from swine were transferred into a vegetable, Jewish, Muslim, and vegetarian consumers may not wish to eat this product.[40] The controversy over such problems has so far remained subdued, however, because producer information on where the inserted genes come from is usually available, and because no products containing problematic genes are currently on the market. In the United States, for example, Muslim and Jewish organizations have so far not objected to existing GE foods. But opposition could intensify quickly if products of the type mentioned above appeared on the market and if producers were unwilling and/or unable to label them effectively.

Finally, the issue of labeling of GE foods has led to a debate about fundamental consumer rights. Advocates of mandatory labeling of GE foods (usually persons more critical of the technology) contend that consumers have the right to know what is in their food and how that food is produced. This right is said to apply irrespective of whether a production technology or the end product pose a risk to human health or the environment. Opponents of labeling (usually proponents of the technology) hold that voluntary labeling would be sufficient to address such concerns. In their view, mandatory labeling would open a Pandora's box. They claim that labeling is costly—with estimates that mandatory GE food labeling could add 10–20 percent to consumer prices. They also hold that such a policy would wreak havoc on the world's food supply system if every minority succeeded in obtaining mandatory labeling with respect to its preferred production technology. The critics of labeling maintain that imposing costs on industry and consumers of this order of magnitude would only be warranted if it reduced public health or environmental risks. They also consider that the high costs of protecting consumers against what they regard as imaginary risks threaten to reduce spending on "real" risks.

FARM-LEVEL PROFITS AND REGULATORY ECONOMICS

This section reviews the available agronomic evidence on farm-level benefits of GE crops and the effects of regulation in this context. The analysis shows that uncertainties over farm-level profits and rising regulatory costs have created dire straights for producers of first-generation GE food crops (GE corn, GE soy). Quite dramatic changes on the supply and demand side would be required to reverse this trend.

Farm-Level Profits

Large-scale planting of GE crops is relatively recent, with the first harvests of GE corn, soybean, and cotton in the United States in 1996. The benefits of agricultural biotechnology for the various actors in the food production chain are thus still difficult to determine.

Table 2.2 shows that US farmers have adopted the new technology at an astonishing pace. In 2002, the shares of GE crops had grown to 34 percent for corn, 75 percent for soybeans, and 71 percent for cotton. Farmers in other countries, with the exception of Argentina, have embraced the technology at much slower speed. Globally, shares in 2001 were 46 percent for transgenic soy, 20 percent for cotton, 11 percent for canola, and 7 percent for corn.[41]

Such figures show that US farmers have cultivated large amounts of GE crops. Contrary to what proponents of the technology frequently claim, they do not per se demonstrate that GE crops are, in terms to be defined, superior to their conventional counterparts. Farm-level decisions on crop production hinge on a variety of factors, including, for example, expected yields, consumer demand, government regulation and subsidies, and the structure of grain-handling systems.

Agronomists have studied the yields, environmental effects (notably, herbicide and insecticide use), and profits associated with individual GE crops in several countries.[42] The results suggest that benefits vary substantially across crop varieties, farms, and other conditions. They also suggest that, on average, the benefits of GE crops currently on the market are modest.[43] The concluding statement in a 2002 USDA report, a source that can hardly be suspected of anti-biotech bias, exemplifies these uncertainties about farm-level benefits of GE crops: "All in all, we conclude that

TABLE 2.2
Percent of US acreage planted with GE crops

	1996	1997	1998	1999	2000	2001	2002
Soybeans	2	13	37	47	54	60	75
Cotton	–	–	45	48	61	69	71
Corn	–	–	25	37	25	26	34

Sources: Carpenter and Gianessi (2001); www.isaaa.org; www.bio.org.

there are tangible benefits to farmers adopting first-generation GE crops. Not all of the benefits are reflected in standard measures of net returns. But in looking at farm-level impacts, it appears that farmers are, at least, not being disadvantaged by the advent of GE pest and herbicide-resistant seed."[44]

Carpenter and Gianessi (2001) estimate that aggregate gains in net revenues in the United States in 1999 amounted to minus (i.e., a loss of) 35 million USD for Bt corn, a profit of 99 million USD for Bt cotton, and a profit of 216 million USD for RR soybeans. They also note that GE crops generally reduced weed-control costs as well as herbicide and insecticide use. A survey of GE crop performance by the USDA published in 1999 indicates that yields from biotech crops were not consistently higher compared to their conventional counterparts. The USDA data suggests some gains for cotton, both in yields and profits—although profits do not seem to be a function of reduced pesticide and insecticide use, which were supposed to be the main benefits. GE soybeans were not associated with increased yields or reduced pesticide/insecticide use. These conclusions hold when controlling for differences in soil, weather, and regional farming practices.

Data compiled by the European Union is largely in line with these assessments. Table 2.3 shows returns (profits) for GE- and non-GE soybeans. Table 2.4 summarizes what I see as "average" findings on yields, seed costs, herbicide and insecticide costs, and profitability of the three most important GE crops in a wide range of agronomic studies.[45] Studies on other GE crop varieties produce a similar picture, with different sorts of benefits varying widely across types of crops.[46]

Such estimates blur the fact that benefits vary enormously also across geographical areas and other conditions. The benefits of GE soybeans and GE corn, for example, are very much affected by variation in the extent and type of weed and pest problems, respectively. Another problem in estimating benefits is that GE and non-GE crop adoption may create interdependencies. For example, widespread use of GE soybeans in the

TABLE 2.3
Returns on GE and non-GE soybeans

Crop	Yield (tons/hectare)	Seed cost (euros/hectare)	Total cost (excluding land, labor) (euros/hectare)	Return on land/labor (euros/hectare)
GE	3.295	57	254	320
Non-GE	3.430	42	274	322

Source: EU (2000a).

TABLE 2.4

Benefits of the three most widely used GE crops relative to their conventional counterparts

Crop	Yield	Seed cost	Herbicide, insecticide cost	Profitability
GE corn	Similar to higher	Higher	Similar	Similar
GE soybeans	Similar	Higher	Lower	Similar to higher
GE cotton	Higher	Higher	Lower	Higher

Sources: Based on Carpenter and Gianessi (2001), EU (2000a), and USDA (1999b, 2002).

United States has created more competition for producers of conventional herbicides. As a result, farmers not adopting GE soybeans have also benefited from reduced weed-control costs. Results may also be biased if early adopters benefit more than late adopters.[47] Finally, virtually all estimates (unrealistically) assume that GE- and non-GE crops are traded at the same price, and they ignore production cost implications emanating from changes in consumer preferences (e.g., demands for labeling and identity preservation (IP)). Such variables can have massive effects on profitability at the farm level and thus farmer decisions on whether or not to plant GE crops.[48] I return to this issue below.

In summary, most agronomic studies suggest some increase in yields for corn and cotton, but not soybeans, some reduction of insecticide and pesticide use for cotton and soybeans, but not corn, and somewhat increased profits mainly for cotton and soybeans. In the case of GE soybeans, most analysts have noted reduced pest management costs, higher seed-costs and somewhat lower yields canceling each other out, thus not resulting in substantially higher profits for farmers. Bt corn yield increases are linked to the extent of infestation by corn borers while higher seed costs and reduced pest control costs tend to cancel each other out. The most consistently positive results obtain only for GE cotton, a non-food product, which appears to involve higher yields, lower herbicide and insecticide use, and higher profits for farmers.[49]

In view of this evidence, it appears that the rapid expansion of GE crop acreage in the United States and Argentina, in particular, has been driven by forces other than short-term farm profits. Such forces include, for example, marketing strategies of technology-input suppliers,[50] a convenience effect,[51] the profile of adopters, costs of segregating GE and non-GE crops, and farmers' assumptions about consumer preferences.[52] Whether GE crops are, on average, more profitable for farmers will only be known once we have long-term studies that take into account yearly fluctuations in yields unrelated to agri-biotechnology per se, variation in prices of seeds and agro-chemical products, costs of labeling and/ or IP, as well as developments on the demand side (e.g., commodity prices, premiums for GE or non-GE crops).

So far we also know very little about the distribution of benefits among the economic actors involved. Some analysts propose that middle to large-size industrialized farms are, and will continue to be, the main beneficiaries of the technology.[53] Others think that agri-biotech companies may acquire enough market power to obtain monopoly or oligopoly rents at the expense of farmers (and also consumers). Recent studies have questioned these propositions. One study shows, for example, that small farmers in China and South Africa have benefited more than larger farmers from growing Bt cotton. In addition, more than 80% of the benefits appear to have gone to farmers.[54] However, the available evidence is too sparse for a reliable assessment. The only compelling result we have is that consumers have not benefited from the first generation of agri-biotech products, because these are exclusively input-oriented. From the perspective of consumers, existing GE corn, soy, and cotton are neither superior in quality, nor are they cheaper.[55]

The evidence discussed here pertains exclusively to GE crops commercially grown at present whose most important traits are increased herbicide tolerance and insect resistance. Short to medium term improvements are concentrating on transferring more than one gene (stacked traits, again for the purpose of insect and herbicide resistance). They are also concentrating on extending the technology to new varieties, for example, wheat, rice, sugarbeet, potato, and on virus and fungus resistance in fruit, vegetables, and wheat. In the longer term, improvements will focus also on output traits, for example, soybeans with improved nutritional traits for animals, corn containing more protein and better amino acid balances, colored cotton, wrinkle-resistant cotton, and nutraceuticals.[56] Many analysts assume that first generation input traits will continue to dominate the global GE crop market, that new generations of GE crops will be adopted more slowly, and that most quality-trait crops will capture mainly niche markets. In addition, we may see some growth in adoption of GE crops for non-food purposes, for example, in the paper and chemical industry, or as an energy source.[57] It is possible but not certain that these future products will be beneficial to farmers (and also other economic actors).[58]

Regulatory Economics

Extant agronomic assessments of agricultural biotechnology are largely blind on the demand side, notably, with regard to consumer acceptance of GE products, regulation, and market prices of GE products. This deficiency is problematic because developments on the demand side have massive implications for profitability on the supply side and therefore also for adoption rates. For example, if demands for mandatory labeling of GE products and IP[59] prevailed, farmers' profits from GE crops, which currently are small, could be eliminated due to segregation, IP, and labeling costs, as well as possible premiums for non-GE products. Agri-biotech and seed industries as well as GE crop farmers and downstream producers (food processors, retailers) have become very vulnerable to this problem because they have concentrated exclusively on the input side.

Not surprisingly then, demands for labeling and IP have been extremely controversial. In a situation where returns on GE crops are not or only slightly superior to returns on non-GE crops, the allocation of labeling or IP costs has a decisive impact on agri-biotech industry profits and farm level adoption of GE crops. Labeling can take two forms: end products (e.g., food in the supermarket) can be labeled as genetically engineered ("positive labeling"), or as not genetically engineered ("negative labeling"). The former solution imposes the costs of labeling on producers of GE products, the latter solution burdens producers of non-GE crops.[60] IP involves labeling and monitoring throughout the food chain and is therefore more expensive than labeling of the end-product alone. Its rationale is twofold: first, to enable public authorities, producers, and consumers to locate and remove public health or environmental problems in the feed or food chain at any point and time (e.g., if a GE food product poses an allergenicity problem, or if unwanted introgression or outcrossing occurs); second, to increase consumer trust in food safety through more public control.

Economists have dwelled extensively on the advantages and disadvantages of imposing labeling or IP costs on GE crop or non-GE crop producers. Many of them advocate labeling of non-GE (or GE-free) products. They claim that there is virtually no evidence for health risks of GE food, and that GE organisms are already widely dispersed in the food chain. In essence, they claim that labeling GE products would not convey useful information to consumers.[61] Based on the same arguments they reject IP for GE foods. They contend that voluntary labeling of GE or non-GE products would be sufficient. Government's role should, in their view, be restricted to protecting consumers against misleading or fraudulent labels.

Analysts who are more critical of agricultural biotechnology tend to dismiss such arguments. They hold that scientific evidence alone cannot be the sole arbiter in this case. Under the banner of "consumer sovereignty," they claim that consumers have the right to know how their food is produced and what it contains, even more so when many consumers feel uneasy about GE products and as long as there are some scientific uncertainties. Agri-biotech critics dismiss the argument that GE organisms are already so pervasive in the food chain that most processed food would have to be labeled as GE food—opponents of labeling in fact argue that this would be excessively expensive and nonsensical. Agri-biotech critics maintain that acceptance of this argument would reward firms that have "contaminated" the food chain with GE organisms without letting consumers know. It would, in their view, encourage more firms to create fait accomplis at the expense of consumers.[62]

Since the late 1990s, many industrialized countries have introduced mandatory labeling of GE products, most notably, all EU countries, Japan, South Korea, China, Russia, and Australia. We do not yet know precisely the costs of this regulation, and who bears these costs. Estimates vary enormously, depending on the country, the GE products covered, thresholds for labeling, and a range of other factors. In my view the most systematic and trustworthy assessment is the one by the EU (2000a), which takes into account a wide range of other assessments, and also IP and labeling costs for (non-GE) specialty crops that have been traded with labeling and IP in niche markets for a long time.[63] IP costs occur in seed production, on the farm, in transport, storage, processing, labeling, and distribution. The EU estimates that IP (the most expensive solution) would increase grain prices by 6–17 percent over the farmgate price.[64]

Under current conditions, costs of this order would clearly make existing GE crops uneconomical for most farmers. Returns of GE crops are, on average, insufficient to cancel out such IP costs, even if we assume that GE and non-GE crops fetch the same price on the market.

If we adopt more realistic assumptions, the commercial prospects of currently marketed GE crops are even worse. Consumers in countries with mandatory positive labeling are usually also more critical of the technology. Producers of GE crops will thus be unable to transfer labeling or IP costs to consumers.[65] On the contrary, figure 2.1 suggests that consumers in many industrialized countries may be willing to pay a substantial premium for non-GE foods.

In other words, under conditions of growing societal demand for mandatory (positive or negative, or both) labeling and IP, farmers producing non-GE crops will find it easier than GE crop producers to shift labeling and IP costs to consumers. Indeed, they need negative labeling and IP to signal the quality of their products to market participants and fetch a premium. Farmers relying on agronomic (input) traits in GE crops are bound to lose. Farmers relying on quality (or output-oriented) traits of GE crops are more likely to benefit (if or when such crops are marketed).[66] This is approximately the situation as it is evolving in Europe and Japan. GE crop farmers and input suppliers in North America appear to understand this development. They have been fighting hard to

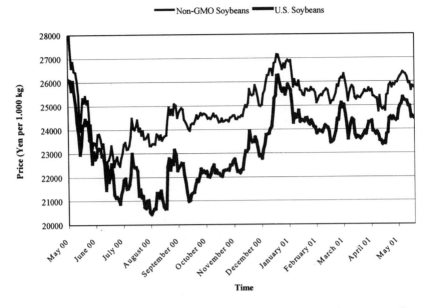

Figure 2.1 Prices of GE (US) soy and non-GE soy. *Source*: Tokyo commodity exchange, www.tge.or.jp/english/market/chart.e/inputpram_m.e.html.

prevent mandatory positive labeling in the United States and abroad and have tried to direct societal demands towards voluntary labeling of non-GE products. Mandatory positive labeling for GE foods alone mainly imposes costs on those producers who tend to fetch a negative premium in the market. It imposes much smaller costs on producers of non-GM crops who currently fetch a premium.

For GE foods to become profitable under a mandatory labeling or IP system, several conditions would have to be met. First, prices of GE seeds and related agrochemical products would have to decrease. Such a development is quite likely because of technological innovation and scale economies. Second, yields of GE crops would have to increase. This is quite possible. Third, labeling and IP costs would have to decrease. Again, this is possible if large quantities are traded and processed and new technologies make IP and labeling more cost efficient. Fourth, GE products would have to involve health or environmental quality traits that are so obvious to consumers that they become willing to pay a premium that cancels out IP and higher input costs.[67] This would imply a reversal of current conditions, where premiums are paid for non-GE foods, and where existing GE foods are neither decisively cheaper nor of superior quality.

Whether these conditions will be met within the foreseeable future remains open. In the short to medium term, GE food producers are in dire straits. Quite dramatic changes on the supply and demand side would be required to reverse this situation.

CONCLUSION

Current controversies over agricultural biotechnology are characterized by an astounding mélange of enthusiastic promises, apocalyptic predictions, wishful thinking, scientific evidence, and moral debate. These controversies, the most important of which are highlighted in this chapter, have centered on health and environmental risks, food security issues, concerns over patenting of the food chain and industrial concentration, ethical concerns, farm-level profits, and regulatory issues.

All of these controversies are ongoing. With regard to health risks, the proponents of agricultural biotechnology appear to have won the upper hand for the time being. Critics of the technology have thus far not been able to come up with widely accepted scientific evidence for such risks. With regard to environmental implications, food security in developing countries, and farm-level benefits, natural and social scientists remain deeply divided over the risks and benefits of the technology. As to other issues, it seems impossible to find objective and/or commonly accepted criteria on which judgments and compromises could be based. Examples include ethical concerns and (in part ideological) concerns over corporate dominance of the food chain and industrial concentration.

Food biotechnology is in a much deeper crisis than most of its proponents tend to admit.[68] It has run into trouble on two fronts. On the demand side, the societal controversies discussed above have depressed consumer (i.e., market-driven) and political support for the technology. On the supply side, uncertainty about farm-level benefits, increasing regulatory costs, and negative consumer reactions have limited, and often reduced, the attractiveness of the technology to farmers, food processors, and retailers. Regulatory polarization and trade tensions over regulatory differences across countries, which are examined in chapters 3–6, have exacerbated this crisis.

In other words, food biotechnology may be heading for a dead end. On the one hand, most investment in food biotech R&D has been, and will continue to be, directed at crops that are most useful to key economic actors in advanced industrialized countries. Developers of these crops, most of them are commercial firms, need large and captive markets with high purchasing power to turn their large investments into profits. This is why these firms have focused heavily on corn, soybeans, and canola and are now anxious to follow up with GE wheat and rice. They have very little incentive to invest in drought-, cold-, salt- or virus-resistant crops that could be useful primarily in developing countries and would be grown there on a smaller scale by less wealthy farmers. Add to that the observation that the precautionary approach to food biotech regulation, adopted by the European Union, appears to be gaining ground also in developing countries (see chapter 3). As a result, the promised new "green revolution" in developing countries may remain a fata morgana entertained by food biotech advocates. On the other hand, in most advanced industrialized countries, where developers of GE crops have much stronger incentives to invest, demand among consumers and the food industry for GE food has remained low and is unlikely to increase in the next few years. The first generation of GE crops has produced some benefits for some farmers in some rich countries, primarily in terms of lower production costs. More nutritious GE feed crops, which may be marketed soon, could be useful to some farmers because they might lower input costs in meat and dairy production. But neither the food industry nor consumers in rich countries are likely to greet more nutritious second generation GE foods with enthusiasm (the first generation of GE crops has not produced any consumer benefits). From the perspective of the food industry, more nutritious GE crops may not be very economical, irrespective of consumer concerns about GE food. Most crops in rich countries are used as food ingredients. And many food producers will find it cheaper and more convenient to add vitamins and other food ingredients during production rather than to use more nutritious GE crops to produce more nutritious food. The retail market for GE nutraceuticals is likely to be too small to compensate for this problem and make large scale R&D in this area worthwhile. In addition, consumers who are fussy about the nutritional quality of food tend to dislike GE food.

To say the least: this combination of large-scale investment in GE crops for rich markets that do not need and/or want these crops and very low levels of investment in GE crops that may benefit primarily poorer countries does not bode well for the future of food biotechnology.

To simplify the argument in this chapter, I have discussed the main controversies over agri-biotechnology in generic terms. In the subsequent chapters I show that the extent and implications of existing controversies have varied strongly across countries. Chapter 3 describes and compares regulatory and market developments in the European Union, the United States, and a range of other countries. Chapters 4 and 5 focus on explaining why observed regulatory and market developments differ very much across countries.

CHAPTER THREE

Polarization

.

IN THIS CHAPTER I examine regulatory and market responses to agricultural biotechnology in a range of countries, including the world's largest economies. The global agri-biotech landscape thus identified is characterized by polarization. The two heavyweights in this system are the European Union, which has imposed severe constraints on the technology, and the United States, which maintains much more permissive policies. The policies of these two jurisdictions are examined in most detail in this chapter. The European Union and the United States are able to develop their regulations relatively independently of each other and of other countries. Regulatory and market responses in most other countries are to a substantial degree driven by developments in the European Union and the United States, the world's largest economies. Some of these other countries, for example, Switzerland, Norway, and many Central and Eastern European countries, have closely aligned with the European Union. Others, notably Canada and Argentina, have aligned with the United States. Yet other countries have been struggling to find some middle ground. Examples include Australia, Brazil, China, Egypt, India, Japan, Mexico, Russia, and South Africa. The analysis in this chapter provides the starting point for chapters 4 and 5, in which I explain why polarization has developed.

REGULATORY RESPONSES IN THE EUROPEAN UNION

At the outset of the regulatory process in the mid-1980s, authorities in the European Union, the United States, and many other countries were divided over whether to restrict or promote the then emerging biotechnology in agriculture. They were also divided over whether to regulate the technology predominantly in terms of products or production processes.[1] Regulating products is based on the assumption that there is nothing unique or particularly risky in applying genetic engineering in agriculture, and that products resulting from such technology are usually the same as comparable products obtained via conventional agricultural methods. Stricter rules apply only when end products (notably, food) are not "substantially equivalent" to conventionally produced counterparts.[2] Regulation of production processes reflects the assumption that genetic engineering poses unique risks, and that the technology as such must be regulated. The latter approach has prevailed in the European Union. The European Union has adopted a range of regulatory measures specifically for agri-biotech applications, with strong emphasis on the precautionary principle.[3] In contrast, the United States, Canada, and a few other countries have embraced a product-oriented approach.

The stringency (restrictiveness) of policies, on which this analysis primarily focuses, will be measured and compared through an assessment of approval and labeling regulations as well as field trials, commercial GE crop production, and imports and sales of GE foods.

Approval and Labeling Regulation

In 1990, the European Council[4] adopted Directive 90/220 on the deliberate release of genetically engineered organisms into the environment.[5] This directive was primarily designed to address environmental aspects of biotechnology. That is, it governed approvals of GE crops for field trials and commercial cultivation. However, until the Novel Foods Regulation was adopted in 1997 (see below) this directive was interpreted broadly to apply also to the approval of GE food. Highly complicated decision-making procedures associated with this regulation implied that imports of GE seeds, field trials, commercial planting of GE crops, and commercialization of GE food and feed products were, de facto, still subject to approval by individual EU member countries.[6]

The limitations of the 1990 directive became apparent when the Competent Authorities of the European Union[7] and the Commission approved a Bt corn variety developed by Novartis (1996), and Monsanto's Roundup Ready soybeans (1996). Disputes among EU countries over the conditions for approval combined with vocal opposition by consumer and environmental groups led to long delays in the approval process, and to uneven implementation of the European Union's approval decisions. Most disturbingly for the European Union, whose internal market provides for the free movement of goods (including agricultural goods), some EU countries imposed unilateral restrictions or bans on GE products that had been cleared by the European Union.

By 1997 the European Union's agri-biotech approval policy was in disarray. Since April 1998, there has been a de facto moratorium on new approvals.[8] As of late 2002, the strongest supporters of this moratorium were Austria, Denmark, France, Greece, Italy, and Luxembourg. These countries maintained that they would not approve any new agricultural GE products until strict labeling and tracing regulations were established. Belgium, Sweden, Portugal, Finland, and Germany adopted somewhat more moderate positions. They emphasized the precautionary principle, arguing that no approvals of new GE products should be issued unless companies could demonstrate that these products did not have adverse effects on the environment and human health. Only the United Kingdom, the Netherlands, and the EU Commission explicitly opposed a formal moratorium.[9]

As shown in Table 3.1, the European Union has approved a relatively small number of GE crops under Directive 220/90 (approval for field trials, commercial cultivation, and import/sale in the form of live GE organisms) and the Novel Foods Regulation (approval for food/feed purposes, primarily in processed form).

In view of this gridlock and the fact that several GE products had, by 1997, already been formally approved by the European Union for commercialization, the European Union intensified its efforts to harmonize approval standards and labeling requirements. In 1997 the European Parliament and the Council adopted Regulation 258/97, the so-called Novel Foods Regulation. This regulation applies to foods hitherto unknown in Europe, including GE foods, and establishes approval procedures in which importers or producers have to show that the food in question is safe for human consumption. In its original version, it requires labeling of GE foods if a genetic modification can be detected. No label is required for products that, in terms of their nutritional or allergenic properties, are "comparable" (substantially equivalent) to conventional products. Virtually all enzymes, vitamins, flavorings and other food additives are exempt from the Novel Foods Regulation as adopted in 1997. Many of these exemptions have been eliminated since.[10]

The 1997 Novel Foods Regulation marks a sea change in the European Union's food safety policy. Thus far, commercialization of food products had been granted without specific approval or notification as long as such products were not incompatible with general or specific regulations (abuse principle). The safety of food products was, by assumption, derived from experience, and not from specific scientific risk assessment. In contrast, the Novel Foods Regulation has imposed legal conditions not only on specific substances but on entire foods. Before 1997, such conditions (e.g., thresholds and risk assessment) only applied to food additives. Since 1997, GE foods (and other "novel" foods) require individual approval before commercialization. Any novel food that is not explicitly approved is prohibited (prohibition principle).

The Novel Foods Regulation (258/97) as such was largely inoperable. It did not define thresholds, testing methods, products subject to testing, and the content of labels. As noted above, it contained many exemptions from approval and labeling rules. And it did not apply to granted or pending approvals: Bt corn and Roundup Ready soybeans, which had been approved by the European Union in 1996, were not covered. Worried about these gaps, some EU countries started to introduce national approval and labeling regulations. Moreover, several states (e.g., Italy) unilaterally blocked imports of several GE products that had been approved through the Novel Food Regulation's simplified notification procedure, which was based on the "substantial equivalence" criterion. These developments risked inhibiting the free flow of goods in the European Union's internal market.[11]

To halt and reverse this trend, the EU Commission and the Council issued several additional regulations. Regulations 1813/97 and 1139/98 required the labeling of food products containing already approved GE soybeans and GE corn, but did not close the other gaps. In January 2000, the Commission issued a standard (49/2000) that mandates labeling if a food product is at least one percent genetically engineered. For such products, the label "genetically modified" is mandatory. An additional regulation (50/2000) has extended the labeling requirement to food ingredients containing GE additives and flavorings if GE organisms can be detected.

In 2001–2003 debate in the European Union focused on how to overcome deadlock in the approval process (notably, the moratorium in place since 1998), and how to implement and extend existing labeling laws.

In February 2001, the EU Council and the European Parliament adopted Directive 2001/18/EC. This new directive superseded Directive 220/90 in October 2002 and is directly applicable in all EU member countries. Like the old directive, the new law governs approvals for field trials, GE crop cultivation, and importation of crops that can propagate (e.g., corn, soy, canola, tomato). Like the old directive it concentrates on environmental risk assessment in this context. Food/feed safety issues are governed by the Novel Foods Regulation, which is also being revised (see below).

The most noteworthy changes include the following. Approvals are limited to a maximum of 10 years. Renewals are possible. The use of antibiotic resistance markers will be phased out between 2005 and 2008. Environmental monitoring of field trials and commercial cultivation will be intensified. The approval process as well as field trials and commercial cultivation will be subject to extensive transparency measures (including, e.g., public registers of trial and production sites). The new directive also contains calls for new and stricter legislation on traceability, liability, and labeling. Decision-making procedures remain largely the same as under the old directive.

The new law was widely regarded as necessary for reactivating the approval process. It is unlikely, however, that it will have this effect in the near future. The decision-making rules in the new directive remain

TABLE 3.1
GE food/feed crops approved by the European Union

Product	Year of approval	Approval of plant	Approval for food and/or feed
Corn			
AgrEvo T25 (Aventis)	1998	Yes: planting, import, processing	Yes (food and feed)
Bt 176 corn (Syngenta)	1997	Yes: planting, import, processing	Yes (food and feed)
MON 810 (Monsanto)	1997	Yes: planting, import, processing	Yes (food and feed)
MON 809 (Monsanto)	1998 (limited approval)	No	Yes (for food additives)
Bt 11 (Syngenta)	1998 (limited approval)	Yes: import, processing, but not planting	Yes (only for food additives)
Soybeans			
RR soybeans (Monsanto)	1996	Yes: import, processing, but not planting	Yes (food and feed)
Canola (rapeseed)			
PGS MS1xRF 1 (Aventis)	1997 (limited approval)	Yes: only seed production	Yes (refined oil)

PGS MS1xRF 1, MS1xRF 2 (two applications) (Plant Genetic Systems N.V.)	1997 (limited approval)	Yes: planting, import, processing	Yes (refined oil)
AgrEvo Topas 19/2 (Aventis)	1997 (limited approval)	Yes: only for import and processing, not for planting	Yes (refined oil)
AgrEvo Falcon GS 40/90 (Aventis)	1999 (limited approval)	No	Yes (refined oil)
GT 43	1997 (limited approval)	No	Yes (refined oil)
Liberator L 62	1999 (limited approval)	No	Yes (refined oil)
MS8xRF3	1999 (limited approval)	No	Yes (refined oil)
Other			
Riboflavin/vitamin B2	2000 (limited approval)	No	Yes
Two types of oil from GE cotton	2002 (limited approval)	No	Yes (refined oil)

Sources: www.transgen.de; www.agbios.com; EU (2001).

Note: Other approved GE products include: Bejo Zaden (RM 3-3; RM 3-4; RM 3-6) Chicorée/Radicchio for seed production, Seita/F tobacco, and several varieties of flowers. Plants were approved according to Directive 220/90. For planting, individual EU country permits are required in addition. Foods were approved according to the Novel Foods Regulation—usually through notification and use of the principle of "substantial equivalence."

largely the same as in Directive 220/90. Applications must be addressed to one or more national authorities. These authorities evaluate applications and send their recommendations to the EU Commission. The Commission submits such applications to all EU member countries for consultation. Scientific committees of the European Union are also consulted. De jure, the Commission has the authority to issue approvals after these consultations unless there is a consensus decision to the contrary in the Council. De facto, the Commission has been, and will continue to be, highly reluctant to overrule member states in this area. Indeed, six EU countries (see above) insist that labeling, traceability, and liability issues, as well as questions relating to exports of GE products to third-world countries and thresholds for acceptable GE contamination of seeds must be resolved first before new approvals are considered. It could easily take two to three years before these problems are fully resolved through new EU laws and their implementation by all EU member states.

In other words, under the moratorium since 1998 each EU country can, de facto, block approvals: if any one EU country objects to a favorable recommendation of any other EU country's Competent Authority, a decision on approval is required at the EU level; at that point, the request for approval runs into the de facto EU moratorium. Moreover, even if the (informal, i.e. de facto) moratorium is abandoned, which could take place in late 2003 or 2004, it is unlikely that the Commission will use its full authority under Directive 2001/18/EC and overrule objecting EU member states. Those overruled would do everything they could to prevent the cultivation and marketing of EU-approved GE crops in their countries. In July 2001 the EU Commission proposed a new law that addresses some of the above mentioned concerns. According to the Commission, this law could enter into force in late 2003 or 2004 and supersede the application of the Novel Foods Regulation to agri-biotech products. It would cover food and feed products. Minimal unintentional and accidental "contamination" with GE organisms not approved in the European Union would be tolerated, with a proposed threshold of 0.5 percent GE content of the ingredient, provided the newly established European Food Safety Authority (EFSA)[12] or other scientific bodies of the European Union granted that such contamination did not pose a health risk. For EU-approved GE products the threshold for mandatory labeling would be 0.9 percent of the ingredient concerned. More generally, the proposed law is to cover foods and feeds with a GE content of one percent or more.

All applications for approval would have to be submitted to the EFSA and would be subject to a comprehensive safety assessment by this authority. This procedure would supersede the notification procedure in which the safety of a product is inferred from "substantial equivalence." In other words, pre-market safety testing will become more elaborate and mandatory. Applicants will have to submit comprehensive documentation. This documentation and the products for which approval is sought could be examined by national or private laboratories. Decisions on approval are to be taken by the EU Commission based on reports by the EFSA. Approvals would be limited to 10 years. Extensions would be possible. All approved foods and additives are to be listed in a publicly accessible registry and detailed documentation would be available on request. Products approved under the Novel Foods Regulation would again have to be approved under the new procedure within nine years of their marketing, and documents would have to be submitted one year after entry into force of the new regulation.

Labeling of GE products would be required not primarily on the grounds of whether GE organisms can be detected in the end product, but on the grounds of how GE products were produced. The principal prerequisite for this measure would be a system in which products can be traced from the kitchen back to the farm. While food additives and aromas would not be subject to the aforementioned approval procedure, they would be subject to the labeling and tracing provisions. These measures would apply to packaged and unpackaged foods sold by retailers and public eateries. Only enzymes produced with GE microorganisms would be exempt from these approval and labeling regulations. GE ingredients are to be indicated individually. Records covering the entire production and trading chain would have to be kept for five years.

Most of these regulations are to apply also to animal feed and feed-ingredients. The Commission's draft does not contain a requirement, demanded by agri-biotech critics, to label meat, milk, eggs, and other products from animals fed on GE feed. But several EU countries have been pushing for such a requirement and the outcome remains uncertain.

Majority approval by the European Parliament and the Council is necessary for the Commission's proposal to enter into force. As of late 2002 the obstacles to such approval remained high. Some EU countries and members of the European Parliament opposed the Commission's proposal because it would transfer decision-making authority from national governments to the Commission and the EFSA. Others demanded thresholds for mandatory labeling below one percent. Most experts believe that a threshold close to zero percent for unlabeled and/or non-approved GE content in food products (and also seed) would make mixed systems of GE/non-GE crop production next to impossible.[13] Decisions on thresholds for labeling and seed contamination are thus crucial to the future of agri-biotechnology in Europe. Thresholds close to zero, possibly in combination with stricter liability laws (another unresolved issue), would make combined GE/non-GE crop production in Europe extremely costly. This would decrease dramatically the attractiveness of agri-biotechnology applications in Europe. Yet others opposed the Commission's proposal because it would impose onerous regulations on European food and feed processors, wholesalers, retailers, restaurants, and other businesses. Indeed, establishing an effective identity preservation system (traceability) along the lines proposed by the Commission would require a large-scale and probably quite costly and time-consuming reorganization of the food supply in the European Union and between the European Union and its trading partners around the world.[14]

Opposition from within and outside the European Union might lead to some "softening" of the Commission's proposal. But the limits to concessions are clearly set by the positions taken by Austria, France, Italy, Denmark, Luxembourg, and Greece. These countries (with some support from Germany and Belgium, and probably tacit support by several other EU states) have stated that they will veto any approval application until stricter regulations are in place. European and non-European biotech as well as food and feed industries thus face a tough choice between no further approvals and regulatory uncertainty on the one hand and approvals subject to stricter regulation and more regulatory certainty on the other.

In view of the above assessment it appears very likely that ongoing regulatory reforms will move the European Union towards stricter agri-biotech policies. However, many elements of the European Union's regulatory system will probably continue to operate in a network-like (decentralized) fashion. Approvals for field trials, commercial cultivation, importation, and sale for food or feed purposes will still begin at national levels and end with majority decisions at the EU level. Risk assessment will remain decentralized and largely in the hands of national authorities. The same holds for implementation and enforcement of approval and labeling regulations. The newly established European Food Safety Authority's functions in these areas will remain largely advisory. Finally, EU countries will maintain considerable room for maneuver in adopting measures that are stricter than harmonized EU standards. I will return to these network-like features of the European Union's regulatory system and their implications in chapters 5 and 7.

Field Trials, Commercial Crop Production, and GE Foods on the Market

The data discussed in this section show that increasingly severe regulatory restrictions on agri-biotech applications in the European Union have had a massive effect on field trials, commercial GE crop cultivation, and GE foods on the market. As shown in figure 3.1, the number of field trials in the European Union is far lower than the number of such trials in the United States.[15] Figure 3.1 also shows that field trials in the European

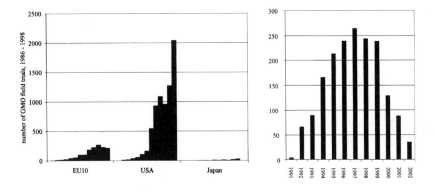

Figure 3.1   GE crop field trials in 10 EU countries, the United States, and Japan, 1986–1998, and approvals for field trials in the European Union, 1991–2002. *Sources:* http://binas.unido.org; http://www1.oecd.org/ehs/; http://biotech.jrc.it; EU 2000. The steep drop in field trials in 2002 (figure on the right) is partly due to the fact that data for 2002 was available only up to July 2002.

Union peaked in 1997 and 1998 and then declined by more than 80 percent until 2002.[16]

These figures mask substantial differences between EU member states. For example, the total number of field trials (1991–2002) varies from 0 in Luxembourg to 510 in France.[17]

Cultivation of GE crops in the European Union is extremely rare. In 1999, when GE crop production reached its peak in the European Union, only Spain (10,000 hectares, around 5000 in 2002), France (<1000 hectares), and Portugal (1000 hectares) were growing GE crops in significant amounts. Non-EU countries in Europe, notably Romania and Ukraine, planted another 3000 hectares. For comparison, in 1999, European GE crop production (including all EU and Central and Eastern European countries, except Russia) amounted to no more than 0.03 percent of the world total. GE crop planting around the same time amounted to 30.3 million hectares in the United States, 10 million hectares in Argentina, and 3 million hectares in Canada (followed by China, South Africa, and Australia). In 2002 worldwide GE crop planting reached 58 million hectares, with the EU share in the world total declining to 0.01 percent.[18]

Approval of GE foods does not necessarily mean that these products are marketed, and that they are sold in substantial quantities. Data on country- and EU-wide GE food sales does not exist. But consumer groups have been collecting some information on GE foods sold in the European Union.[19] This data suggests that since winter 1999/2000 the amount of marketed GE food (or food containing GE ingredients) subject to mandatory labeling has declined dramatically as a result of EU labeling requirements and consumer group campaigns (see also chapter 4).

Indeed, any consumer in the European Union will, as of late 2002, be hard pressed to find any GE food labeled as such. Testing of foods and feeds for GE content is being carried out on a large and growing scale by governments and consumer groups. In dozens of cases where unlabeled products tested positive for GE content, these products were quickly withdrawn from the market by food processors or retailers, no matter whether or not the GE organisms concerned had been approved by the European Union. Thousands of products on the EU market still contain GE organisms or ingredients produced through genetic engineering, above all enzymes (which remain unregulated) and small traces of GE organisms (e.g., soy or corn). But GE content is usually very low and not subject to mandatory labeling.

In summary, the European Union has moved from a situation of no regulation of agricultural biotechnology in the early- to mid-1980s to very strict approval regulation for GE crops, foods, and feeds, and to increasingly strict and harmonized labeling requirements. As a mirror image of that regulation, the number of GE crop field trials, which reached a peak in 1997, has declined rapidly thereafter. Commercial cultivation of GE crops is virtually non-existent in comparison to the United States, Argentina, Canada, and a few other countries. Very few GE crops and GE foods and feeds have been approved for commercialization in the European Union. And virtually none of these approved GE products has been marketed in substantial amounts.

AGRI-BIOTECH POLICY IN THE UNITED STATES

US agri-biotech policy is built on the assumption that applications of biotechnology in agriculture involve innovation in how food or feed is produced, but usually do not lead to substantially different properties or increased riskiness of food/feed products themselves. In following this product-orientation, the US Food and Drug Administration (FDA), the US Department of Agriculture (USDA), and the US Environmental Protection Agency (EPA) have approved most industry requests for field testing and commercialization of GE seeds, crops, foods, and feeds. This permissive policy is reflected in a relatively large number of approved GE products as well as large-scale field testing and commercial cultivation of GE crops.

Approval and Labeling Regulation

In the early- to mid-1980s different parts of the US government, in particular the EPA, USDA, and FDA, competed for regulatory authority in biotechnology policy. Similar to Europe, they were divided over whether to restrict or promote this new technology, and whether to adopt a product- or process-oriented approach to regulation. The White House Office of Science and Technology Policy (OSTP), USDA, and FDA sought to promote biotechnology and advocated a product-approach, whereas EPA argued in favor of developing new risk assessment procedures for GE organisms and process-based regulation.[20]

In 1984, responding to increasing criticism, notably by industry, of lack of coordination of biotech policy among government institutions, the Executive Office of then US President Ronald Reagan created a Cabinet Council Working Group with representatives from fifteen agencies. The Reagan administration thus prevented a takeover of regulatory authority by the EPA,[21] more active involvement of the US Congress, and more public scrutiny of the regulatory process in general.[22]

In 1986, this working group issued a Coordinated Framework for the Regulation of Biotechnology. The Coordinated Framework provided for the establishment of a Biotechnology Science Coordinating Committee (BSCC), assigned the primary responsibilities for regulation to EPA, USDA, and FDA, and set forth principles for coordination and cooperation among these authorities.[23] Most importantly, it firmly established the product-orientation of US biotech policy and denied the necessity of new legislation and new regulatory agencies exclusively for agri-biotechnology. Thus it locked in the prevailing assumption that agri-biotechnology should not be viewed as posing special risks to human health and the environment. This position was supported and legitimized by a 1989 report of the US National Research Council.[24] Broader social or political implications of biotechnology were not addressed at that stage.[25] In the United States, all GE products have ever since been regulated on the basis of pre-existing legislation and the Coordinated Framework.

In more general terms, the US approach to agri-biotech regulation can be described as administrative and based on what the technology's advocates call "sound science." Indeed, the US Administrative Procedure Act stipulates that regulation must be based on a clear policy rationale, scientific evidence for risks, and legal authority. Regulation is frequently subject to legal review and litigation. And the US judicial system creates ample opportunities for liability litigation over product safety issues. All these elements have pushed regulators and industry towards approaches that are closely tied to scientific evidence.[26]

Transportation, cultivation (for field testing or commercial production), and propagation of GE crops are governed by the USDA's Animal and Plant Health Inspection Service (APHIS) under the Federal Plant Pest Act. APHIS is the lead agency if a GE plant is not intended for human consumption and is not modified to contain a pesticide. It issues de facto commercial permits stating that a given GE plant is not a pest and needs no further regulation. It also carries out an environmental assessment of the plant under the National Environmental Policy Act.[27]

EPA is responsible for regulating pest-resistant GE crops under the Federal Insecticide, Fungicide and Rodenticide Act, the Toxic Substances Control Act, and the National Environmental Policy Act. Such crops are subject to a risk assessment regime under which producers must submit testing data to the EPA. These data are publicly available during a 30 days notice and comment period before approval.

The FDA has regulatory authority for GE foods, food additives, processing aids, and biotech medical products. It also has primary responsibility for labeling, with the exception of meat and poultry products (governed by the USDA). Most analysts note that, of the three agencies, the FDA has had the greatest influence because most biotech products on the US market are food or health care products.[28] The FDA's approval procedure is based on consultations with producers and summaries of tests submitted by producers. The information exchanged in the approval process is not public.

In the course of the 1990s, the USDA and the FDA gradually moved toward more permissive implementation of approval standards initially set under the Coordinated Framework. In 1993, the USDA (APHIS) introduced a notification (instead of permit) procedure for six transgenic crops (corn, soybean, cotton, tomato, potato, and tobacco).[29] In 1997, it extended this notification policy to the majority of GE crop varieties cultivated in the United States and simplified notification procedures for imports, release into the environment, and transportation of GE organisms.[30] Thus it has removed an increasing number of GE plants from its oversight (56 GE crop varieties, as of December 2002).[31]

In 1990, the FDA approved the first food-ingredient produced with biotechnology, chymosin, an agent that helps milk clot in making cheese. This approval was followed by rennin, which is also used in cheese production, and recombinant BST, which is used to increase milk output in cattle. In 1994, in accordance with its 1992 interpretation of the Federal Food, Drug, and Cosmetic Act,[32] the FDA introduced a simplified approval procedure for GE foods, starting with Calgene's FLAVR SAVR™ tomato.[33] Under this procedure applications for approval of GE foods are not subject to comprehensive scientific review because the production process as such is thought to pose no significant risks. GE foods are "generally recognized as safe" (GRAS) unless, in the judgment of the manufacturer, there is a reason for concern (e.g., allergy problems).[34] Foods considered GRAS are not subject to pre-market risk assessment by the FDA.[35] In essence, this system allows biotech firms to decide on their own whether a GE product is safe. The FDA is only consulted.

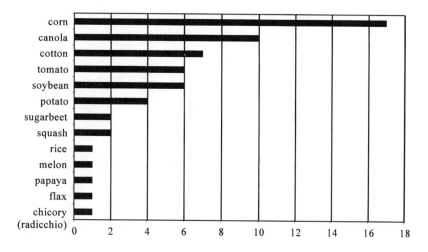

Figure 3.2 Approved agricultural GE products, as of 12/2002. *Sources*: www.agbios.com; www.ucsusa.org; www.fda.gov. Some of these products (e.g., StarLink corn and FlavrSavr tomatoes) are no longer sold. These websites also list firms to whom approvals were issued, engineered traits of these products, sources of the new genes, and other information. ISAAA refers to 51 GE products commercialized in the United States, but it remains unclear from www.isaaa.org what types of products are included in this count.

As of December 2002, the three agencies responsible had issued approvals for around 59 GE crop varieties, among them 51 that are used for food purposes (Figure 3.2).

The permissive policy just described is also reflected in US policy on labeling. GE foods are subject to the same labeling requirements as all foods on the US market.[36] Labeling is only mandatory if a particular GE food is no longer "substantially equivalent" to the corresponding conventional food in terms of composition, nutrition, or safety.[37]

In 1992, the FDA ruled that if any of the most common allergens (e.g., milk, eggs, wheat, fish, crustacea, tree nuts, legumes, especially peanuts) are added to food via biotechnology, the producer must either provide scientific evidence that the allergen is not present in the new food or label the product. Such products are subject to additional risk assessment. The label does *not* have to indicate that the food was produced with biotechnology. It must only state that the food contains a potential allergen.[38] Labeling is also required if a food product is transformed through biotechnology so that its nutrient content does not conform to what is normally expected.[39] Consequently, the vast majority of GE foods on the US market do not require labeling, and no GE food product is labeled as such. The FDA has full legal and regulatory authority to remove food from the market even after approval if it is considered to be unsafe or incorrectly labeled. Its authority is immediate and final.

The EPA has favored a more process-oriented approach to agri-biotech regulation than the FDA and the USDA.[40] In late 1994, it proposed a set of regulations for GE plants designed to resist pests, treating such plants as if they were pesticides. Due to opposition from other parts of the US government, industry, and scientists, the proposed rules were not adopted.[41] In 1999, more intense public debate and NGO involvement were triggered by research suggesting that Bt corn caused harm not only to pests (notably, the corn borer), but also Monarch butterfly larvae. In response, the EPA again examined whether to subject certain GE crops to pesticide regulations. In January 2000, it asked farmers cultivating Bt corn to plant buffer zones with conventional corn to protect the Monarch butterfly and safeguard against other potentially negative environmental effects.[42] Continuing opposition has thus far prevented process-oriented regulation beyond such ad hoc measures. No US agency systematically monitors the ecological impacts of deregulated GE crops.

In the late 1990s, more intense public debate on labeling of GE foods developed. Opinion polls suggested that around 80–90 percent of US respondents favored mandatory labeling of GE foods. In November 1999, 49 members of Congress sent a letter to the FDA requesting mandatory labeling on the basis of the Food, Drug and Cosmetic Act. In March 2000, more than 50 US consumer groups filed a legal petition against the FDA calling for a moratorium on GE product approvals until stricter procedures were installed.[43] Two bills on labeling of GE foods, and two bills on safety testing were introduced in the US Senate and House in 1999 and 2000.[44] Moreover, NGOs launched several lawsuits[45] to bolster requests for mandatory labeling and have also stimulated legislative activity at the US state-level.

The FDA has remained largely immune to this pressure. Its policies have been protected by the courts.[46] Thus far, all national and state-level attempts to introduce mandatory labeling have failed. The most prominent effort to date, a 2002 ballot initiative in Oregon, resulted in a 73 percent rejection by voters of mandatory labeling.[47] In January 2001, the FDA formally reaffirmed its product-oriented approach. It also introduced two measures for strengthening its regulatory oversight.[48] First, it made hitherto voluntary consultation between biotech firms and the FDA in the approval process mandatory. Thus it reactivated a similar proposal made in 1993 but dropped due to opposition from scientific and professional groups.[49] This new measure will not substantially change the FDA's permissive approval policy: producers have thus far subjected all GE foods or feeds marketed in the United States to the FDA's consultation program installed in 1994, probably to reduce liability risks. Second, the

FDA issued guidelines for voluntary labeling of GE/non-GE foods. These guidelines are similar to the ones currently applied to organic and kosher foods.[50]

Field Trials, Commercial Crop Production, and GE Foods on the Market

Figure 3.3 shows a rapid increase in the number of US field trials with GE crops. The first field test in the United States was conducted in 1987. The total number of field trials, around 1000 per year since the late 1990s, is far larger than that of any other country (see also figure 3.1).

Table 3.2 conveys a similar picture for agricultural land sown to GE crops. Worldwide GE crop production (58.7 million hectares, or 145 million acres, planted in 16 countries in 2002) is heavily dominated by the United States, with US farmers responsible for two-thirds of worldwide GE crop production. Adding Argentina (23 percent) drives that share up to 90 percent. This percentage increases to 99 percent when we add Canada (6 percent) and China (4 percent). GE soybeans and GE corn account for around 80 percent of worldwide GE crop production, with one US firm (Monsato) supplying the technology for around 90 percent of the world total. GE cotton follows with 12 percent and GE canola with 5 percent of the world total of GE crop acreage. In 2002, the GE shares in US crop production were 75 percent for soybeans, 71 percent for cotton, and 34 percent for corn. Worldwide, they were 51

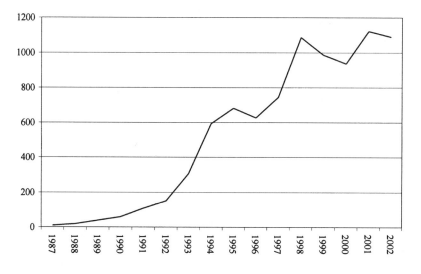

Figure 3.3 Permits and notifications issued by the USDA for field trials in the United States. *Source*: www.aphis.usda.govt.

TABLE 3.2
Agricultural land sown to GE crops (million hectares, percentages)

	1996	1997	1998	1999	2000	2001	2002
USA	1.5	7.2	20.8	28.7	30.3	35.7	39.0
Other countries	1.2	4.4	7.8	11.2	13.9	16.9	19.7
US share (%) in world total	56	62	73	72	69	68	66

Sources: www.isaaa.org; www.usda.gov; www.transgen.de.

percent for soybeans, 20 percent of cotton, 12 percent for canola, and 9 percent for corn.[51]

The extent to which the US food supply contains GE organisms is impossible to determine with precision, not least because GE food or GE food ingredients are not subject to mandatory labeling. Such measurement is also impossible because the US food supply contains not only 51 approved GE food crop varieties, but also a range of other GE ingredients, for example GE enzymes. Consumer groups and scientific associations claim, however, that 70–90 percent of processed food products sold in the United States in 2002 contained GE organisms.[52]

GE soy and GE corn account for the largest share among GE products in the US food supply. Other GE food products have thus far been much less successful. GE tomatoes, the first GE crop to be commercialized, have been abandoned. GE potatoes were withdrawn from the market by Monsanto in 2001. GE tobacco and GE flax, two non-food GE products, have met the same fate. Aventis has thus far refrained from commercializing its herbicide resistant GE rice. GE sugar beet has not been adopted on a significant scale by US farmers. The introduction of GE wheat by Monsanto has been delayed to 2004 or 2005 due to uncertainties about the market response. The commercialization of GE fish (notably salmon) remains steeped in controversy and is unlikely to take place anytime soon.[53]

In summary, in stark contrast to EU policy, US agri-biotech policy has relied on permissive approval and labeling regulation, an administrative approach to regulation based almost exclusively on the "substantial equivalence" criterion and "sound science," and on managing risks through technical means and product liability.[54] This policy is reflected in a comparatively large number of approved GE crops, a large number of field trials, large-scale GE crop cultivation (in absolute figures and shares of the world total), and the presence of GE organisms in most processed foods sold in the United States. Moreover, whereas EU policy-making has followed a decentralized, network-like pattern, US agri-biotech regulation has been issued, implemented, and enforced by three federal agencies. In a nutshell, the European Union has pursued a model of very restrictive but somewhat heterogeneous regulation within a decentralized, network-like pattern of decision-making, implementation, and enforcement. Centralized and homogenous laxity has prevailed in the United States.

OTHER COUNTRIES

As noted above, the European Union and the United States are the two heavyweights in terms of global effects of their agri-biotech regulation. They are at opposite ends as regards the stringency of their agri-biotech regulation. The following review, covering a wide range of other countries, shows that some of these countries have clearly aligned with the European Union or the United States, whereas others have positioned themselves in between the European Union and the United States. Because most developing countries and transition economies are still at an early stage of agri-biotech policy-making it remains unclear whether the tide will eventually turn towards the EU or the US regulatory model. At present it appears that more countries are moving at least some distance towards the EU model and away from the US model. In a superb analysis, Paarlberg (2003) attributes this trend to superior influence by the European Union, primarily via four channels: international organizations, NGOs, development assistance, and international commodity markets.

Approval and Labeling Policies

Table 3.3 indicates the number of approved GE products and the presence/absence of mandatory labeling for a range of developing and industrialized countries.[55] These figures must be interpreted with great caution. The policies of many countries are very much in flux and information (especially on approved products) is often incomplete or contradictory. The number of approvals is only a rough proxy for the permissiveness of a country's agri-biotech policy because it does not distinguish approvals for marketing as food/feed and commercial cultivation. I will look at crop production further below. Moreover, approval and labeling policies, even where they are in place, vary very much in terms of stringency—notably also in regard to implementation and enforcement.

Table 3.3 shows that most countries have approved only very few or no GE crops.[56] Exceptions are the United States, Canada, Japan, Australia, the European Union, and Argentina. Of these countries, only the United

TABLE 3.3
Approvals and mandatory labeling worldwide, 2002

Country	Number of approved GE products	Mandatory labeling
Argentina	9	No
Australia	22	Yes, since 2002
Bolivia	3	No
Brazil	0	Yes, expected for 2003
Bulgaria	NA	No
Canada	52	No
China	4	Yes, since 2002
Czech Republic	NA	Yes, since 2002
Egypt	0	No
European Union	14	Yes, since 1998
Hungary	NA	Yes, since 1999
Hong Kong	NA	Yes, expected for 2003
India	3	No
Indonesia	1	Yes, since 2002
Japan	34	Yes, since 2001
Kenya	0	No
Malaysia	1	Yes, expected for 2003/4
Mexico	4	Yes, expected for 2003
New Zealand	NA	Yes, since 2002
Norway	NA	Yes
Poland	1	NA
Philippines	0	No
Romania	3	NA
Russia	4	Yes, since 2002
South Korea	1	Yes, since 2001
Saudia Arabia	NA	Yes, since 2001
South Africa	3	No
Sri Lanka	0	No
Switzerland	4	Yes, since 1999
Taiwan	NA	Yes, expected for 2003
Thailand	0	Yes, since 2002
United States	59	No
Uruguay	1	No

Sources: www1.oecd.org/ehs/biobin; www.agbios.com; www.greenpeace.org; www.transgen.de; www.binas.unido.org/binas; www.isaaa.org.

Note: The list includes countries for which some information was available. All 13 countries currently applying to join the European Union will have to adopt the EU's mandatory labeling regulations. NA, not available. Figures on approval are quite unreliable because sources often do not specify whether approval was granted for marketing as food or feed, and/or for commercial cultivation. The figures shown in this table refer predominantly to approval for marketing as food or feed. In some cases, notably some developing countries, zero approved products may simply indicate that the respective country does not have functioning approval regulations. GE food processing aids and GE food additives are not included in the count.

States, Canada, and Argentina grow GE crops in substantial amounts (see below). Moreover, there is a worldwide trend towards mandatory labeling. This trend is led by the European Union. The group of countries not moving in that direction is led by the United States.

In other words, the global agri-biotech landscape is shaped by two blocks. One is dominated by the European Union and includes non-EU countries in Western Europe (notably, Norway and Switzerland) as well as most transition economies in Central and Eastern Europe (above all, countries applying for European Union membership). The other is dominated by the United States and includes in particular Canada and Argentina.

Other countries, to the extent they have adopted operational agri-biotech policies, have been struggling to find some middle ground. Most of them (with the exception of Japan and Australia) have approved very few or no GE products for marketing and/or cultivation. Approvals for cultivation have been issued primarily for GE cotton, that is, a product serving largely non-food purposes (limited quantities of cotton seeds are used in food oil production). Most of these countries have adopted mandatory food labeling requirements, although usually in forms that are less strict than corresponding EU rules.

Japan, the world's third largest economy, started out with US-style agri-biotech regulation and then moved towards the EU model. Australia, which cultivates some GE crops, has introduced mandatory labeling. Brazil has installed a provisional ban on GE product imports and cultivation and will probably introduce mandatory labeling in 2003/2004. China, which cultivates some GE cotton, has introduced mandatory GE food labeling in 2002. In 2002 India permitted cultivation of GE cotton but not GE food crops. Mexico, which has very close economic ties to the United States, has adopted a more cautious approach to GE crops than its large neighbor. South Africa, which is the only country on the African continent with substantial GE crop production, has thus far resisted calls for mandatory labeling.[57]

Field Trials and GE Crop Production

In 1998 (the last year for which comparable figures are available) 71 percent of the entries in the OECD's BioTrack database were by the United States, 15 percent by EU countries, 9 percent by Canada, 2 percent by Australia, 0.7 percent by Japan, and 0.6 percent by New Zealand. These figures can serve as rough proxies for the relative extent of field testing in advanced industrialized countries other than EU countries and the United States. Judging from the more eclectic evidence from a range of other sources,[58] these proportions have probably not changed much since 1998.

Data on field testing in developing countries remains scarce and unreliable (the OECD's BioTrack program covers only OECD countries). A cursory review of the available evidence suggests that the number of field tests in developing countries is dwarfed by the number of such tests in the OECD world. Developing countries reporting GE crop field tests include Argentina, Belize, Bolivia, Brazil, Costa Rica, Chile, China, Colombia, Cuba, Dominican Republic, Egypt, Guatemala, India, Indonesia, Kenya, Malaysia, Mexico, Nigeria, Peru, South Africa, Thailand, Uganda, the Philippines, Venezuela, and Zimbabwe. The most extensive testing has taken place in Argentina, Brazil, China, and South Africa, with China far ahead of all other developing countries. In Central and Eastern Europe, only Bulgaria, the Czech Republic, Romania, and Russia have reported some field tests.[59]

Somewhat more reliable data exists for GE crop cultivation.[60] Table 3.4 shows that, in countries other than the United States and European Union, only Argentina and Canada produce GE crops on a larger scale. GE crop production in China, South Africa, and Australia, which is also quite substantial, is largely restricted to GE cotton (a non-food crop).

TABLE 3.4

GE crop cultivation outside the United States and the European Union (million hectares)

	1996	1997	1998	1999	2000	2001	2002
Argentina	<0.1	1.5	3.5	5.8*	10.0	11.8	13.5
Australia	0	0.2	0.3	0.3	0.2	0.2	0.2
Brazil	0	0	0	1.2*	NA	NA	NA
Bulgaria	0	0	0	0	<0.1	<0.1	<0.1
Canada	0.1	1.7	2.8	4.0	3.0	3.2	3.5
China	1.0	1.0	1.1	1.3	0.5	1.5	2.1
Columbia	0	0	0	0	0	0	<0.1
India	0	0	0	0	0	0	<0.1
Indonesia	0	0	0	0	0	<0.1	<0.1
Honduras	0	0	0	0	0	0	<0.1
Mexico	0	0	<0.1	<0.1	<0.1	<0.1	<0.1
Romania	0	0	0	<0.1	<0.1	<0.1	<0.1
South Africa	0	0	<0.1	0.2	0.2	0.2	0.2
Uruguay	0	0	0	0	<0.1	<0.1	<0.1
World total	2.6	11.5	28.6	41.5	44.2	52.6	58.7

Sources: EU (2000) for 1996–1999; www.isaaa.org for 1999–2002.

*This figure reflects EU estimates of GE cultivation in Brazil based on illegally imported GE seeds from Argentina. Such illegal seed imports are assumed to increase GE crop production in Brazil and decrease the one in Argentina. See also www.greenpeace.org (background information 03/02).

Countries not listed in this figure do not permit commercial cultivation of GE crops.

CONCLUSION

The analysis in this chapter has shown that an increasing divide has been developing between agri-biotech promoting and agri-biotech restricting countries, both in terms of approval and labeling regulation and at the market level (crop production, GE food/feed sales). The former group of countries clusters around the United States. It includes in particular Canada and Argentina. The latter group clusters around the European Union. It includes most non-EU states in Western Europe, such as Norway and Switzerland, and many Central and East European countries.

Many other countries (e.g., Australia, Brazil, China, India, Japan, Mexico, Russia, and South Africa) have moved towards stricter approval procedures. And many of these countries have adopted mandatory labeling requirements. These regulations differ very much in terms of their stringency. However, they position these countries somewhere in between the European Union and the United States. On average, more countries worldwide appear to be moving at least some distance towards the EU regulatory model than towards the US model, although this process is still very much in flux.

These "tectonic shifts" in the global landscape of agri-biotech regulation have thus far not generated much pressure for reform of US approval and labeling regulation (nor that of Canada and Argentina). But they have affected markets. First, most analysts note a chilling effect on GE corn and GE soybean cultivation. The exception to this trend, GE cotton, is largely a non-food product. Second, polarization has contributed substantially to delaying the commercialization of new GE crops, such as GE wheat, rice, sugar beet, potato, and fish. Third, polarization has contributed to upheaval in the biotech industry. Large life sciences firms, for example, Novartis, Dow, DuPont, and Pharmacia have spun off their agri-biotech divisions. The financial performance of the giant in the agri-biotech business, Monsanto, has been very poor since 2000. Fourth, polarization is affecting world agricultural trade. Moreover, it has all but promoted public funding of agri-biotech R&D in developing countries, where the technology could be most useful. Chapters 4 and 5 explain why polarization has emerged. Chapter 6 examines international trade implications.

CHAPTER FOUR

Interest Group Politics

PROPONENTS of agri-biotechnology believe that the polarizing trends shown in chapter 3 will fade away once GE products with more apparent consumer benefits enter the market, longer-term risk assessments show no negative but rather positive effects of GE products on consumer health and the environment, and food security problems in developing countries become more acute. The critics refer to the same factors when predicting that the technology will follow the example of nuclear energy in terms of a risky technology that most societies do not want and do not need.[1]

As a starting point for this chapter and chapter 5, I argue that such predictions are little more than wishful thinking of one or the other side as long as they are not grounded in a systematic explanation of why polarization has emerged. Only on the basis of such an explanation can we assess whether the factors highlighted by proponents or critics will in fact move agri-biotechnology towards breakthrough or stagnation in the medium to long term. The same holds for assessments of whether particular public or private sector strategies for promoting the technology will or will not be effective. In chapter 6 we will also see that more knowledge on how strongly committed particular societies are to specific levels of regulatory stringency is required to assess the likelihood of international trade conflict over agri-biotechnology and the possibilities for resolving such conflict.

Empirically, the explanation developed here and in chapter 5 focuses primarily on the European Union and the United States, the two opposites in worldwide agri-biotech regulation. It relies on two theoretical approaches.

The first approach concentrates on explaining differences in countries' reactions to agricultural biotechnology from the "bottom up," that is, in terms of interest group politics. This approach centers on the struggle for political and market influence among competing interest groups, notably consumer or environmental groups (more generally, NGOs) and producer groups (biotech firms, farmers, grain handlers, food processors, retailers, wholesalers). It explains which types of interests dominate in the regulatory process in pluralistic (democratic) societies when and why. The *collective action capacity* of particular interest groups, which derives from a distinct set of determinants, is the key factor in this explanation. The interest group politics model tells us why agri-biotech adverse consumer and environmental groups have been able to gain the upper hand in the European Union and successfully push for severe constraints on the technology. It also tells us why the regulatory process in the United States has been dominated by agri-biotech promoting producer groups.

The second approach, applied in chapter 5, involves a "top-down" perspective. It explains outcomes in terms of interactions among governments (member states in the European Union, states in the United States). It regards both the European Union and the United States as federal political systems in which political authority is divided between a central government (the EU Commission, the European Parliament, and the European Court of Justice in the European Union; the federal government and other federal institutions in the United States) and other political units (EU member states; US states). The institutional setting (e.g., division of authority, decision-making rules) in which bargaining over proposals for regulation takes place differs across the two political systems. For reasons explained in chapter 5, the European Union's system of regulatory policy-making has contributed to a "ratcheting up" effect, which has increased regulatory stringency. Such an effect has not materialized in the United States.

These two explanations, in combination, suggest that polarization is likely to persist for the foreseeable future. They go against predictions that regulations and de facto adoption of agri-biotechnology will converge internationally, either in favor or not in favor of the technology. As a corollary, we will see in chapter 6 that coercion by the United States through the World Trade Organization or unilaterally is very unlikely to yield substantial concessions (a relaxation of agri-biotech regulation) from the European Union.

EXPLAINING REGULATORY POLARIZATION "BOTTOM UP"

The most popular political economy theory of regulation holds that, in regulatory processes, concentrated interests dominate over diffuse interests, and that regulatory outcomes thus tend to reflect the preferences of concentrated interests.[2] As a corollary, the theory predicts that most regulations will reflect the preferences of producers rather than consumers. To the extent that consumers benefit from regulation (or the absence of regulation, or deregulation), these benefits are usually coincidental.[3]

Because the global agrochemical and agri-biotech sector is highly concentrated[4] whereas NGOs have large and diverse memberships, we should expect permissive agri-biotech policies in accordance with industry preferences. US policy—permissive approval regulations and no mandatory labeling—seems to fit that prediction. Biotech input suppliers in the United States have received the regulations they want. In contrast, in the European Union the agri-biotech sector has been overwhelmed by a very heterogeneous coalition of agri-biotech adverse interests. This development is particularly striking because national and supranational regulators in Europe are widely assumed to maintain close ties with the industries they regulate.[5] How can we explain the European Union's deviation from the outcome predicted by the conventional theory of regulation?

The following explanation assumes that variation in the stringency of agri-biotech regulation results primarily from variation in the collective action capacity of consumer/environmental and producer interest groups. First I concentrate on when and why environmental and consumer groups are able to campaign effectively for stricter regulation. The subsequent section focuses on producer interests. I also consider the role institutions may play in affecting the collective action capacity of interest groups.

Collective Action Capacity of Environmental and Consumer Interests

The starting point for an answer to why the producer dominance hypothesis appears to be inconsistent with the empirical evidence on agri-biotech regulation (particularly in the European Union)[6] can be found in Mancur Olson's "Logic of Collective Action."[7]

Olson hypothesized that large (latent) groups are difficult to mobilize. The underlying logic, applied to the agri-biotech case, is as follows. Consumer and environmental organizations are pressure groups that offer a "collective good," that is, consumer or environmental protection. The production of collective goods is usually plagued by a free-rider problem. Everyone can benefit from such goods promoted by a pressure group, no matter whether she or he joins or in other ways actively supports the group. Assuming that the average person is a rational egoist, even those persons who welcome and benefit from a particular collective good (e.g., more consumer protection) have a strong incentive to let others pay and do the work. Consumer or environmental groups usually involve large numbers of people, which worsens the free-rider problem: in large groups, free riders are harder to identify, single out, punish, or reward with selective incentives. Moreover, the heterogeneity of interests is likely to increase with the number of people involved. This is why larger groups are more difficult to mobilize for a common purpose.[8]

I pick up at this point and assume that environmental and consumer interest groups are usually aware of their collective action problem. To mitigate or solve that problem, they frequently focus on issues that allow for maximum mobilization of membership and financial resources. Issues that provoke *public outrage* are crucial in this regard. Public outrage can be defined in terms of the fear or anger a particular risk generates among a relatively large part of a country's population. Its extent depends on specific characteristics of a given risk and a range of other factors that are exogenous to my argument here.[9] In the empirical analysis I capture public outrage in terms of public risk perceptions and trust in regulatory authorities.

In terms of its issue characteristics agricultural biotechnology has a considerable public outrage potential. However, the extent to which this potential becomes politically relevant is largely a matter of public perception. If the public in a given country is more critical or fearful of a particular technology, in ways and for reasons to be identified, NGOs are likely to be more successful in mobilizing their memberships if they decide to campaign for more regulatory restrictions on this technology. Because NGOs know this, they are more likely to campaign for such restrictions. In other words, I expect that NGO campaigns for regulatory restrictions on agricultural biotechnology will be more extensive and more successful in countries where public concerns or fears about the technology are greater.

Note that this argument cuts against the conventional view in pro-biotech industry circles of "who is in the driving seat." Most agri-biotech supporters assume that NGOs have been the principal instigators of public concerns over agricultural biotechnology. The theory outlined here tends to argue the other way around: that NGOs are opportunistic actors piggy-backing on pre-existing negative public perceptions of agri-biotechnology. Who is right is an empirical question and will be addressed further below.

Public outrage increases the capacity of environmental/consumer groups to influence regulatory processes via markets and via politics. The underlying logic is as follows.

Focusing on issues with a high public outrage potential enables environmental/consumer groups to obtain or enhance their reputation as defenders of important public interests, activate existing members of their respective group, receive attention by the media, attract more members, mobilize non-members (latent supporters of a cause), and raise more funds. If public outrage is strong enough to significantly raise environmental or consumer groups' collective action capacity along these lines they can take more effective action against producers. They can, for example, organize boycotts of specific products, firms, or even entire industries, and launch public campaigns aimed at tarnishing the image of firms, industries, or products.[10] Through such action, environmental/consumer groups can bring about changes in producers' preferences and behavior in the market place, with evident implications for regulatory processes.

NGOs can influence not only markets, but also policy-making. Particularly in decentralized and multilevel regulatory systems, which provide more access points for NGO campaigns, public outrage tends to shift political influence from producers to environmental and consumer groups. Decentralization refers to the horizontal division among equals of authority in regulatory processes (e.g., among EU member countries or US states). Multilevel systems are systems where authority is divided between the national (federal) or supranational level on the one hand and the sub-national or national level on the other hand. Once environmental/consumer groups have overcome their collective action problem by exploiting public outrage, their liability of large numbers turns into an asset: by virtue of their large membership, they can exert substantial political influence on politicians and regulators since consumers are also voters.[11]

In summary, the theoretical argument sketched here holds that public outrage grows with negative public perceptions of a given technology and low public trust in regulatory authorities. Public outrage boosts the collective action capacity of environmental and consumer groups. Thus it increases these groups' capacity to influence the market for a given technology and the preferences of producers operating in this market. Moreover, public outrage in combination with institutional structures favorable to environmental/consumer group involvement (in particular, decentralized and multilevel regulatory policy-making) shifts political influence from producer to environmental/consumer interests.

Collective Action Capacity of Producer Interests

The conventional political economy model of regulation holds that stricter environmental or consumer protection standards are more likely to be enacted if producers can benefit economically from the particular regulation. In principle, stricter regulation can yield at least two types of benefits to producers.

1   *Protectionist benefits.* Environmental and consumer protection will tend towards greater stringency particularly in areas where regulation can be designed to shield import-competing domestic firms from foreign competition. The assumption here is that producer demand for import-restricting regulation is likely to attract more political support if justified in terms of protecting public health and the environment, rather than in terms of protecting domestic firms. The latter is more difficult to justify and defend because it transfers wealth from domestic consumers to domestic producers.[12]

2 *Domestic economic benefits.* Similar to the argument on protectionist
   rents, this argument assumes that firms' interests are shaped by industrial structure and that firms seek to improve their competitive position through regulation. But in contrast to the regulatory capture and
   rent-seeking argument in conventional economic theories of regulation[13] it does not assume that there is a single industry with homo-
   geneous interests within a given country. Individual firms or groups
   of firms within a specific industry may lobby for stricter or laxer
   regulation, and for harmonized or particularistic regulation, depending on differences in industrial structure and competitive position.
   For example, some large firms may lobby for stricter environmental
   or consumer regulation that would be too costly for smaller firms to
   implement, whereas smaller firms within the same industry and the
   same country oppose such regulation.[14]

I now connect these rent-seeking arguments to the above propositions
on the collective action capacity of environmental and consumer NGOs.
In this combined argument public outrage and associated campaigns by
environmental and consumer groups can exert "pull" and "push" effects
on producers (industry).

First, public outrage and NGO campaigns can act as facilitators for
rent-seeking by producers. "Strange bedfellow" coalitions of environ-
mental/consumer and producer interests that lobby for the same stricter
regulation but for different reasons are expressions of this possibility.
Such pull effects may weaken producer coalitions to the extent that incentives to "piggy-back" on public outrage and NGO campaigns differ
across firms or types of producers in a given industry. In agri-biotechnology, for example, the collective action capacity of pro-biotech producers,
who seek lax regulation, will decrease if some firms in the food industry
experience strong incentives to support more restrictive regulation. To
identify differences in industrial structure (competitive position of firms)
that may account for variation in rent-seeking incentives I will distinguish
between agri-biotech firms (upstream producers), farmers, and retailers
and food processors (downstream producers).

Public outrage and NGO campaigns cannot only reduce producers'
collective action capacity by acting as facilitators for rent seeking by
some producers (the "pull" effect). They may also exert a "push" effect
by coercing producers that do not expect to benefit from stricter regulation into supporting or tolerating such regulation. Again, differences in
industrial structure and competitive position are likely to determine the
extent to which particular producers in a given industry are more or less
susceptible to push effects. For example, some producers may be more
vulnerable to public outrage and NGO campaigns than others because

they have valuable brands to protect, or simply because they are bigger, which makes them a more attractive target for NGOs. In addition, organizational and economic rigidities in particular economic sectors may also shape the extent to which push effects translate into industry behavior. For example, low economic concentration and poor political organization may, paradoxically, make certain industrial sectors less vulnerable to NGO campaigns.

In summary, the argument outlined here holds that variation across countries in public outrage and NGO campaigns generates variation in the extent of pull and push effects on producers. Contingent on differences in industrial structure, the extent to which these effects weaken producers' collective action capacity will vary across countries.

COMPARING EU AND US REGULATORY POLICY

The following analysis focuses on a straightforward comparison of market responses and regulatory policies in two jurisdictions, the European Union and the United States, through case studies. In chapter 3 I observed particular market responses and regulatory outcomes in the two political systems. Below I will now examine whether the empirical observations for the explanatory variables are congruent with the more abstract theoretical argument just outlined.[15]

More specifically, we have observed that the European Union has imposed severe restrictions on agricultural biotechnology, whereas the United States has maintained an open market and a permissive regulatory policy in this field. In the European Union, we should thus observe more negative public perceptions of the technology and lower public trust in regulatory authorities (i.e., a higher extent of public outrage) than in the United States. We should also observe more access for environmental and consumer NGOs to agri-biotech policy-making in the European Union than the United States. Moreover, in the European Union we should observe a decline in producers' collective action capacity due to strong pull and push effects that emanate from public outrage, NGO campaigns, and differences in industrial structure. In the United States, these pull and push effects should be much weaker than in the European Union.

The analysis will indeed show that regulatory policy in the European Union can be traced back to two driving forces: high collective action capacity of NGOs due to public outrage and an institutional environment favorable to agri-biotech adverse interests (notably, decentralized and multilevel policy-making); and fragmentation of producer interests due to NGO campaigns and "push-effects" facilitated by particular industrial structures (notably, high concentration in the retail food sector and low concentration in the farm and grain handling sectors). US agricultural biotech politics has been dominated by a strong and cohesive coalition of pro-biotech up- and downstream producers and farmers.

Low public outrage has made mobilization of NGOs in the United States difficult. In combination with an institutional environment less favorable to NGOs (notably, centralized regulatory policy-making) it has resulted largely in the exclusion of biotech adverse interests from agri-biotech policy-making. Rigidities emanating from lower concentration in the retail food sector and higher concentration in the seed, grain handling, and farm sectors have helped in locking in agri-biotech promoting policies.[16]

EU Policy

While some analysts had already warned of growing opposition to agricultural biotechnology in the early to mid-1990s, no one anticipated the coming upheaval that would virtually shut down the European Union's market for GE crops and GE foods. Ex post, the strong trend towards stricter agri-biotech regulations in the European Union can be explained in terms of an increasingly broad and influential agri-biotech adverse coalition. This coalition includes environmental and consumer groups as well as many farmers, food processors, and retailers. I examine the emergence of this coalition along the lines set by the theoretical framework just described.[17] To simplify the analysis I consider the European Union largely as one political unit and do not explore differences across EU countries (e.g., in terms of consumer perceptions). Such differences and their effects are examined in chapter 5.

Environmental and Consumer Interests

European environmental/consumer groups have focused very strongly on biotechnology issues ever since the mid- to late-1980s, when the regulatory process in the European Union began. Benefiting from public aversion to agri-biotechnology and low public trust in regulatory authorities, they have been able to mobilize their membership against the technology, and to launch major anti-agri-biotech campaigns against input suppliers, food processors, and retailers. These NGO activities have divided producers and have thus reduced producers' collective action capacity. They have also influenced the decisions of regulators.

Survey results show that a large part of the European public holds negative views on green biotechnology and GE foods in particular. With the exception of nuclear energy, agricultural biotechnology has been the most unpopular technology among EU consumers. Table 4.1 shows some survey results obtained in 1999, the most recent year for

TABLE 4.1
Consumer acceptance of GE foods in the European Union, 1999

	Mostly agree	Mostly disagree	Do not know	Maximum
Would buy GE fruit if it tasted better	22%	66%	11%	Mostly agree: Netherlands, 30% Mostly disagree: Greece, 88%
Would pay more for non-GE food	53%	36%	11%	Mostly agree: Greece, 83% Mostly disagree: United Kingdom, 51%
Willing to buy cooking oil containing a little GE soy	22%	62%	16%	Mostly agree: Netherlands, 37% Mostly disagree: Greece, 88%
Willing to eat eggs from hens fed on GE corn	19%	66%	15%	Mostly agree: Netherlands, 33% Mostly disagree: Greece, 88%

Source: Eurobarometer (1999). The most comprehensive and systematic analysis of EU consumer perceptions of biotech applications is Gaskell and Bauer (2001). The authors of that volume also examine media and focus group responses.

which comparable data for the European Union and the United States is available.[18]

Consumer surveys after 1999 have produced very similar results. In a 2001 Eurobarometer survey of all 15 EU member countries, for example, 57 percent of the respondents believed that GE food was dangerous. Ninety-five percent of the respondents stated that they must have the right to know whether or not GE products are in their food, and that they must have the right to choose. Seventy percent stated that they do not want this type of food. Consumers in Finland and Spain viewed the technology in somewhat more positive terms, consumers in Sweden, Denmark, France, Austria, and Greece held the most negative views. In comparison to the United States, consumers in Europe perceive higher risks in GE food than US respondents. Analyses of media reporting and focus group studies report similar results. For example, media reporting on agricultural biotechnology tends to be more positive in the United States than in the European Union.[19] The most recent Eurobarometer survey, carried out in 2002 and published in 2003, shows that opposition to GE food has slightly decreased in a few EU countries but, on average, remains very strong. Even when potential benefits of GE food are clearly highlighted in survey questions (e.g., less pesticide residues, favorable environmental properties, better taste, less fat, lower price) 45–65 percent of the respondents would refuse to buy such products. Interestingly, consumers in the European Union appear to be least attracted by potentially lower prices of GE food.[20]

The theoretical argument above assumes that NGOs have profited from rather than instigated negative public perceptions of agri-biotechnology. The available survey data is largely congruent with this assumption. It shows that consumer acceptance of green biotechnology in the European Union was already rather low before 1996, when GE foods first appeared on the EU market and extensive NGO campaigns began. For example, from 1991 on surveys indicate rapidly declining optimism about biotechnology among EU respondents (from 0.55 in 1991 to 0.25 in 1999 on a 0–1 scale). In 1995, 33–50 percent of European respondents regarded GE food as a health hazard (as compared to 27 percent in the United States in 1999). European consumers also appear to have been concerned about labeling before 1996. In a Eurobarometer survey conducted in late 1995/early 1996, for example, 75 percent of respondents disagreed with the statement "it is not worth putting labels on GE foods."[21]

In view of these survey results the relatively positive consumer response to Sainsbury's GE tomato puree in the United Kingdom (see chapter 2) should not be viewed as representative of EU-wide public opinion on agri-biotechnology in 1996. The Sainsbury's case is frequently used by agri-biotech proponents to claim that consumers were enthusiastic about the technology in 1996, and that this enthusiasm was subsequently destroyed by NGO campaigns.

To demonstrate more systematically that NGOs have benefited from rather than created negative public views on GE food we would need more comparable time series data on public opinion—ideally, annual survey data for all EU countries for the years 1990–2002, based on identical questionnaires. Such data does not exist. However, with reference to the somewhat sketchy evidence we have, I largely concur with the conclusion by Gaskell and Bauer (2001:111–112), the authors of the most comprehensive and sophisticated survey of public perceptions of agri-biotechnology in the European Union to date:

> We would argue that while the NGOs were successful in mobilizing support amongst a European public that held them in high regard, they were not the instigators of European concerns about agricultural biotechnology. The Euro-barometer surveys show that as early as 1991 there were widespread concerns of the same type as in 1999. The NGOs capitalized on existing, if vaguely articulated, opposition. Over the years this was amplified and transformed into a considerable political moment.

The survey results discussed here also challenge two other popular explanations of restrictive EU regulations on agri-biotechnology. One regards the BSE[22] crisis as the principal cause. Pre- and post-1996 consumer surveys show that there is no sudden drop in consumer acceptance of agri-biotechnology around 1996, when the BSE crisis erupted in full, but a slow decline. I revisit this point further below. The other explanation sees general technophobia in Europe as the principal cause. Again, the survey data do not support this claim. European consumer perceptions across a range of technologies are, on average, not more negative than US consumer perceptions.[23]

Social scientists have thus far provided only sketchy answers as to why public acceptance of GE foods varies so much across the European Union and the United States. Explanations range from arguments about food culture, eating habits, and agricultural traditions to arguments about environmental and consumer group influence on public opinion.[24] Many of these explanations are neither theoretically nor empirically plausible,[25] others are more convincing.

Gaskell and Bauer (2001) identify moral concerns, concerns about risks, and perceptions of low benefits as the three principal driving forces of negative consumer views of agri-biotechnology in the European Union, with moral concerns acting as a veto factor. In their analysis of 1999 consumer survey data, these three variables account for 70 percent of variation in consumer support for the technology. Although leftist governments dominated in Europe when the technology was first marketed, Gaskell and Bauer argue that opposition to agri-biotechnology was, at least in Austria, Denmark, and Greece, less government than consumer driven. In France, Germany, the Netherlands, and Sweden, governments appear to have played a more important role. Interestingly also, the level of consumer knowledge about biotechnology has virtually no influence on the level of support for the technology. I will revisit this point in the concluding chapter.

Another very compelling finding is that public perceptions of authorities regulating and actors using the technology in question account in part for deviations between scientific risk assessments and public risk perceptions.[26] Survey results indicate that people who do not trust that biotechnology is adequately regulated are more concerned about possible risks and perceive smaller benefits from the technology. They show that Europeans trust regulatory agencies and politicians much less than North Americans.[27] Similarly, while US consumers trust scientific associations and the FDA as sources of information on food safety issues, Europeans express more trust in consumer and environmental groups. The most recent Eurobarometer survey demonstrates that in the European Union differences in levels of trust in particular societal organizations have remained remarkably stable between 1991 and 2002.[28] In brief, consumer support for agri-biotechnology appears to decline with perceptions of higher risk and lower public trust in regulators.[29]

Low levels of public trust by Europeans in their regulatory authorities have been attributed to a variety of influences, notably, general features of EU regulatory policy-making and specific food safety crises.

The EU does not have a scientific apparatus of its own. The Commission works with a wide range of committees, whose members are government officials, university scientists, and scientists from the private sector. This so-called commitology system has been widely criticized as nontransparent and open to political influence. Many analysts believe that this system is ultimately responsible for the severe mistakes in handling the BSE crisis and subsequent food scandals in the 1990s.[30] Public trust in the regulatory capacity of the European Union and its member states received an additional blow by corruption scandals and other management failures in the EU Commission in the late 1990s.[31]

The EU has in recent years engaged in a variety of reforms to restore public confidence in its regulatory capacity. These are reflected in the 1997 New Approach to Consumer Health and Food Safety, the 1997 Green Paper on the General Principles of Food Law in the European Union, and the Commission's 2000 White Paper on Food Safety. The aim of these reforms is to establish a more transparent and science-based approach to risk assessment, risk management, and risk communication. The recently established European Food Safety Authority has no regulatory powers of its own, but provides scientific advice, collects and analyzes information, and communicates with the public on issues of risk.[32] Whether this new system will create greater public trust in the European Union's food regulation system remains unclear. I will return to this issue in chapter 7.

As shown above, the BSE crisis may not have been a key determinant of negative perceptions of agri-biotechnology in Europe. However, it is widely assumed that the BSE crisis and other public health and safety scandals (e.g., the dioxin scandal in Belgium in 1999, and HIV contaminated blood in France and elsewhere[33]) in the second half of the 1990s have dealt another blow to public trust in regulatory authorities and the scientific expertise on which they rely.[34] These crises have also increased the receptiveness of the media to public health and environmental issues. Thus, they have contributed indirectly to more negative press coverage of agricultural biotechnology, with obvious implications for public perceptions.[35]

Social scientists do not yet fully understand the complex interactions between consumer perceptions, scientific evidence on risks, public trust in regulators, NGO campaigns, and their effects on regulatory processes. We know, however, that European environmental and consumer groups have focused on agri-biotech issues earlier and more extensively than their North American counterparts.[36] We also know from surveys that European consumers hold more negative views on agri-biotechnology and trust regulators less than their North American counterparts. It appears, moreover, that campaigns by environmental and consumer groups have contributed to increasing media coverage and public awareness of biotechnology issues. Thus, they seem to have reinforced the "right to know" justification for labeling, which tends to thrive in situations of widespread public concerns over food safety and low trust in regulators.[37] The same applies to negative public perceptions of GE foods.

On balance, the evidence suggests that public aversion to GE food and low public trust in regulatory authorities have helped NGOs in Europe in mobilizing their members and other (latent) supporters of their cause. NGOs have acted as amplifiers rather than instigators of the European consumer revolt that began in 1996. They have transformed latent consumer opposition into a powerful political movement with strong ties to environmental and anti-globalization movements. Due to their high collective action capacity, agri-biotech adverse NGOs have been able to shape societal responses to agri-biotechnology through market-oriented strategies (pressure on producers) and lobbying of policy-makers. I discuss political pathways of NGO influence in this section and focus on market pressure in the section on producers.

Some early interest in biotech issues notwithstanding, agri-biotechnology rose to the top of the agendas of European environmental and consumer groups only in 1996.[38] NGO campaigns were sparked particularly by the European Union's authorization of Roundup Ready soybeans in May 1996 and Bt corn in December 1996. With the benefit of hindsight, we now know that the European Union's regulatory authorities (and also producers) misjudged the extent of opposition when they approved these two GE crops without first putting in place effective labeling requirements and post-marketing controls (e.g., tracing and liability regulations).[39]

Greenpeace and Friends of the Earth Europe (FOE), the largest environmental interest groups in Europe, made agricultural biotechnology one of their top priorities and have invested heavily in campaigns ever since. The same applies to the European Bureau of Consumers' Unions (BEUC), a Brussels-based federation of independent national consumer organizations from all European Union and other European countries. While BEUC has lobbied mainly for stricter labeling of GE foods, Greenpeace and FOE have adopted strong anti-agri-biotech positions. All three groups, as well as many other environmental and consumer groups in Europe[40] have persistently and sharply exposed and criticized inadequacies in the European Union's agri-biotech regulations and their implementation.[41]

NGOs were not at the negotiating table when agri-biotech regulations were designed by the EU Commission and adopted by the Council and European Parliament. But one can spot their influence at several key points in the regulatory process. NGO influence on regulatory decisions has been facilitated in particular by well-developed access to the Commission and the European Parliament—in addition to access to national level institutions and decision-makers.

In the European Union most regulatory activity is initiated by the Commission. Analysts of European policy-making have shown that the Commission has deliberately promoted (and also financially and organizationally supported) NGO participation in many policy areas over the past two decades. It has done so for two reasons: first, to increase its constituency and thus counteract growing influence of the Council, the Parliament, and the European Court of Justice; second, to counteract persisting complaints about the democratic deficit of the EU.[42]

More specifically, in the second half of the 1980s, the European Union's Directorate General for Environment, Consumer Protection, and Nuclear Safety emerged as the leading agency for the regulation of agri-biotechnology. This Directorate's key role in developing Directive 90/220 and also the Novel Foods Regulation adopted in 1997 opened an important door for environmental and consumer group influence on the European Union's regulatory policy.

Historical accounts of the regulatory process[43] show that the leading role of the European Union's environmental directorate and the influence of NGOs were in large measure responsible for moving the European Union's agri-biotech policy from a system of monitored self-regulation towards process-oriented regulations that were grounded in the precautionary principle and emulated Danish and German consumer and environmental policies.[44] Similarly, the NGO-led public outcry over the Commission's approval of GE soy and GE corn in 1996 and its initial decision not to require labeling of these products strengthened the position of the European Union's environmental directorate within the Commission. The 1996 decision not to require labeling was consistent with the Novel Foods Regulation, as it was then under discussion.[45] Yet, strong opposition by environmental and consumer groups combined with concerns on the part of food processors and retailers (see below) enabled the European Union's environmental directorate to make a technical adaptation to Directive 90/220 in June 1997. This adaptation in effect overturned some provisions of the Novel Foods Regulation and required mandatory labeling for all GE foods.

Opportunities for environmental and consumer groups to influence the European Union's regulatory policy grew further with the 1986 Single European Act, the 1993 Maastricht treaty, and the 1997 Amsterdam

Agreement. These three agreements strengthened the European Parliament (EP). The co-decision procedure, which also applies to agri-biotech regulation, requires majority support for new regulations (or regulatory reforms) from both the Council and the Parliament. The EP, eager to ascertain in practice its formally expanding authority, has been particularly open to NGO influence. Many analysts in fact claim that the EP has become a champion of European consumer and environmental concerns.[46] Motivated in large part by NGO lobbying, the EP has repeatedly and successfully challenged proposals by the European Commission and the Council of Ministers that would have led to a relaxation of approval and labeling regulations.[47]

Producer Interests

Most farm interest groups as well as food processors and retailers have been driven into supporting stricter regulation by a combination of several factors: persistently negative public perceptions of agricultural biotechnology and regulatory authorities; concerted anti-agri-biotech campaigns by NGOs; particular features of industrial structure; and growing regulatory restrictions on the technology imposed by the European Union and individual member states. Biotech firms have found it impossible to stop this trend.

Concerned about growing differences in regulation among EU countries, the agrochemical, pharmaceutical, and food industries in the European Union began to argue in the mid-1980s that there was a need for EU-wide harmonization of biotech regulation.[48] Surprisingly, such statements were, in the early phase of the policy process, not accompanied by more concrete initiatives. Greenwood and Ronit (1995) and Patterson (2000) provide the following explanations.[49]

First, European firms were accustomed to organizing along product rather than production process lines. Thus, they did initially not regard themselves as biotech firms with a common interest. They were also concerned that organizing along process lines would invite regulators to install process-oriented regulations ("horizontal" regulations in the European Union's terminology). Second, the large number of medium- or small-size firms that had only recently entered the biotech field, combined with substantial economic competition among these firms, made collective action difficult. Notably, expectations differed between small or medium firms and large multinational firms as to the need for harmonized regulations and the cost implications of regulation. Third, the biotech industry overestimated the influence of EU directorates other than the environmental directorate, which opposed process-oriented (horizontal) regulation of agricultural biotechnology and had previously succeeded in excluding a wide range of products from drafts of Directive 220/90. Only in June 1989, when biotech firms realized that the tide was moving against them, did they create a Senior Advisory Group for Biotechnology (SAGB).[50]

Most analysts thus claim that the unwillingness or inability of input suppliers to organize in time is responsible for the industry's inability to prevent the European Union's 1990 decision to focus on process-oriented agri-biotech regulation. Input suppliers had viewed agri-biotech regulation largely as a means to facilitate the operation of the European Union's internal market through harmonization of regulations. But Directive 90/ 220 in fact put the European Union on a trajectory where agri-biotech regulation installed base standards for environmental and consumer protection. With reference to the very slow and cumbersome reforms of Directive 220/90 in 2001 and 2002, analysts claim that the path dependency of the European Union's complex regulatory system has, ever since, made it extremely difficult to return to the regulatory approach of the early to mid-1980s.[51] The latter approach had focused more strongly on science-based and monitored self-regulation. The outcome of efforts to reform Directive 90/220 (see chapter 3) demonstrates indeed that attempts by biotech firms and other agri-biotech proponents to obtain a relaxation of existing approval and labeling rules have been entirely unsuccessful.

The above explanation focusing on the timing of the industry's political organization accounts rather well for why producers were unable to prevent Directive 90/220. But the path dependency argument explains only in very vague terms why biotech firms and their supporters have never been able to reverse the regulatory trajectory the European Union entered in 1990. The theoretical argument outlined at the beginning of this chapter helps in filling the gap.[52]

Over the years the agri-biotech sector in Europe has become highly concentrated (as it has in the United States).[53] The conventional economic theory of regulation suggests that this market concentration should bolster the collective action capacity of biotech firms and translate into successful lobbying for less restrictive agri-biotech regulations. Alternatively, one might also claim that large European biotech firms will lobby for stricter agri-biotech regulation if such regulation can be designed to protect or enhance their competitive position—notably, vis-à-vis US biotech firms. The evidence disconfirms both propositions.

First, persistently negative public perceptions of the technology and campaigns by NGOs have neutralized virtually all attempts by European biotech firms and EuropaBio, the European Association of Bioindustries, to lobby for a relaxation of approval regulations and to prevent or relax mandatory labeling requirements. Activists from Greenpeace and Friends of the Earth, as well as many smaller groups, have engaged in a large number of media-effective anti-agri-biotech activities, for example, uprooting of GE crop fields, attempts to prevent the unloading of ships with US GE crops, and campaigns against leading agri-biotech firms.[54]

NGO campaigns against large agri-biotech firms have been particularly effective because these firms are vulnerable to problems of reputation. NGO campaigns have targeted firms headquartered in Europe, such as Novartis, Syngenta, and Aventis, but also firms headquartered outside Europe and active in the European market, most notably Monsanto. Because they supply GE-seeds, these firms are ultimately the sources of all GE products.

NGO campaigns have turned large agri-biotech firms into highly visible targets onto which the wider public has been able to project agri-biotech related fears, but also more diffuse fears about globalization, technological innovation, corporate control of the food supply, and US dominance over Europe. With slogans such as "Monsanto is trying to force-feed Frankenstein food to Europeans," activist groups have conceptualized GE products as a risk imposed on Europeans by powerful American firms and their government. In the late 1990s the United States inadvertently helped such campaigns with its efforts to pressure the European Union into lifting its ban on growth hormones used in meat production.[55] Similar to the growth hormones case, US pressure on the European Union to relax its restrictions on GE products has been widely perceived in Europe as an effort to impose, for parochial commercial reasons and against the will of consumers, a risky technology. Social science research on risk suggests that people are more willing to accept risks imposed by nature, but are likely to react unfavorably when forced to expose themselves involuntarily to man-made risks.[56]

Monsanto, Novartis, Syngenta, Rhone-Poulenc, AgrEvo, Aventis, Zeneca, and other leading agri-biotech firms have found it extremely difficult to defend against this onslaught.[57] Most biotech firms active in Europe as well as EuropaBio eventually adapted their position to NGO demands and have reluctantly supported mandatory labeling of GE food ever since. Permissive approval regulations and no mandatory labeling were (and still are) their preferred policies. But in view of strong consumer concerns over the technology, stern opposition by NGOs, and increasingly heterogeneous regulatory responses by individual EU countries, stricter and harmonized approval and labeling regulations became their second-best option.[58]

As to the second proposition, from standard economic theories of regulation we can derive the hypothesis that stricter agri-biotech regulation in Europe reflects protectionist demands by the European biotech industry. Restrictive regulations in the European Union may, for example, reflect attempts to provide some breathing space for the European Union's agri-biotech industry that could eventually allow this industry to catch up with US-based competitors. This assumption is in fact widely shared by supporters of the technology, particularly in the United States.[59]

The available evidence does not support this proposition. European biotech firms have persistently lobbied for laxer approval and labeling regulations and have spoken in favor of mandatory labeling only when they had no other choice. Moreover, it is difficult to see how European agri-biotech firms could derive economic benefits from stricter regulation. First, with very few exceptions (e.g., Syngenta) European biotech firms have focused more on medical than on agri-biotech applications. Second, even if they had engaged much more in agri-biotechnology, it is unclear whether and how the European Union could have designed regulations so that these would have benefited the European Union's agri-biotech industry at the expense of foreign competitors. Protectionist regulations would not have helped the European Union's agri-biotech industry with its key problems, namely, low public acceptance of GE products, regulatory constraints on the technology, and shortages of venture capital.

There are some possible indications for protectionist incentives among input suppliers. The European Union, for example, provides considerable funding for agri-biotech research while maintaining severe restrictions on the commercialization of the technology. Brazil's ban on Monsanto's GE soybeans is interpreted by some analysts as an attempt to provide breathing space for EMPRADA's indigenous R&D on GE soybeans. Syngenta (a Swiss firm), which makes much higher profits on pesticides than on GE crops, might benefit from the European Union's strict agri-biotech regulation because this regulation keeps substitutes for some pesticides (i.e., GE crops producing their own pesticides) out of the European market. Some agrochemical firms that use developing countries as a dumping ground for products banned in industrialized countries could see those markets disappear if GE crops substituting for traditional pesticides were adopted in poorer parts of the world. I would argue, however, that those assertions are insufficiently backed up by evidence. They do not provide a convincing argument that the European Union's strict regulation is driven by protectionist interests of the European agrochemical and biotech industry.

Let us turn to farmers, the second producer group on which this analysis focuses. Assuming large economies of scale in GE crop cultivation, many analysts predicted fierce opposition by EU farm interests to the introduction of the technology.[60] They assumed that large industrialized farms would benefit more from agri-biotechnology. Farms in the European Union, which on average are much smaller and less industrialized than US farms, would thus experience major disadvantages. From this argument, analysts and also many policy-makers, notably in the United States, have jumped to the conclusion that the European Union's biotech restrictions are the result of an "unholy alliance" between protectionist farm interests and environmental and consumer groups. The available evidence disconfirms such claims.

In the mid- to late-1990s, some farm interest groups in the European Union, for example, the European Farmers Coordination, expressed concerns about GE crops. But the majority of European farmers did not actively lobby regulators to impose restrictions. Lack of direct economic competition between imported GE crops and European farm produce appears to be the principal reason. Import and export data support this claim.

Imports of soybeans and corn from the United States have, since the mid-1990s, declined, to some extent probably due to regulatory restrictions (see also chapter 6). The US share in the European Union's corn imports dropped from 86 percent in 1995 to below 10 percent in 2000. US soybean exports to the European Union fell from around 2.6 billion USD to less than one billion USD in 2000. However, imports of these crops from other non-EU countries as well as total EU imports of soybeans and, to a lesser extent, also corn increased at the same time.[61] Whereas the European Union is largely self-sufficient in corn, EU production of soybeans amounts to less than 10 percent of domestic consumption. Because most of the corn and soy consumed in the European Union is used for animal feed, premiums for imported non-GE soy and, to a much lesser extent, corn may even have imposed additional costs on EU farmers. In other words, the European Union's agri-biotech regulations have not improved the competitive position of EU farmers vis-à-vis their US counterparts. On the contrary, they may have worsened their competitive position.

More active support by EU farm interest groups since the late 1990s for more restrictive agri-biotech regulation stems primarily from concerns about turmoil in European food markets. These problems have resulted from the BSE and other food safety crises, and also from more general problems associated with food surpluses[62] and massive restructuring and concentration in European agriculture. In this context, support for stricter agri-biotech regulation, and in some cases explicit support by farmers for anti-agri-biotech campaigns by NGOs, must be viewed as part of an overall effort to address consumer concerns and stabilize markets through stricter food safety regulation across the board.[63] Anti-agri-biotech views among EU farmers have also been bolstered by Monsanto's and other biotech firms' strategies of market entry—notably, their purchases of many seed companies and controversy over the "terminator" gene—

both of which raised the specter of corporate dominance over the European food supply. In particular, European farmers fear being squashed between oligopolistic pricing by biotech and seed firms (which would raise farmers' input costs) and oligopolistic pricing by food processors and retailers (which would reduce farm-gate prices). Finally, European farmers' turn against GE crops received an additional boost from the imposition by the United States of trade sanctions of over 100 million USD per year against EU agricultural products in the trade conflict over growth hormones.

Increasingly negative views on agricultural biotechnology among EU farmers have also been reinforced by cases in several EU countries where fields were accidentally planted with GE contaminated seeds.[64] NGOs and farmers have accused governments of being incapable of ascertaining that imported seeds are GE free. More generally, and similar to the BSE crisis, these cases have reinforced the view among consumers and also farmers that governments have lost control in food safety matters. In most of these cases, GE-contaminated crops were destroyed and farmers were compensated by their respective government—an implicit acknowledgement of problems in controlling seed imports.

Although opposition to agricultural biotechnology among EU farmers has so far not been driven by protectionist incentives, some analysts anticipate that such incentives could become stronger once new GE products with more direct competitive effects on EU farmers enter the world market on a larger scale (e.g., GE wheat, rice, fruit, meat).

Let us assume that biotech firms and seed developers come up with a new GE crop variety that produces radically higher yields than conventional crop varieties (e.g., wheat or corn). EU farmers would then face a dilemma. They could press the European Union to approve this crop variety. This choice would help in safeguarding the competitive position of EU farmers domestically and globally. But it would risk antagonizing EU consumers and NGOs. Falling prices due to increased supply would also accelerate the concentration process in European agriculture, with negative political repercussions in most EU countries. Or they could press the European Union not to approve this new crop variety (or GE crops in general). This choice would satisfy the majority of EU consumers and NGOs. It would also protect farmers from cheaper imported crops. But it would reduce EU farmer's competitiveness on a global scale. And it would increase trade tensions with the United States and other biotech-promoting countries. The above analysis suggests that EU farmers will tend towards the latter option due to consumer aversion, NGO opposition, and oversupply problems in European agricultural markets.

European farmers thus seem to be set on a trajectory towards stronger opposition to the technology. If at some point in the future the competitiveness issue dominated over the issue of consumer confidence and food safety, stricter labeling regulations would not solve the problem for EU farmers. In that case, farmers would lobby more strongly for more severe restrictions on GE crops and GE foods.

The European Union's agricultural policy has had ambivalent effects on farmers' incentives in this context. On the one hand, the Commission has proposed the approval of certain GE crops and tends to regard agri-biotechnology as potentially useful in increasing the global competitiveness of European farmers. On the other hand, increasing agricultural output (and thus falling prices) through GE crops would exert additional pressure on the Common Agricultural Policy (CAP). Subsidies to farmers under the CAP are, to a substantial degree, still tied to farm output. Increased output would thus strain the CAP's budget, which is already in trouble because of the European Union's expansion to Eastern European countries with large agricultural sectors. This might create incentives among EU policy-makers not to push for GE crop adoption., Moreover, ongoing agricultural policy reforms in the European Union are redirecting subsidies from intensive to extensive forms of agriculture, notably organic farming. This trend may create additional disincentives for European farmers to adopt technologies (such as GE crops) that potentially increase productivity.

The third producer group on which this analysis focuses includes food processors and retailers (downstream producers). Food processors and retailers in the European Union initially tried to resist demands for mandatory labeling. They were concerned about the cost implications and the possibility that consumers may shy away from food carrying GE labels. But since 1996 they have adjusted swiftly to the demands of environmental and consumer groups.[65] While most downstream producers have, in principle, not opposed GE products, they have given in to market pressure and have accepted demands for segregation, tracing, and labeling.[66]

This response by downstream producers to consumer and NGO demands has been facilitated by high concentration in the food retail sector in the European Union and low concentration in the farm and grain-handling sectors. Here lies one of the key differences between the European Union and the United States in industrial structure.[67] This difference helps in accounting for the weak collective action capacity of pro-biotech producers in the European Union but not in the United States.

Available indices of market concentration suggest that in 1996, when the controversy over biotech food began, the top 20 retail firms in the European Union controlled around 40–60 percent of the EU market.[68] In several EU countries, market concentration was as high as 60–80 percent. Dominance by one firm or a duopoly was (and still is) a dominant pattern.

The available data also suggests that concentration in the US retail food market was lower at that point in time.

Concentration of the retail sector in the hands of fewer firms in the European Union, and particularly their efficient organization through Eurocommerce, a Brussels-based association of the European retail and wholesale sector, has made it easier for European downstream producers to switch position in line with consumer and NGO demands.

Moreover, lower concentration of the European farm, seed, and grain handling sectors has facilitated the downstream industry's support for mandatory labeling. It has done so by offering a larger variety of segregated supply chains that can be effectively and efficiently controlled by individual processors, wholesalers, and retailers.[69] In contrast, higher concentration and vertical integration/coordination in the United States of the farm, seed, grain, and oilseed handling, and food processing sectors has led to rapid adoption of GE crops. But the concentrated bulk commodity system in grain and oilseed handling in the United States, combined with the absence of mandatory labeling, has made it much more difficult for US downstream producers to obtain non-GE produce. Reorganizing supply chains and segregating GE and non-GE products is much costlier in the United States than in the European Union because large parts of the US production chain are now "contaminated" with GE products.

However, the strategy of European downstream producers of differentiating products along GE/non-GE lines and stopping the anti-agri-biotech trend half way by accepting labeling quickly ran into problems. Under fierce pressure from NGOs labeled GE foods have gradually disappeared from the market, whereas thousands of products containing GE organisms in forms or quantities not subject to mandatory labeling remain on the EU market. By the end of 2000, almost all major food retailers and food manufacturing companies in the European Union had announced that their products would be non-GE.[70]

The first to adjust were large food processors worried about valuable brands. In 1997, Nestlé, a Swiss company that was initially opposed to GE food labeling, began to label its GE products in Europe without being legally required to do so. Unilever, a company based in the Netherlands and the United Kingdom, did the same in 1998. At that point in time, Nestlé was the world's largest food processor, Unilever the third largest. Both firms justified labeling with consumers' right to know, but emphasized that GE foods did not pose any health risks. In August 2000, Novartis, a Swiss firm, which in October 2000 spun off its agricultural business (now Syngenta), declared that it would no longer use GE ingredients in any of its food products worldwide. Many other food processors have followed this practice.

Similar to biotech firms, changes in the behavior of food processors have also been prompted by concerns over increasing differences in the regulatory policies of individual EU countries. Such differences threatened to reduce economies of scale advantages of large food processors. Concerns of this nature have, for example, been expressed by the Confederation of Food and Drink Industries (CIAA), the most important association of the food and drink industry in the European Union. Food processors have thus come to prefer stricter but uniform EU labeling and also approval regulations over permissive but increasingly heterogeneous regulations.[71]

Retailers have followed the same trajectory for the same reasons.[72] Under pressure from NGOs and consumers they have embraced mandatory labeling and, in many cases, have gone further and have withdrawn GE products altogether.[73] In response to the slow pace of EU-wide harmonization of labeling rules they have also issued joint standards to reduce uncertainty among consumers and producers, establish a level playing field, and reduce transaction costs in cross-border trade.[74]

From 1999 on, a fairly consistent pattern of interaction between NGOs and processors and retailers emerged. Producers labeled a variety of GE foods in conformity with declarations by individual firms, joint standards issued by producer associations, and finally EU regulations issued from May 1997 on. Examples are tomato sauce made from GE tomatoes and Nestlé's "butterfinger" (a peanut butter and cornflakes candy bar). NGOs then singled out labeled products, such as Nestlé's "butterfinger," for massive public campaigns. In response, retailers and processors withdrew these products. In other words, producers' support for labeling produced a "Catch-22" situation: if they labeled a GE product, they were attacked by NGOs and were forced to withdraw the product; if they did not label a GE product, they risked exposure through NGO campaigns plus legal action for violation of EU or national regulations. This pattern of interaction resulted in a rapidly declining number of labeled GE products on the EU market.[75] In brief, consumer demand for GE foods would probably not have collapsed without mandatory labeling.[76]

Public pressure on food processors and retailers has grown further due to the increasing extent of testing by NGOs and public authorities for undeclared and/or non-approved GE organisms. This has gone hand in hand with increasingly precise and decreasingly costly testing methods.[77] Whenever GE organisms have been discovered in food products, even if below the European Union's threshold, retailers have, in most cases, quickly withdrawn these products, particularly if they had previously declared that they would stop selling GE foods. While the costs of EU regulations had thus far fallen primarily on producers outside the European Union (US agricultural exporters, biotech firms), the cost implications of stricter agri-biotech regulations for producers in the European Union have begun to rise to some extent.

These costs vary across GE products. Significant problems for processors and retailers in the European Union have resulted primarily from soybean imports. For climatic reasons, the European Union produces only around one percent of the world supply of soybeans and imports around 14 million tons of soybeans annually. It also imports more than 10 million tons of shredded soybeans and other soy products. The European Union's own production amounts to a total of 1.6 million tons of soybeans, produced mainly in France and Italy. The largest part of the European Union's imports comes from the United States, Argentina, and Brazil, the first two of which are major producers of GE soybeans.[78]

Processors and retailers in the European Union have encountered much smaller problems with regard to GE corn. Segregation and certification that only the four GE corn varieties approved by the European Union are present,[79] or that, in the case of EU countries that have banned Bt corn, no Bt corn is present, is difficult and costly. The European Union's corn imports from the United States have thus decreased sharply. However, there is an abundant supply of non-GE corn from within the European Union and other countries. Premiums for GE-free corn have thus remained low, whereas premiums of 6–17 percent have been paid for non-GE soybeans. Because of low world market prices for soy and corn over the past few years, the overall effect of premiums on European consumers of imported soy and corn has been quite small.[80]

Despite these (rather small) problems with soybean imports it is very unlikely that processors and retailers will reverse their position and seek to re-establish a market for GE foods in the European Union within the next few years.[81] Their principal problem now is enzymes, vitamins, and food additives produced through biotechnology. These GE ingredients are used for and/or contained in thousands of food products on the EU market, usually in forms and quantities currently not subject to formal approval and mandatory labeling.[82] If all these products had to be formally approved, labeled, and subjected to an IP system under EU legislation, the food supply in the European Union would experience major disruptions. The strategy used by processors and retailers since 1999, to remove GE foods from the market rather than label them, would in many of these cases be extremely costly. Not surprisingly, producers who have declared their products GE free have implemented this commitment only with regard to soy and corn ingredients subject to mandatory labeling under current EU regulation. Governments, EU authorities, and NGOs, for their part, have so far largely refrained from coercing processors and retailers into accepting approval and labeling of *all* GE organisms in food products and *all* products produced through GE organisms. Whether this delicate balance can be maintained for long is anything but certain.

US Policy

In the United States permissive regulation has been installed and sustained by a broad and cohesive pro-agri-biotech coalition. This coalition comprises the large majority of input suppliers, processors, retailers, as well as farmers. Lobbying on the part of environmental and consumer groups for stricter agri-biotech regulation has remained relatively weak, primarily due to substantial consumer acceptance of GE products and trust in regulatory authorities. In addition, compared to the European Union stronger centralization of regulatory authority has made US regulators more immune to NGO pressure. These permissive regulatory conditions have also been sustained by (compared to the European Union) lower concentration in the retail sector and higher concentration in the farm, grain and oilseed handling, and food processing sectors. This industrial structure, which makes segregation and labeling costlier and harder to organize, has motivated downstream producers and farmers to resist (limited) consumer demands for stricter regulation.

Environmental and Consumer Interests

Some public controversy over biotech issues arose in the United States after the Asilomar conference in 1975,[83] when rBST (a biotech hormone that increases milk production in cattle) was marketed in the 1980s, and when first field trials of GE crops were carried out in California in 1987. But public concerns, to the extent they existed, were successfully addressed through scientific risk assessment and the courts. The latter protected the industry against virtually all legal challenges to biotech applications. By the mid-1990s, the US public appeared to have lost interest in environmental issues and, related to that, biotech issues.[84] Only in the late 1990s did US NGOs revisit the issue and begin to lobby on a larger scale for mandatory labeling of GE foods and stricter environmental and health risk assessment in the approval process.[85] Turning points are marked by the cloning of a sheep in 1997 and by the claim, published in 1999, that Bt corn may kill not only pests but also the Monarch Butterfly. The latter quickly became a symbol for the environmental risks associated with GE crops. Other indications are Jeremy Rifkins (1998) book, *The Biotech Century*, and protests against a USDA proposal to allow GE foods to be classified as organic. Since 1999 one also observes a larger number of US media reports on the agri-biotech controversy in Europe.[86]

However, in comparison to Europe, the proportion of US NGOs not fundamentally opposed to agricultural biotechnology is much larger. Consumers Union, for example, the largest US consumer interest group, has advocated mandatory labeling, but has not questioned the safety of GE food as such.[87] Similar positions have been adopted by the Environmental Defense Fund, the Union of Concerned Scientists, and the Center for Science in the Public Interest. Again, these three NGOs are not fundamentally opposed to agricultural biotechnology.[88] They have concentrated on allergens, labeling, and specific environmental effects of agri-biotechnology, have criticized the FDA's labeling policy, and have lobbied for mandatory labeling. Most NGO activity has consisted of lobbying of policy-makers on the basis of scientific arguments, and lawsuits against regulatory agencies, such as the FDA, and individual biotech firms. Fundamental opposition to the technology has been voiced chiefly by smaller and more radical NGOs.[89]

The evidence discussed below suggests that substantial public support for agricultural biotechnology and the broad and cohesive pro-agri-biotech coalition of producers and government agencies have made US environmental and consumer groups very reluctant to campaign against the technology. While the interaction effects of public risk perceptions and NGO campaigns are difficult to assess,[90] it appears that NGOs are willing to invest heavily in anti-agri-biotech campaigns only when they see a substantial public outrage potential or when public aversion is already high. Neither is the case in the United States.

Table 4.2 shows that, compared to Europe, US consumers view GE foods more favorably. Research that assesses the willingness of consumers to pay a premium for non-GE products and thus captures the intensity of consumer preferences more accurately than the data in table 4.2 confirms this assessment. Jutta Roosen, for example, finds that in the year 2000 French, German, and British consumers were willing to pay a premium of $9.3, $7.7, and $6.3, respectively, for beef not fed on GE corn. US consumers were willing to pay only $3.3.[91] Other data not shown here demonstrates that US public support for agri-biotechnology has remained quite high over time.[92] It is interesting to note that, whereas consumer perceptions on agri-biotechnology differ very much between the European Union and the United States, Europeans are not generally more pessimistic about new technologies (e.g., medical biotechnology) than North Americans.[93] Frequently voiced claims that stricter EU regulations on agri-biotechnology derive from greater technophobia in Europe are clearly wrong.

Surveys are no more than snapshots at a particular point in time; and it appears that US consumer opinion on the issue is quite volatile. Much depends on the wording of questions.[94] Some survey results suggest lower

TABLE 4.2
Consumer views in the United States and the European Union, 1999

	United States	European Union
Should GE food be encouraged (index, with a mid-point between positive and negative at 2.5)	2.7	2.1
Even if it has benefits, GE foods are fundamentally unnatural	49%	69%
If anything went wrong with GE foods it would be a global catastrophe	40%	57%
The risks of GE foods are acceptable	39%	21%
GE foods would bring benefits to a lot of people	65%	28%

Source: Gaskell and Bauer (2001:108–9).

US public support for agri-biotechnology than the survey results shown in table 4.2. Yet others show that consumer preferences for labeling are rather weak.[95] Nonetheless, even a conservative comparison of the large number of available survey data[96] allows for the conclusion that US consumers view agricultural biotechnology more favorably than consumers in the European Union.

As in the European Union, the driving forces of public opinion remain disputed. Some analysts point to differing levels of public awareness. Yet, the hypothesis that low levels of awareness make consumers less critical of the technology is hard to support. While some surveys show that US consumers are less aware and less critical of GE food than EU consumers, other surveys do not find differences in public awareness of the technology across the Atlantic.[97] It is equally difficult to find evidence for whether positive or negative press coverage or NGO campaigns are driving public option, or vice versa.[98] The same holds for arguments about deep-seated cultural differences, which crystallize in differing concerns about the "natural-ness" of food and concerns about environmental consequences.

One of the most evident differences between EU countries and the United States, and thus one of the most convincing explanations of transatlantic differences in consumer perceptions, is the degree of consumer trust in biotech information sources. US consumers trust the American Medical Association, the FDA, university scientists, registered dietitians, and farmers most, whereas Europeans put greater trust in consumer and environmental organizations and the medical profession.[99] Trust of US consumers in regulators and scientists has been sustained in the absence of major food safety scandals in the 1990s. In contrast, EU consumers have experienced a range of major food safety crises, most notably BSE and the Belgian dioxin scandal. These crises have dealt a large blow to the credibility of regulators and scientists in the European Union. In the United States, recent controversies over StarLink corn and the ProdiGene case (see chapter 2) have not significantly affected public support for agricultural biotechnology.[100]

As noted above, most NGOs in the United States have focused predominantly on the labeling issue, while survey results indicate that US consumers hold somewhat ambivalent views with regard to mandatory labeling. In the late 1990s these developments began to influence US regulatory policy and the behavior of producers. I discuss regulatory issues at this point and examine market developments (influence on producers) further below.

Until the late 1990s biotech policy in the United States was shaped almost entirely by the scientific community, industry, and the three US government bodies responsible for regulation (USDA, FDA, EPA). For example, NGOs were not substantively involved in the development of the FDA's agri-biotech approval and labeling policy. Their lobbying for mandatory labeling and stricter risk assessment gained some ground only when the StarLink problem emerged in September 2000 (see chapter 2).

A wide range of environmental and consumer NGOs, for example Greenpeace, Friends of the Earth, the Organic Consumers Association, the Genetically Engineered Food Alert, the Pesticide Action Network, Sustain, the Center for Food Safety, and many others seized that opportunity.[101] Most of these groups have severely criticized the FDA's January 2001 proposal on notification and voluntary labeling. They have requested more rigorous safety and toxicological testing for all GE foods and food additives and an end to what they have called the FDA's "no labeling, not safety testing" policy. Similarly, NGOs have criticized the inadequacy of EPA-mandated measures against cross-pollination of GE crops, as well as the EPA's environmental risk assessment practices for the technology.

In terms of its scale and intensity, this NGO activity has remained much smaller than its counterpart in Europe. Its overall effect on regulators has also been small. As reflected in its 2001 proposal, the FDA has stuck firmly to its permissive approval and product-oriented labeling policy. Aware that there is some public support for labeling, the FDA has sought to restrict labeling to a voluntary, market-driven process, and to make sure that it works in orderly fashion. As long as public acceptance of agricultural biotechnology and public trust in regulatory authorities do not decline dramatically it is unlikely that US regulations will become much stricter. Efforts to obtain stricter regulation via US state legislatures or referenda have been unsuccessful. The US regulatory system for agri-biotechnology remains far more centralized at the federal level and harder for NGOs to access than its EU counterpart.[102] Attempts to force regulatory changes through legal action have also failed. It thus seems that the future of GE crops and GE food in the United States will be decided in the market rather than through the regulatory process. The outcome will ultimately depend on reactions by food processors, retailers, and farmers to consumer pressure (in the United States and abroad), possible liability issues, and in the case of farmers also productivity gains that can be achieved through the technology.

Finally, it is interesting to note that European NGO campaigns against GE food have had little effect on US NGO's ability to launch similar campaigns. Efforts to create or amplify spill-over effects, for example through the Transatlantic Consumer Dialogue and similar forms of trans-atlantic interaction among consumer and environmental NGOs, have been largely unsuccessful.[103] This again confirms the proposition that NGOs cannot create public outrage, but that they tend to piggy-back on it. NGOs also need particular institutional structures to translate political campaigns into policy changes. Low public outrage and adverse institutional structures (from an NGO viewpoint) ultimately account for why NGOs have not been able to shape US agri-biotech regulation.

Producer Interests

In contrast to Europe, producers in the United States have been able to form and maintain a cohesive and well-organized pro-agri-biotech coalition that includes input suppliers, food processors, retailers, and farmers. Big agri-biotech firms have been the leaders in this coalition. The latter have coop-erated closely with regulators in what can be defined as a "boardroom" structure of biotech policy making.[104] Only since the late 1990s has this system become somewhat more open to influence by the US Congress and environmental and consumer groups. I focus again on three types of produ-cers: input suppliers, farmers, and food processors and retailers.

Boosted by large-scale government funding, a well-functioning venture capital market, favorable patent rights, and strong cooperation between industry and universities, the US biotech industry has developed into the world's largest.[105] As noted in chapter 2, the US firm Monsanto controls around 80–90 percent of the world market for GE seeds. To recuperate its enormous R&D costs, the US biotech industry needs biotech friendly regulation.

The large majority of input suppliers in the United States are organized in a single association, the Biotechnology Industry Organization (BIO).[106] In addition, large biotech firms have also become involved individually in the regulatory process.[107] BIO and its members have persistently supported permissive approval regulations and have strongly opposed mandatory labeling.[108] Thus they have backed the FDA's regulatory policy.[109]

Homogenous interests of its membership, substantial scientific expertise, and strong financial and other support from large biotech firms (e.g., Monsanto, Pioneer Hi-Bred, Astra Zeneca, Novartis) have equipped BIO with a high collective action capacity.[110] BIO maintains close relationships with the FDA and other US regulatory agencies. A large part of BIO's staff consists of former government officials. Many observers have also pointed to a "revolving door" policy in which employees move back and forth between regulatory authorities and biotech companies.[111] Industry views on biotechnology, notably with regard to economic competitiveness and pressure for fast commercialization to recoup R&D costs, have thus quickly found their way to US biotech regulators. To enhance consumer acceptance of GE products and safeguard against a "spill-over" from Europe, seven large biotech companies and BIO formed the Council for Biotechnology Information. They are investing around 50 million USD per year, and possibly up to 250 million USD over 3–5 years to build public support for biotech foods.[112]

This symbiotic relationship between input suppliers and regulators corresponds to a pattern that political scientists have defined as "boardroom" policy-making.[113] This pattern of policy-making is the most susceptible to regulatory capture by industry. Indeed, Henry Miller, a former FDA official and vocal agri-biotech advocate, once stated that "in this area, the US government agencies have done exactly what big agribusiness has asked them to do and told them to do."[114]

Negative public perceptions of GE foods, particularly in Europe, and to a much smaller extent also in the United States have, thus far, affected the cohesion of input suppliers only at the margin. Most notably, in combination with a variety of other factors they have encouraged several large firms (e.g., Novartis, Astra Zeneca, Pharmacia, Aventis) to divest or separate their agri-biotech parts. This development has contributed to a divergence of interests between firms engaged in agricultural biotechnology and firms engaged in medical biotechnology—with the latter blaming the former (notably Monsanto) for negatively affecting the overall biotech market.[115]

Data on GE crop cultivation (see chapters 2 and 3) shows that US farmers have adopted the new technology at a rapid pace, although adoption to date remains limited to a few, albeit important, crops—most notably, soybean, corn, and cotton. Why they have done so remains disputed. In principle, the benefits of GE crops include increased yields, lower production costs, easier management, and reduced pesticide use.

But the agronomic evidence discussed in chapter 2 (e.g., the data on profits) casts some doubt on the frequent assertions that GE crops have been highly beneficial to US farmers. In the absence of clear-cut evidence of higher yields and profits, analysts have often referred to more convenient pest management and vertical integration of the grain handling system as motivating factors.

The available data suggests that middle- to large-size farms have embraced GE crops more rapidly than other farms.[116] In contrast, the growing organic food market has provided an important niche for small farmers. We should thus expect operators of larger farms to favor more permissive approval regulation and oppose mandatory labeling. We should also expect them to support US trade policies designed to open world markets to GE products. Smaller family farms, which have been slower to adopt GE crops or have not adopted this technology (e.g., organic farmers), are likely to benefit more from stricter agri-biotech regulations that impose costs on larger producers. We should thus expect owners of smaller farms to favor stricter agri-biotech approval regulations and mandatory labeling. This difference in interests, driven by differences in industrial structure, should be most pronounced in the case of corn and soybeans, which account for the largest share in GE crops.

The evidence is largely congruent with these assumptions. The American Farm Bureau Federation (AFBF), the largest US farm organization, is dominated by large agricultural producers. It has fully supported the FDA's approval and labeling policy.[117] The National Family Farm Coalition (NFFC), a network of grassroots organizations working on family farm issues, opposes vertical integration of agriculture and corporate agriculture more generally. It has criticized US agri-biotech approval policy and has requested mandatory labeling.[118]

The American Soybean Association (ASA) and the National Corn Growers Association (NCGA) represent export-oriented producers with a large stake in GE crops.[119] Because producers of GE soybeans and GE corn are more export-dependent than other members of AFBF, ASA and NCGA have adopted even stronger pro-agri-biotech positions. Predictably also, concerns of ASA over problems of consumer acceptance and regulatory restrictions in other countries have been stronger than concerns of NCGA: US soy producers are more dependent on export markets than US corn producers: in 1996, when the agri-biotech controversy began, 37 percent of US produced soybeans or soybean products were exported, compared to 19 percent of US produced corn.[120] However, both associations are strong supporters of a permissive approval policy and oppose mandatory labeling.[121] The US Grains Council, which develops export markets for US crops, has adopted very similar positions.[122] The American Corn Growers Association (ACGA) represents smaller family farms. In contrast to the ASA and NCGA, ACGA has recommended stricter approval policies and mandatory labeling of GE foods.[123] Pointing to decreasing demand for GE food and feed since 1999, uncertainty over the costs of segregation, and liability problems with GE crops, it has encouraged farmers to opt for non-GE crops.[124]

Diverging interests due to differences in industrial structure, but also the fragmentation of the US agricultural association system more generally, have limited the collective action capacity of farmers. More than 200 interest groups are involved in US agricultural policy issues, and these groups specialize in different issues (general commodity associations, single commodity associations, and specialized associations). US agri-biotech regulation therefore corresponds to the interests of groups representing larger and export-oriented farmers, but not so much due to the collective action capacity of the latter. It does so because these groups have allied with biotech firms and food industry associations. Smaller farmers producing for the domestic market and favoring stricter approval regulations and mandatory labeling have only recently gained some more influence in alliance with environmental and consumer groups.[125]

This constellation of farm interests and its implications for US agri-biotech policy have been quite stable since the mid-1990s. Whether they will remain so in the medium to long term depends largely on the benefits of GE crops to farmers, many of whom survive on a narrow margin of profitability. These benefits are virtually impossible to predict. Estimates of current agronomic benefits from GE crops, as discussed in chapter 2, remain disputed. This holds even more for benefits from future GE varieties. Moreover, estimates of agronomic benefits do not take into account consumer acceptance, which may vary over time, countries, and crops. Consumer opposition to GE foods in the European Union, Japan, and other countries has increased between 1995 and 2002, and so has the stringency of approval and labeling regulations outside the United States. As a result, demand for non-GE corn and non-GE soybeans has grown and US soy and corn exports to countries with stricter regulations have suffered.[126]

The effects of these changes in consumer acceptance and foreign regulation on US farm interests have thus far been mitigated by several circumstances. Most notably, due to high costs of segregation and identity preservation as well as large government subsidies (which reduce commercial risks), export-oriented US farmers have responded only very slowly to changes in public risk perceptions and foreign regulation. GE soy and GE cotton acreage continued to expand through 2002, whereas GE corn acreage (where consumer and regulatory responses have been more negative) leveled out or declined. It is likely that differences in consumer reactions across countries and crops as well as US policies designed to mitigate the effects of consumer reactions on farm income will increase the heterogeneity of US farm interests with regard to GE crops. Under these circumstances, input suppliers and the FDA are bound to remain the leaders of the pro-agri-biotech coalition. The only serious risk to the coherence of this coalition could emanate from food processors and retailers.

Until the late 1990s, US food processors and retailers encountered very little consumer opposition to GE foods, which began to appear on the US market on a massive scale in the mid-1990s. They have not benefited much from the first generation of GE foods because this generation involves input rather than output traits. But many of them expect larger benefits from following generations of GE foods, some of which are likely to involve output traits such as enhanced nutritional qualities.[127] However, food processor and retailer interests have diverged to some extent since the late 1990s, primarily between smaller and larger firms and between firms serving the organic and non-organic food market.

The vast majority of large processors and retailers have supported the existing US approval and labeling policy, arguing that labeling would stigmatize their products and brands, and that it would be costly to implement. Grocery Manufacturers of America (GMA) and the National Food Processors Association (NFPA), the two largest associations of the US food processing industry, have been the most influential representatives of such interests. GMA represents primarily processors of branded foods, NFPA represents firms that process and package fruits, vegetables, meat, fish, specialty food, and beverage products.[128] In contrast, many smaller, specialized food processors and retailers, notably those in the organic food business, have supported stricter approval and labeling regulation. In their lobbying efforts, they have frequently allied with consumer NGOs, for example, Consumers Union, the Center for Food Safety, or the Alliance for Bio-Integrity.

While smaller producers, especially those catering to the organic food market, have sought to capitalize on somewhat increased consumer concern over GE foods by selling non-GE food, GMA and NFPA have, since the late 1990s, sought to reverse that trend through intensified lobbying of policymakers and public campaigns.[129] For example, pro-GE food processors and retailers have founded the Alliance for Better Foods (ABF), which so far has invested several dozen million USD in public relations activities and election campaign contributions.[130] Their efforts have focused particularly on preventing mandatory labeling. Indeed, they seem to have learned from Europe and Japan that labeling can have significant effects on consumer behavior. A May 2001 survey by the Center for Science in the Public Interest, a consumer NGO, shows that, while the intensity of consumer preferences for mandatory labeling is rather low, consumers would still hesitate to buy GE food if it were so labeled.[131]

These efforts have been somewhat weakened by defections from the pro-agri-biotech coalition of several large food processors and retailers.[132] In spring 1999, for example, Greenpeace sent letters to major baby food companies, asking if they had taken any steps to ensure that they were not using GE ingredients. In response, Gerber and Heinz, two large baby food producers, switched to non-GE-ingredients.[133] Firms such as McDonalds, McCain Foods, Frito-Lay, IAMS pet foods, Whole Foods Market, Wild Oats Markets, Seagram, and a range of others also claim to have reduced or eliminated GE foods from their US business in response to NGO campaigns.[134] The StarLink controversy has led to another wave of adjustments in corporate strategies. Archer Daniels Midland, for example, which purchases around 30 percent of all corn, soybeans, and wheat in the United States announced that it expected US farmers and grain elevators to start separating and segregating GE and non-GE crops. Other firms, such as ConAgra, ADM, and Cargill have made similar announcements.[135] Some analysts thus regarded the StarLink controversy as the "beginning of the end" of GE crops.[136]

The evidence is far too ambiguous to justify such a sweeping conclusion. First, it remains unclear to what extent these declarations and announcements have in fact been implemented. Moreover, a cautious interpretation of survey data (see above) suggests that US consumers do, in principle, value more choice and the right to know what is in their food. But they do not appear to be fundamentally unhappy with the current regulatory system, which does not include mandatory labeling. Public trust in regulatory agencies and public support for GE food do not seem to have suffered very much from the StarLink and the ProdiGene controversies. Both episodes have shown, after all, that US regulatory authorities, backed by strong national liability laws, were able to solve the problem quite effectively in a rather short time-frame. As long as consumer opposition does not grow further and (related to that) the intensity of NGO campaigns for mandatory labeling does not increase, food processors and retailers are unlikely to move further towards mandatory labeling and GE-free products.

In more general terms, the available evidence suggests that (compared to the European Union) lower economic concentration in the US retail sector, greater heterogeneity of interests among downstream producers, and the absence of a unified institutional structure for coordinating individual firm and industry positions (the equivalent of Eurocommerce) have made downstream producers more resistant to (rather low) consumer pressure. Resistance on the part of downstream producers has also been reinforced by higher concentration in the farm, grain and oilseed handling, and food processing sectors. These sectors operate largely on the basis of non-segregated bulk commodities, which makes it costlier to reorganize supply chains and segregate GE and non-GE products.[137]

CONCLUSION

This chapter has shown that the collective action capacity of agri-biotech adverse European environmental and consumer groups has been higher than the capacity of their US counterparts. This difference can be traced back to transatlantic differences in consumer perceptions of agri-biotechnology and public trust in regulatory agencies (public outrage). Differences in the extent and nature of NGO's agri-biotech campaigns reflect this variation in collective action capacity. Agri-biotech adverse groups in Europe have been more successful in shaping market responses and producer behavior than agri-biotech adverse groups in the United States. Public outrage in combination with more access to the regulatory process due to decentralized and multilevel policy-making has also enabled agri-biotech adverse interests in Europe to exert more influence on regulation. In the United States low public outrage and the centralized regulatory system for agri-biotechnology have acted against agri-biotech adverse interests. In chapter 5 I will expand on the effects of institutional differences between the European Union and the United States.

The evidence discussed above also shows that the collective action capacity of pro-agri-biotech producers has varied substantially between the European Union and the United States. Interestingly, "push" effects have played a more important role than the "pull" effects highlighted by conventional theories of rent-seeking (protectionism). Public outrage and NGO campaigns have divided producers in Europe and have thus reduced their political influence. But the pro-biotech producer coalition in Europe has been weakened not primarily because of protectionist "piggy-backing" by some producers (input suppliers, farmers). It has been weakened because those producers most vulnerable to market pressure by NGOs (notably, retailers and food processors) have been pushed towards support for stricter regulation. In contrast, in the United States a cohesive and well-organized pro-biotech producer coalition has prevailed due to lower public outrage and weaker campaigns by agri-biotech adverse NGOs.

The analysis demonstrates furthermore that, besides transatlantic differences in public risk perceptions and NGO behavior, differences in industrial structure play a substantial role in explaining why the pro-biotech producer coalition has become very weak in the European Union but not in the United States. Retailers, food processors, and grain handlers have been pivotal actors in this regard. Due to higher concentration of the retail sector in the European Union, both in economic and organizational terms, downstream producers in the European Union have found it easier than their US counterparts to coordinate and adjust their business strategies to changing consumer and NGO demands. In addition, the US farm, grain and oilseed handling, and food processing sectors are more concentrated than their European counterparts. And they rely primarily on non-segregated bulk commodities. This has made it costlier for US downstream producers to reorganize their supply chains and segregate GE and non-GE products. These structural rigidities in US agricultural, food processing, and retail systems make it likely that pro-agri-biotech policies in the United States will survive the ongoing decline of Monsanto, by far the world's largest supplier of GE seeds, and widespread divestment of agri-biotech divisions in the life sciences industry (e.g., by Novartis, Dow, and DuPont).

CHAPTER FIVE

Regulatory Federalism

THE INTEREST group (or "bottom-up") perspective applied in chapter 4 views influence exercised by NGOs and firms in markets and regulatory processes as the principal driving force of regulation. It largely ignores interactions among governments and their effects on regulation. Chapter 5 fills this gap. The "regulatory federalism" approach employed here regards agri-biotech policies as outcomes of interactions among political subunits (member states in the European Union, states in the United States) within a federal political system in which these subunits can to some degree act autonomously. The explanation concentrates on whether political subunits within the federal system can, by unilaterally installing stricter or laxer regulation of agricultural biotechnology, push the stringency of system-wide regulation up or down. The theoretical foundations of this explanation are briefly outlined in the following section. The analysis of agri-biotech policy-making in the European Union and the United States then shows that in the European Union we observe a substantial "ratcheting-up" effect, whereas such an effect is absent in the United States. These differences, which have been pulling EU and US agri-biotech policy in different directions, are likely to persist and produce a range of negative consequences for other countries and agricultural biotechnology as such. These consequences are identified in the conclusion.

EXPLAINING REGULATORY POLARIZATION "TOP DOWN"

The argument outlined here combines several propositions from the political economy literature on regulation and federalism.[1] Some authors claim that regulating the quality of products is more likely to lead to regulatory differences between jurisdictions than regulating production processes. One of the reasons is that product regulations can be used more easily and directly for protectionist purposes, that is, to shield domestic producers from foreign competition. Process regulations have only indirect effects on trade flows—they primarily affect production costs, the competitiveness of firms, and investment flows. They are harder to use for protectionist purposes. For example, food-packaging regulations are more effective in restricting certain food imports than regulations governing working conditions on farms.

Moreover, in most regional and global trading systems differences in production processes are, with very few exceptions (e.g., prison and slave labor), viewed as expressions of legitimate comparative advantages. Process-based trade restrictions are thus largely illegal under the WTO as well as most regional trade agreements. In contrast, international trade agreements allow for import-restricting product regulations under a variety of circumstances, for example, to protect public health and the environment.

In other words, international trade regulations are quite congruent with prevailing incentives with regard to product and process regulations. International law provides states with less leeway in imposing trade-restricting process regulations, and states usually have a smaller economic incentive to do so. International legal constraints on imposing trade-restricting product regulations are weaker, while states have a stronger economic incentive to use such regulations to shield domestic producers from foreign competitors.

In fully integrated product markets, such as those of the European Union and the United States, where agricultural and other goods are by law allowed to flow freely across the boundaries of the subunits (EU member states, US states), differences in product and process regulations can be problematic. Differences between subunits in process regulations, for example, worker protection, air quality standards, or corporate taxation, can lead to differences in production costs and thus competitiveness, which some governments and firms may regard as illegitimate. But as noted above, such effects on trade flows are more indirect and long term. Subunits are also more reluctant to address such differences system-wide (e.g., by harmonizing regulations) because they fear opening a Pandora's box: there is no objective boundary between regulatory differences that constitute legitimate comparative advantages and regulatory differences that constitute illegitimate market-distortions.[2]

Differences in product regulations between states located in an economically integrated federal system tend to be more problematic than differences in process regulations. Regulatory diversity in product regulations does not automatically lead to effective federal regulation (i.e., harmonization). But integrated markets and federalism often combine to discipline conflicts among subunits because non-agreement (i.e., continuing regulatory differences) would result in market fragmentation, something that all subunits usually want to avoid.

In some cases, conflicts over regulatory differences can be solved through mutual recognition: that is, each subunit grants access to goods lawfully produced in any other subunit within the same federal system (see chapter 6). In other cases, regulations are harmonized at the federal level. If each subunit subscribes to the same rules, goods can again flow freely. Harmonization instead of mutual recognition occurs primarily in policy areas where subunits with stricter regulation are unwilling to accept products produced in countries with more lax regulation. For example, countries that require catalytic converters in domestically produced cars will, for environmental and economic competitiveness reasons, be reluctant to allow imports of cars without such devices.

In principle, harmonization of product regulation can occur at any level of stringency, as long as the subunits in a federal system can come to an agreement. Three variables are primarily responsible for determining whether harmonization of product regulation occurs at lower or higher levels of stringency:

1   the extent of autonomy of subunits in a federal system with regard to a given regulatory issue;
2   the extent to which the electorate in states with stricter regulation would tolerate downward harmonization;
3   the extent of economic damage that would result from non-agreement.

Thus, the likelihood of harmonization at higher levels of stringency increases with the extent of autonomy of the subunits, the extent of opposition against downward harmonization in subunits with stricter regulation, and the extent of economic damage that would result from non-agreement. Note that this argument cuts against a popular proposition in the environmental policy literature. That proposition holds that devolution promotes regulatory laxity.[3]

The dynamics of upward harmonization are illustrated in figure 5.1.

Anti-agri-biotech state Pro-agri-biotech state	Strict regulation	Lax regulation
Strict regulation	4 3 (I)	1 1 (III)
Lax regulation	3 2 (II)	2 4 (IV)

Figure 5.1   Upward harmonization.

In this stylized situation, a pro-agri-biotech and an anti-agri-biotech state are located within a federal system that maintains a fully integrated market for agricultural goods. Each state has sufficient autonomy to establish, at least to some extent, its own agri-biotech regulation. That is, the federal government does not have full authority to impose uniform regulation. To simplify the argument, we assume that each state can adopt either strict or lax regulation. The pro-agri-biotech state prefers lax agri-biotech regulation, the anti-agri-biotech state prefers strict regulation. The benefits of each state range from 1(worst) to 4 (best). The benefits of the pro-agri-biotech state are depicted in the lower left of each quadrant, the benefits of the anti-biotech state in the upper right.

Let us assume that stricter agri-biotech regulation does not produce protectionist benefits, but that some states are genuinely concerned about public health and environmental effects of the technology—this assumption appears plausible in light of the evidence for the European Union (see chapter 4). Consequently, both states prefer harmonized regulation to differing regulation, but would prefer harmonization at different levels of stringency if they could decide in isolation of each other. The pro-agri-biotech state would, in principle, prefer harmonization at low levels of stringency (both states adopt lax standards), the anti-agri-biotech state would prefer harmonization at high levels of stringency (both states adopt strict regulation).

Because both states find themselves in an integrated market they cannot decide in isolation. If both states pursued the policies they like most the common agricultural market would be disrupted. Let us assume that, if this happened, the economic damage would be high—a plausible assumption given the high volumes of agricultural and food trade within the European Union and the United States. In quadrant II of the figure, the pro-agri-biotech state would receive a benefit of 2 instead of 4. It could cultivate and sell GE crops in its own market, but could not export such products to the other state because that state would not let such products into its market. The anti-agri-biotech state's imports of agricultural products from the other state would be disrupted. However, it could stick to its preferred policy and could continue to export its non-GE products to the other state. Its benefit would thus be 3. Outcome III would be highly unattractive to both, because each would regulate against its preferences and trade would be disrupted.

This leaves us with outcomes I and IV. Here we assume that the average voter and consumer in the anti-agri-biotech state strongly prefers strict regulation. If the pro-agri-biotech state stuck to lax regulation, the anti-agri-biotech state would, under pressure from voters (consumers), adopt strict regulation and risk a breakdown of the common market (outcome II) rather than agree to downward harmonization (outcome IV). Once the anti-agri-biotech state opts for strict regulation and credibly signals to the other state that it will not back down, the pro-agri-biotech state has a strong incentive to adjust its regulation upward because it benefits more from outcome I than outcome II.[4] It cannot obtain the maximum benefit from outcome I, but it will prefer harmonization to non-agreement. The following section shows that the dynamics illustrated in figure 5.1 are clearly observable in the European Union, but not in the United States.

COMPARING EU AND US REGULATORY POLICY

The evidence supporting the interest group explanation (see chapter 4) does not differentiate between individual EU countries and US states. This simplification facilitates explanation but misses out on the implications of variation in interests and policies across jurisdictions. A quick review of such variation illustrates this point. Table 5.1 shows that in 1996–1999 (the last year for which such data is available) public support for agricultural biotechnology varied strongly across EU countries. For example, while consumers in Austria, Luxembourg, and Greece were very critical of the technology, consumers in Spain, Portugal, the Netherlands, and

TABLE 5.1
Consumer acceptance of agricultural biotechnology in EU countries, 1996–1999, 2002

	GM crops	GM food
Austria	− 2 (− 1)	− 2 (− 1)
Belgium	+ 1	− 1
Denmark	− 1	− 2 (− 1)
Finland	+ 1	+ 1
France	− 1	− 1 (− 2)
Germany	+ 1	− 1
Greece	− 1	− 2
Ireland	− 1 (+ 1)	− 1 (+ 1)
Italy	+ 1 (− 1)	− 1
Luxembourg	− 2 (− 1)	− 2
Netherlands	+ 1	− 1
Portugal	+ 2 (+ 1)	− 1 (+ 1)
Spain	+ 2	+ 1
Sweden	− 1	− 2 (− 1)
United Kingdom	− 1 (+ 1)	− 1

Sources: Nature Biotechnology 18 Sept. 2000:938; Gaskell and Bauer (2001:58).
Note: Countries are ranked from most negative (− 2) to most positive (+ 2). The values for 2002 are in parentheses if different from 1996–99 averages. See Gaskell et al. (2003).

TABLE 5.2
Public perceptions, media coverage, and policy in the European Union, 1996–1999

	Facilitative	← .... →	Constraining
Public perceptions	Finland, Netherlands, Italy, Portugal (United States, Canada)	Germany, United Kingdom	Austria, Greece, Sweden, Denmark, France (Switzerland)
Media coverage	Germany, Italy (United States, Canada)	Finland, Netherlands, France	Austria, Sweden, United Kingdom, Denmark, Greece, Portugal (Switzerland)
Policy	Germany, Finland, Netherlands, (United States, Canada, Switzerland)	Portugal	Austria, France, Sweden, United Kingdom, Greece, Denmark, Italy

Source: Gaskell and Bauer (2001:121).

Finland held more positive views. Additional data not shown here indicates that negative public views of agri-biotechnology increased strongly over time in Greece, Luxembourg, Belgium, France, and the United Kingdom, and that public acceptance of the technology remained persistently positive in the Netherlands and Finland.

To provide a broader picture of the "public sphere" in which agricultural biotechnology is situated, Gaskell and Bauer (2001) compare perceptions, media coverage, and policy. Table 5.2 again indicates substantial variation across EU countries.

In 1996–1999, in Finland, the Netherlands, and Germany, the three elements of the "public sphere" were more favorable to agricultural biotechnology than in Austria, Denmark, France, Greece, Sweden, and the United Kingdom. Countries where the three elements did not line up include Portugal and Italy (and also Switzerland). From 1996 to 1999 the level of controversy—measured by an analysis of media reporting—decreased in the United Kingdom, Germany, Italy, and Austria, but increased in Greece, France, Portugal, Denmark, and Finland.

These findings are largely congruent with policy positions with regard to the European Union's 1998 moratorium on new approvals of GE crops (with the exception of the United Kingdom, which opposed the moratorium). Denmark, France, Greece, Italy, and Luxembourg have strongly backed this moratorium. Belgium, Sweden, Austria, Portugal, the Netherlands, Finland, and Germany have adopted somewhat more moderate positions. The United Kingdom and the Netherlands have explicitly opposed a formal moratorium.[5]

Unfortunately, the available survey data on consumer perceptions of agricultural biotechnology does not allow for a systematic assessment of differences between US states. Neither does the available information permit a comparison of policy and media reporting differences between US states. Consequently, we do not know for sure whether or not variation across US states exists to the extent it does in the European Union. However, this information gap is no coincidence. It reflects an assumption among social scientists that differences across gender, education level, etc. are more important than differences across US states.[6] It also reflects the fact that agri-biotech regulation is firmly in the hands of the US federal government, with very little interaction between US states (see below). Differences in agri-biotech policy positions of individual US state legislatures, governments, and consumers appear to have been largely inconsequential for policy-making in this area at the federal level. In the European Union, such differences have been crucial, with obvious incentives for social scientists to collect data.

In principle, differences across EU countries (and to some empirically unobservable extent perhaps also across US states) may lead to a competition in laxity among jurisdictions. In that case, jurisdictions that install laxer regulation may drag everyone's standards down to the lowest common denominator. We have also seen, however, that there are conditions under which subunits imposing stricter regulation are likely to drag everyone's standards up. The following analysis demonstrates the latter trend for the European Union. In contrast, the institutional setting in which US agri-biotech policy is made has rendered that system largely immune to such pressure.

"Ratcheting Up" in the European Union

The dynamics illustrated in figure 5.1 correspond quite closely to what has happened in the European Union. On the one hand, EU countries are bound by supranational rules that guarantee the free flow of agricultural goods. On the other hand, they maintain considerable autonomy in closely related policy areas, such as environmental and public health regulation. In particular, individual EU countries have in many areas safeguarded the right to establish regulations that are stricter than harmonized EU standards, or that deviate from the principle of mutual recognition. Predictably, this autonomy has caused more conflict with respect to product than process regulation. The European Court of Justice (ECJ) has repeatedly upheld national regulations that deviated from EU norms.[7] Its rulings are in many ways reminiscent of comparable WTO verdicts (see chapter 6). Stricter national regulations that have trade-restricting effects are usually upheld by the ECJ as long as they do not discriminate between imports from different EU countries, do not favor domestic over foreign producers, and can be justified from a scientific viewpoint (at a minimum in terms of the precautionary principle).[8]

The constraints of partial national autonomy have been felt in EU decision-making on agri-biotech issues. Authority in EU agri-biotech regulation is divided between the Council (the key EU body where national representatives interact), the European Commission, and the European Parliament (the latter two are supranational EU bodies). The Commission holds a monopoly in proposing new regulation. To become effective, its proposals must obtain a majority of votes in the Council and the Parliament. In the Council votes are weighted by country size (e.g., Germany has 10 votes, Luxembourg 2). As of late 2002 (before the expansion of the Union from 15 to 25 countries, scheduled for spring 2004), majority decisions required 62 votes in favor, 26 votes constituted a blocking minority (the total number of votes was 87). Voting in the Parliament was by simple majority among MEPs present and voting (626 total).[9]

When we combine the above overview of national policies (tables 5.1 and 5.2) and the decision-making rules just described we see that there is no clear majority either for stricter or for laxer agri-biotech standards. Germany, Italy, Finland, and the Netherlands (which favor a more facilitative policy) hold 28 votes. France, Greece, Austria, Sweden and Denmark (the most agri-biotech constraining countries) hold 26 votes. If we add the United Kingdom (which tends to favor restrictive agri-biotech policies), the votes in favor of stricter rules increase to 36. In other words, both groups hold sufficient votes to block policy changes. Even if EU countries were not allowed to impose stricter than harmonized agri-biotech rules it would be hard to find 62 votes in favor of a relaxation of existing standards. Moreover, the agri-biotech critics would find it difficult to muster enough votes for stricter rules. In this scenario, there would simply be deadlock. Because agri-biotech issues are highly controversial, EU countries may also decide to apply the consensus rule to avoid implementation problems—overruled countries tend to drag their feet when it comes to implementing decisions. In that case the likelihood of deadlock is even higher.

Partial national autonomy combined with domestic pressure, preferences of the EU Commission, and the co-decision procedure (majority requirement in the Council and the European Parliament) account for why a "ratcheting-up" trend, rather than deadlock, has occurred. Particularly at times when EU decision-making bodies were deadlocked on the issue individual EU countries favoring stricter regulation introduced or threatened to introduce national rules, thus increasing regulatory heterogeneity. This heterogeneity has been amplified by rules that retailers or food processors have set for themselves (e.g., labeling standards) to reduce market uncertainty pending EU regulation. In the food sector, where the EU maintains a highly integrated market, this heterogeneity in product regulations has been felt very quickly and directly.

Driven by domestic public perceptions, media attention, and lobbying from agri-biotech adverse interest groups, EU countries with stricter regulations have refused to relax those rules. Even in cases where one or more EU states unilaterally imposed stricter rules and those rules appeared to violate EU regulations, neither the Commission, nor pro-agri-biotech governments, nor agri-biotech firms took these countries to the ECJ.[10] Even if they had it would have been far from clear that the disputed regulations would have been invalidated by the ECJ. Moreover, countries found guilty would probably have done everything to avoid compliance with a negative verdict.[11]

The Commission has usually given in to pressure from agri-biotech adverse countries. It has generally favored more permissive agri-biotech policies. But facing disruptions in the European Union's internal market, it has consented to stricter and harmonized standards to avoid (on average) laxer but heterogeneous rules. Many food processors and retailers, notably those that operate in many EU countries, have held similar preferences. Some analysts also claim that the Commission has supported higher standards because harmonized standards transfer authority to the supranational level, and to the Commission in particular. Finally, the Parliament, the majority of whose members present and voting must also back proposals by the Commission to relax or tighten agri-biotech rules has generally supported stricter consumer standards.[12]

The EU Commission's and the Parliament's positions have also been shaped by other considerations. The European Union's treaties commit supranational policy makers to the highest possible standards of consumer and environmental protection and the precautionary principle. In view of widespread public skepticism about European integration and low trust in regulatory authorities, EU policy makers have had little incentive to lower protection standards, even when such standards appeared to apply to perceived rather than scientifically proven risks.

These dynamics of EU agri-biotech decision-making have led to a "ratcheting-up" trend. Deadlock in EU decision-making has led to regulatory heterogeneity as individual states and food industries have adopted their own rules. Heterogeneity has then motivated the establishment of harmonized minimum standards at the EU level. Unilateral imposition of regulation (or industrial self-regulation) stricter than existing minimum standard has subsequently induced EU countries to raise the respective base standards closer to the stricter national standards. And so on. This ratcheting-up effect can be illustrated with two examples.

First, beginning in the mid-1990s some EU countries unilaterally introduced mandatory labeling for GE foods in the absence of EU-wide legislation, whereas other EU countries opted for laxer rules. For example, Denmark required full disclosure of any GE ingredients, whereas the United Kingdom did not require labeling of substantially equivalent foods. In other cases, some countries unilaterally banned the marketing of GE corn and soy despite EU approval of the respective products. For example, Austria, Italy, and Luxembourg invoked the safeguard clause in directive 90/220 to ban the import of Bt corn into their countries. In another case, the French government first prohibited the cultivation of Bt corn although it had been approved by the European Union. In 1998, it approved the planting of Bt corn, but under opposition from Greenpeace and other NGOs, reversed its decision. None of these unilaterally imposed regulations has been challenged in court, be it by the Commission, pro-agri-biotech governments, or private-sector firms. Instead, growing heterogeneity has translated into intensified efforts at EU-wide harmonization of rules and has resulted in stricter standards.

Second, a call in 1998 by Greece for other countries to sign a statement in favor of a freeze of new GE product approvals pending stricter approval and labeling regulation by the European Union snowballed into an EU-wide moratorium on new approvals. This happened when it became clear that around half of the European Union's member countries would unilaterally impose such a moratorium in the absence of a Council decision to that end. De jure, the Commission can still issue approvals against the will of individual EU member countries. De facto, its authority to that effect has been suspended and taken over by the EU member states since 1998.

Centralized Laxity in the United States

In the United States the authority of individual states to install agri-biotech regulation that is more restrictive than federal rules is heavily constrained. First, decision-making occurs exclusively at the federal level and within very few institutions. Rules are issued and enforced by the FDA, the USDA, and the EPA—with the FDA holding the dominant position.[13] In contrast, EU rules are adopted in a decentralized and multi-level procedure.[14] They are proposed by the Commission and must be adopted by majority by the Council and the European Parliament. In the United States, the equivalent would be that proposals by the FDA, USDA, EPA, or the US President would require majority support from a body composed of state governors (or states' environmental or agriculture ministers) and the US Congress. In other words, decision-making is far more centralized in the United States than in the European Union.[15]

Second, even though agri-biotech rules have thus far been set exclusively at the federal level, US states may have some legal or de facto authority for unilaterally issuing and enforcing higher than federal standards. In the past, this has happened in a variety of environmental policy areas.[16] Indeed, legislatures in several US states, for example North Dakota, Montana, Oregon, Minnesota, and California have debated proposals for agri-biotech restrictions. The most prominent proposals were meant to ban specific GE crops and introduce mandatory labeling of GE food. But thus far, no proposals that would impose substantial constraints on GE crop cultivation or sale or would introduce mandatory labeling have been adopted. In late 2002, for example, voters in Oregon rejected a ballot initiative for mandatory GE food labeling with a majority of 73 percent.[17] Three proposed bills on labeling and moratorium issues in Vermont got nowhere. A recent survey shows that in 2001–2002, 158 pieces of legislation on agri-biotech issues were submitted in 39 US states. Forty-five pieces of legislation were adoped, two-thirds of which dealt with criminal enforcement against GE crop destruction by protesters. Other pieces of legislation dealt with liability issues. None of the legislation that passed imposed mandatory labeling or restrictions on GE crop cultivation or marketing.[18]

If such legislation was adopted at some point in the future it would almost certainly be challenged in court. Legal opinion on the issue remains divided. Some lawyers claim that unilateral state restrictions would violate the interstate commerce clause of the US constitution. This clause gives Congress the power to regulate commerce among US states and prohibits state regulations that benefit in-state economic interests by burdening out-of-state producers. Other lawyers claim that carefully designed agri-biotech restrictions may not violate that clause.

Court decisions in other environmental and consumer protection cases provide some, albeit limited, guidance. State statutes that were discriminatory or had an extraterritorial reach were usually invalidated. Moreover, the burden on interstate commerce must not outweigh local benefits, and no other less trade-restrictive means should be available to advance a legitimate local interest.

In principle, restrictions on agricultural biotechnology imposed by individual US states could be protected by the courts if they imposed similar burdens on in-state and out-of-state producers (e.g., seed suppliers) and did not in other ways unduly advantage in-state interests. They might also be upheld if discriminatory aspects of a statute could be defended by evidence that local interests were of great economic, public health, or ecological importance and no other means could achieve the same purpose. Legitimate local interests might include protection of local farmers from cross-pollination or other forms of crop "contamination" by GE organisms and from associated liability problems, protection of the environment from genetic drift, or protection of farmers and states' grain handling industry from export losses. Restrictions might be legitimized particularly if new GE crops could permanently alter the environment and farmers' competitiveness. Agri-biotech restrictions would also be more likely to survive challenges in court if they did not control conduct beyond the respective state's boundaries (extra-territorial effect). That could be the case if statutes were limited to restricting in-state cultivation and sale of GE seeds or crops. Other measures such as bans on GE food sales or mandatory labeling requirements would be much harder to defend because they would directly affect farmers and input suppliers in other states. In 1996, for example, Vermont's labeling law for BST (a hormone used to stimulate milk production in cows) was invalidated in court.[19]

The legal limits of US states' autonomy in agri-biotech regulation have not yet been tested to a substantial degree. From the above arguments, however, it appears that the autonomy of US states in this area is smaller than its counterpart in the European Union. The fact that very few US states have even attempted to restrict the technology might be an expression of these constraints.[20] Alternatively, it might simply be the result of low public ("bottom-up") pressure for restrictions, relatively homogenous producer interests, and massive industry lobbying against such rules (see chapter 4).

The ballot vote on labeling in Oregon and other attempts to impose restrictions on agri-biotechnology at the state level suggest that all of the aforementioned factors can play an important role. In Oregon, for example, the rejection of mandatory labeling is attributed by many analysts to aggressive lobbying by the biotech industry, a rather low intensity of consumer preferences for restrictions on GE food, and concerns over the political and legal feasibility of unilateral state legislation in this area.

Whether the characteristics of US regulatory federalism or other factors are primarily responsible for locking in the current US system of regulatory laxity in agri-biotechnology is impossible to determine with precision at this stage. In the same vein, we do not know to what extent regulatory federalism in the US would make current US agri-biotech regulation resilient against potentially growing bottom-up pressure in important US states. Systematic analysis by other authors of all failed attempts to impose state-level restrictions on GE food in the US will hopefully contribute to closing this research gap in the near future.

However, let us assume that public pressure for restrictions grew in some US states; that these states imposed some restrictions; and that these restrictions were upheld by the courts. Even in that case, which at present appears unlikely, a "ratcheting-up" trend would probably emerge much more slowly than in the European Union. As noted above, agri-biotech regulation is centralized at the federal level with no formal opportunities for state governments to ratchet up federal regulatory stringency through majority decision-making. The most likely scenario would then be that some large states introduce restrictions, and that these restrictions have negative effects on other states' agricultural exporters. Farmers in the latter states, perhaps followed by their governments, would thus have an incentive to meet the higher standards in their export markets if they cannot defeat these stricter standards in court. Eventually, this "trading-up" effect, the best known example of which are auto emission standards in the United States,[21] would spread throughout the United States and would eventually motivate federal agencies to tighten their agri-biotech regulation. We are still far away from this scenario.

CONCLUSION

The analysis in chapters 4 and 5 has shown that a combination of interest group dynamics and particular characteristics of regulatory federalism has increased regulatory restrictions on agricultural biotechnology in the European Union. These forces are much weaker in the United States, which accounts for regulatory laxity there. Will regulatory polarization between the European Union and the United States persist? The evidence points to a resounding Yes.

The combination of low public acceptance of GE foods and low trust in regulators, pressure by NGOs, growing opposition against GE crops among farmers, strong incentives for processors and retailers to withdraw from the market for labeled GE foods, and institutional inertia in EU policy-making make a reversal of the trend against agricultural biotechnology in the European Union very unlikely. To the contrary, mandatory labeling is a solution for those consumer concerns that center on information asymmetry, but not a solution for consumer concerns centered on risk-shielding of entire societies or moral/ideological issues. Moreover, mandatory labeling does not solve problems of agricultural excess capacity and inferior competitiveness of European farmers on a global scale. Mandatory labeling may thus be only an intermediary step on the way to even more severe restrictions on GE crops and foods in Europe.

The dominance of agri-biotech adverse interests in the European Union is bolstered by the characteristics of regulatory federalism in Europe. Decision-making structures in the European Union allow agri-biotech adverse minorities to block attempts at relaxing existing restrictions. In addition, the combination of decentralized and multi-level decision-making, substantial regulatory autonomy of EU countries, and concerns about safeguarding the European Union's internal market encourage a "ratcheting-up" of agri-biotech regulations through majority decision-making.

If it is very unlikely that the European Union will move towards the US regulatory model of centralized laxity in agricultural biotechnology, will US policy move towards the EU model? The evidence suggests it will not. Slightly growing public concern over GE food since the late 1990s, and the StarLink controversy in particular, have produced some cracks in the pro-agri-biotech coalition. Several large biotech firms have divested their agri-biotech divisions and interests between firms engaged in medical and agricultural biotechnology have begun to diverge. Some food processors and retailers have moved towards GE free products and voluntary labeling. This development has weakened pro-agri-biotech campaigns. The StarLink and ProdiGene controversies as well as disputes over technology fees have led to conflicts between farmers and input suppliers. However, these cracks have thus far been much to small to pose a serious threat to the cohesion and political influence of the pro-agri-biotech producer coalition in the United States. Potential conflicts between US farmers and input suppliers in view of precarious export opportunities for GE crops have been largely drowned in government subsidies for US farmers. These subsidies, which were massively expanded in 2002, have disproportionately benefited large soybean and corn farmers, many of which cultivate GE varieties. More subsidies lead to lower commercial risks associated with GE crop cultivation, and this increases incentives to adopt the technology. Moreover, as shown in chapter 4, rigidities inherent in industrial structures (notably, lower concentration, in economic and organizational terms, of the retail sector; higher concentration in the farm, grain handling, and food processing sectors) make it more difficult for US than for EU producers to adjust to consumer and NGO demands for segregation and labeling.

In addition to low interest group ("bottom-up") pressure for stricter agri-biotech regulation, the characteristics of US regulatory federalism act against more restrictive agri-biotech policies. The above analysis shows that even in the unlikely event that consumer pressure for tighter rules grew low regulatory autonomy of US states in agri-biotech matters combined with centralized decision-making at the federal level would slow down any "contagion" effect that may emanate from individual US states trying to unilaterally impose more restrictive policies.

Persisting regulatory polarization poses problems not only for the world's two largest economies alone. It also affects other countries and hampers the further development of agricultural biotechnology in a variety of ways.

First, it limits the policy options of other countries, particularly those that are economically dependent on the European Union, the United States, or both. For some countries, there appears to be no other choice than to align their policy with that of a dominant neighbor. Switzerland, Norway, and Central and Eastern European countries have thus aligned with the European Union, Canada with the United Stated. Yet other countries' economic dependence on the European Union or the United States is small enough to allow for some room for maneuver, but large enough to prevent autonomous decision-making. Many of these countries, for example, China, Brazil, India, Japan, Mexico, and Russia, have thus adopted regulations whose stringency lies somewhere between the EU and the US models. Agri-biotech policy in these countries is very recent and very much in flux.

Both the European Union and the United States are currently battling for influence on the regulatory policies of these countries by trying to entice, coerce, or cajole these nations into one or the other policy. Whether these countries will eventually move more towards the EU or the US model of agri-biotech regulation remains open. In any event, regulatory polarization makes it much harder for many countries to decide, according to their own local or national economic, ecological, or humanitarian needs, on whether to promote or restrict agri-biotechnology.

This problem became particularly visible and disturbing when, in 2002, controversies over US food aid to sub-Saharan Africa arose. This food aid included GE crops and was therefore refused by some recipient countries, notably Zambia. The US government and other proponents of agri-biotechnology quickly accused the European Union as well as some African countries of Luddite and immoral positions that contributed to starvation in developing countries. They also called for trade sanctions against the European Union, claiming that the Europeans were forcing African states to refuse US food aid on the grounds of imaginary risks. Agri-biotech critics, for their part, accused the US government of trying to force-feed starving Africans on GE food with the aim of opening new markets for the technology.

Second, regulatory polarization reduces returns on investment in the technology. It thus deters further private investment in agri-biotech

R&D, not only in Europe and countries with similar restrictions, but also in agri-biotech promoting countries like the United States, Canada, and Argentina. Regulatory polarization has clearly increased commercial risks, notably for US input suppliers, farmers, food processors, and retailers because of higher uncertainty over export markets and fears of a spill-over of agri-biotech aversion from the European Union to the United States. Leading agri-biotech firms have invested heavily in the technology, but have become hesitant to direct more investment into this area. Negative effects can also be observed with regard to commercialization of new GE varieties and adoption of GE crops by farmers worldwide.

Third, regulatory polarization deters public and NGO support for agri-biotech R&D in developing countries where this technology could potentially contribute most to alleviating food supply problems. To improve their image and raise political support for the technology, some input suppliers have provided free access to patented GE crops to some developing countries. But such gifts are ad hoc and selective. Commercial incentives of input suppliers are biased towards OECD markets, where purchasing power is much higher. Intensified ties between private sector and university R&D (which are driven by narrow financial interests), particularly in the United States but also Europe, have reinforced that bias. Government and NGO support is unlikely to fill the gap. In Europe and elsewhere, governments, NGOs, and universities are highly reluctant to sponsor agri-biotech R&D in developing countries, primarily because of the anticipated political backlash. Many developing countries, for their part, are reluctant to accept help in this area because of fears of declining agricultural exports to the seemingly growing number of agri-biotech adverse markets.

Finally, regulatory polarization creates conflict in the global trading system. Such conflict exacerbates the three aforementioned problems. This issue is examined in the next chapter.

CHAPTER SIX

International Trade Conflict

THIS CHAPTER shows that regulatory polarization in agri-biotechnology, which was described and explained in chapters 3–5, creates tension in the world trading system. It explores whether and how this tension could develop into full-blown trade conflict, and what the consequences of major trade conflict would be.

In an open world economy, the economic and political implications of national or regional (in the case of the European Union) agri-biotech regulation reach far beyond the countries adopting such regulation. In particular, differences in agri-biotech regulation across countries can have strong effects on international trade flows. GE crops produced in one country cannot be exported to another country if the latter does not approve the marketing of such crops. Or, if a destination country requires mandatory labeling of GE food, exports of GE food by other nations to that country may decline; labeling tends to increase the production costs of GE technology adopters and the price of their products; and consumers may shun products identifiable as GE products because of health, environmental, or ethical concerns.

The costs and benefits that flow from the effects of regulatory differences on international trade can vary substantially across countries. Such variation creates distributional conflict among and within states in regional and global trading systems. Conflict of this nature may range from minor disagreements to full-blown trade wars.

In this chapter I focus on explaining the potential for escalation of tensions emanating from regulatory polarization in agri-biotechnology. These tensions emerged in 1997 with complaints by US exporters and biotech firms about the European Union's slow and non-transparent approval process and about individual EU countries' bans on GE products approved by the European Union. They intensified with the European Union's introduction of mandatory labeling and the moratorium on approval of new GE crops in 1998–99. In mid-May 2003, when this book went to press, escalation appeared ever more likely with a formal request by the United States for consultations under the WTO's dispute settlement procedure.

First I explore the distributional implications of regulatory polarization, concentrating on export revenues and broader effects on economic welfare. I then examine the effectiveness of current policy tools for coping with distributional conflicts between economic winners and losers of regulatory polarization, particularly between the European Union and the United States. These policy approaches include voluntary means, such as mutual recognition of standards, compensation, multilateral harmonization of agri-biotech regulations, and unilateral "trading up" (adaptation of regulation and/or export practices in exporting countries to the preferences of importing countries with stricter rules). They also include coercive approaches, notably, third-party arbitration and punitive economic measures.

I conclude that current policies for mitigating or eliminating tensions in transatlantic trade are of limited effectiveness. The world's first and second largest economies, which also account for the largest bilateral trading relationship in the world, remain on a collision course in this area. The final chapter of the book outlines policy options that may help in avoiding a full blown trade war and giving agricultural biotechnology a fair chance to prove its value in the medium to long term.

ON COLLISION COURSE

Many observers of the world economy have predicted a transatlantic trade conflict over agricultural biotechnology on a scale that would dwarf other disputes in the world trading system, such as those over export subsidies, anti-dumping policies, hormone use in beef production, or bananas.[1] Such predictions have been stimulated by a variety of statements by high US government officials suggesting that an escalation of the dispute is likely.

In 1999, Stuart Eizenstat, then US Under Secretary of State, argued before the US Congress that the agri-biotech issue was "the single greatest trade threat that we face systemically with the European Union." He also claimed that "almost 100 percent of our agricultural exports in the next five years will either be genetically modified or combined with bulk commodities that are genetically modified."[2]

Very similar statements have been made by members of the Bush administration, which entered office in 2001. In January 2003, US trade representative Robert Zoellick stated "The European anti-scientific policies are spreading to other corners of the world. ... I think that is a rather serious development. ... I find it immoral that people are not being able to be supplied food to live in Africa because people have invented dangers about biotechnology. That puts it rather high on my scale to deal with."[3]

An even more aggressive tone was adopted by the *Austin American-Statesman* (January 27, 2003): "The United States is in the middle of a war that receives little notice, and one in which former European allies again are standing in the way of progress. It's the war on hunger, and it's being thwarted by European Union nations that oppose genetically modified (GM) crops developed in the United States. ... EU members are warning other nations—some with starving populations—not to accept GM food sources from the United States or risk losing foreign aid and markets for their goods. It is an outrageous act of blackmail that forces the governments of poor nations to choose between maintaining friendly relations with Europe and letting their people starve." Similarly, the US based Center for Global Issues accused the European Union and agri-biotech critics in general of "technological apartheid".[4]

In mid-May 2003 the US Administration decided to launch the WTO's dispute settlement procedure. As a first step, it formally requested consultations. This request was supported by Canada and Argentina (two other exporters of GE crops). When this book went to press, these consultations were beginning. While the US complaint appeared to focus primarily on the European Union's moratorium on new approvals, the United States had not presented its legal case in detail.

The transformation of the General Agreement on Tariffs and Trade (GATT) into the World Trade Organization (WTO) in 1994 has gone hand-in-hand with a reform of dispute settlement procedures. WTO rules now prohibit the unilateral imposition of trade sanctions in trade disputes. Such sanctions can only be imposed if the WTO issues a "guilty verdict," the defendant country refuses to comply, and the WTO explicitly approves punitive economic measures requested by the plaintiff country. If the United States decided to fully escalate current tensions over agri-biotechnology it would thus have to operate through the WTO's dispute settlement system. Imposing sanctions on the European Union outside the WTO framework would cause such damage to the world trading system by undermining its institutional foundation that the United States is highly unlikely to pursue this option.

However, even if the United States escalated transatlantic trade tensions over agri-biotechnology in conformity with WTO rules, such escalation would burden the WTO with an almost impossible task. It would disrupt efforts to liberalize global trade, particularly in agricultural products. It would probably involve an escalation of punitive economic measures and countermeasures that could cost farmers, input suppliers, food processors, retailers, consumers, and taxpayers in the European Union, the United States, and other countries billions of dollars. It would also exacerbate already existing challenges to agri-biotechnology (see chapter 2).

Are current transatlantic trade tensions over agri-biotechnology in fact likely to escalate into a full-blown trade war? Research in political science and economics has thus far not produced empirically robust explanations of when and why which types of trade conflicts are more likely to escalate.[5] Explanations and predictions of this sort are indeed difficult because escalation processes are usually shaped by a wide range of variables many of which are difficult to measure and integrate into explanatory models. Drawing on a large body of statistical analyses and case studies I submit, however, that the likelihood of escalation of trade tensions over differences in agri-biotech regulation depends primarily on:

1   the international distribution of economic costs and benefits flowing from agricultural biotechnology and regulatory restrictions on this technology;
2   the effectiveness of non-coercive policy measures for coping with regulatory diversity; these include measures negotiated and accepted voluntarily by the countries involved—notably, mutual recognition by countries of each others agri-biotech regulations, compensation for export revenue losses paid by countries with stricter agri-biotech regulations to countries with laxer agri-biotech regulations, and multilateral harmonization of agri-biotech regulations; they also include unilateral measures, notably, adjustment of regulation and export-practices in exporting countries to stricter regulation in importing countries ("trading up");
3   the anticipated effectiveness of coercive policy measures, notably, the (potential) plaintiff's chances of winning a legal case in the WTO's dispute settlement system, and the likelihood of the defendant backing down before a WTO panel decision or after a "guilty" verdict.[6]

In other words, the United States is more likely to launch a trade war against the European Union on this issue if its economic losses resulting from the European Union's agri-biotech restrictions are large, non-coercive policy measures for resolving the problem are ineffective, and the prospects of winning the case through the WTO are good. This chapter examines each of these three influences.

First I explore the extent to which the European Union's regulatory restrictions have imposed costs on US agricultural exporters. I then discuss estimates of economic benefits and costs of agricultural biotechnology at the international level under different policy scenarios, thus identifying winner and loser countries in a broader sense.

The analysis of trade data suggests that US exporters are currently suffering losses in the order of several hundred million dollars per year. It also shows that this loss could increase to several billion USD in the years ahead if regulatory constraints in the European Union were to grow further, other countries followed the EU regulatory model, and new GE crops were approved by the United States but not the European Union.

A quantitative analysis of broader welfare implications of agri-biotechnology under different regulatory scenarios produces results that are broadly consistent with the aforementioned findings based on trade data. It shows that US agricultural exporters suffer from the European Union's restrictions. However, parts of the overall welfare loss caused by EU restrictions may fall on the European Union itself. The analysis of trade data and welfare implications also suggests that EU farmers have, so far, not benefited from restrictive EU regulation of agri-biotechnology. The available evidence does, therefore, not support the US claim that the European Union's constraints in this area constitute agricultural protectionism disguised as consumer and environmental protection.

The history of protectionism and trade conflict shows that governments frequently do not act in the interest of their respective country's overall welfare, but cater to politically influential interest groups, firms, or industries. The results discussed here highlight that, in terms of overall US economic welfare, it may be nonsensical for the United States to escalate transatlantic trade tensions over agri-biotechnology. They also suggest, however, that the concentration of costs on particular economic actors in the United States is such that escalation of the dispute by the US government is likely.

Second, I outline the principal voluntary policy measures for coping with regulatory polarization and its economic effects. None of these most widely used policy tools for mitigating or eliminating negative effects of differing national product standards on international trade is likely to be effective with regard to agricultural biotechnology.

In the agri-biotech case, the most common international approach to dealing with differing standards, mutual recognition, is unacceptable to the European Union. Mutual recognition implies that countries grant market access to products approved by the authorities of their trading partners. This solution would open the EU market to GE food approved in the United States (and perhaps elsewhere) but not in the European Union. In essence, current GE product approval rules in the European Union would thus apply only to EU producers. The analysis in chapters 4 and 5 has shown that the opposition to such a solution would be overwhelming. Moreover, mandatory labeling of GE products, which would probably be required to make mutual recognition work efficiently and make it even remotely acceptable to the European Union, appears unacceptable to the United States.

Another solution, financial compensation[7] by the European Union for American producers negatively affected by the European Union's restrictions, is virtually impossible for the same reasons. Such compensation would mean asking European taxpayers to compensate US producers in the order of hundreds of millions and possible billions of dollars for EU regulations that most Europeans regard as fundamentally legitimate and justified.

Harmonization of regulation through negotiation and formal agreement is yet another policy option that is frequently used in global and regional trading systems. This solution has been employed extensively in the European Union, including for agri-biotechnology. As regards food biotechnology, this is the most ambitious policy tool because it seeks to eliminate trade tension by eliminating regulatory polarization very directly. In the transatlantic context, bilateral efforts to harmonize approval and labeling standards have so far failed for the same reasons that have prevented mutual recognition and compensation. So have the two principal multilateral harmonization efforts: those by the CODEX Alimentarius Commission, an international body co-sponsored by the UN Food and Agricultural Organization (FAO) and the Word Health Organization (WHO), and those under the Biosafety Protocol to the UN Convention on Biodiversity.

As to unilateral measures, trade tension could be mitigated or eliminated through "trading up"[8] in the United States. Such trading up could come in two forms. The United States could formally tighten its approval and labeling regulation so that US exports produced under US law would generally meet European regulatory standards as well ("regulatory adjustment"). This would also pave the way to a formal transatlantic system of mutual recognition in agri-biotechnology (see above). Alternatively, individual US exporters may decide to comply on their own with European standards in the absence of stricter US regulation ("market adjustment"). I show that regulatory adjustment has occurred to a very minor extent, but is far from sufficient for mitigating trade tensions. The analysis also shows that some market adjustment has taken place but is reaching its limits.

Third, I examine coercive measures, in particular whether the United States could achieve its policy goals through the WTO's dispute settlement system. The analysis suggests that it is far from clear whether the United States would win a WTO case from a legal viewpoint. Even if it did, it is very unlikely that the European Union would make substantial concessions. The European Union is also unlikely to make concessions before a WTO verdict, or to acquiesce to WTO approved punitive measures by the United States as it has done in the case of beef hormones.

How likely is escalation of the current conflict into a full blown transatlantic trade war? Escalation could range from launching formal dispute settlement in the WTO to punitive economic measures against the European Union, if the US position was endorsed by the WTO, and countermeasures by the European Union. The evidence for the first and second driving force referred to above suggests that the potential for escalation is high. The external costs of EU regulations are concentrated on a politically influential group of US producers, and these costs are rising. Voluntary measures for mitigating transatlantic trade tensions have so far been ineffective, with the partial exception of market adjustment.

The evidence on the effectiveness of coercive measures is somewhat inconclusive. Legal opinion is divided on whether the United States could win a WTO case over agri-biotech regulation. The analysis in chapters 4–6 suggests, moreover, that the European Union would not make concessions, either in the shadow of a pending WTO verdict or afterwards (with or without punitive measures imposed by the United States). This should deter the United States from escalating the dispute much beyond the WTO's consultation procedure. I argue, however, that uncertainty about ultimately winning a WTO case may not deter such escalation. The main reason is that escalation may produce short-term gains for the US administration (e.g., political support by important constituencies), whereas the costs of escalation would be dispersed and would materialize over the longer term (e.g., destabilization of the WTO, negative effects on the further development of agricultural biotechnology). In conclusion I examine contextual conditions that also affect the likelihood of escalation.

ECONOMIC WINNERS AND LOSERS

Capturing the economic consequences of regulatory polarization at national and international levels is complex and full of uncertainty. Estimates quoted by policy-makers usually relate to export revenue lost as a result of agri-biotech regulations in destination countries that reduce or bar market access. Attempts to identify in overall welfare terms the economic winners and losers of regulatory polarization rely on general equilibrium models of the global economy. These models assess the "global GMO dividend" and its distribution across countries or geographic regions, contingent on different policy scenarios. They are useful in exploring future GE crop production, prices, trade patterns, and economic welfare under different European agri-biotech policy scenarios. In this section, I review both approaches in an effort to assess the costs imposed on agri-biotech adopting countries by countries with stricter agri-biotech regulation.

Export Revenues

Arguably the most obvious economic effects of regulatory differences are those on exports and imports of agricultural produce. Approval of a particular GE crop variety by an exporting country, but not by its trading partners, imposes costs on the exporter—products not approved abroad cannot be exported. If regulation in a trading partner country requires the labeling of GE food this may reduce demand for the exporter's products: if a product with a GE label does not offer a clear quality or price benefit over the conventional counterpart, risk averse consumers are less likely to buy this product; if exporters adjust by exporting non-GE products they incur costs in segregating GE and non-GE products and labeling them. Traceability requirements designed to track agri-biotech products throughout the production and distribution chain, which are to be implemented in the European Union within the next few years, add further costs. As noted in chapter 2, such costs can easily reduce or neutralize productivity gains from agricultural biotechnology. When production costs for exporters rise, exports decrease. Export revenue thus decreases or, to be more precise, is smaller than it would have been under conditions of laxer agri-biotech regulation in importing countries.

To what extent have US agricultural exports to the European Union suffered from regulatory differences? The following assessment concentrates on corn and soy. These two crops are among the three most important field crops in the United States and are most directly affected by the European Union's regulations: in 2002, around 34% of US corn and 75% of soy was genetically modified.[9] Ideally, this assessment should establish what the value of US corn and soy exports to the European Union would have been had the European Union adopted the same agri-biotech regulation as the United States, holding all other influences (e.g., exchange rates, supply from other countries) constant. Such an assessment is impossible and we have to rely on a cruder analysis that looks at trade flows and makes an informed guess as to why they have varied over time.

Figure 6.1 indicates that US corn exports to the European Union declined from around 420 million USD in the mid-1990s to around 3 million USD in 2002.[10] The decline of corn by-product exports (where the European Union consumes around 60% of such US exports) was less pronounced but also substantial (from around 670 to 370 million USD). Argentina, which does not grow GE corn, has replaced the United States as the European Union's main supplier of corn. The US share in the European Union's corn imports had dropped from 86 percent in 1995 to below 10 percent by 2000. Figure 6.1 shows that US soybean exports to the European Union have also decreased, from a peak of 2.6 billion USD in 1996 to 1.1 billion USD in 2002. Soybean meal exports have fluctuated

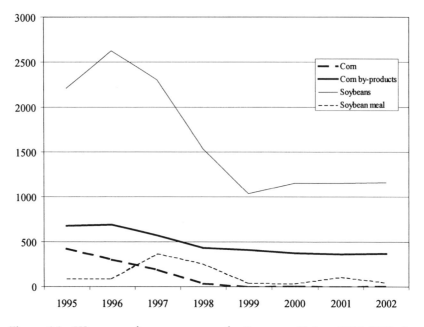

Figure 6.1 US corn and soy exports to the European Union, 1995–2002, in million USD. *Source*: FATUS database (Foreign Agricultural Trade of the United States, USDA/ERS, www.fas.usda.gov). The figures for 2002 are estimates.

at far lower levels. Brazil (which does not permit domestic GE soy production) and Argentina (which does) have become the main suppliers of the European Union.[11]

Trade flows of a particular commodity between the United States and the European Union are affected by many variables (e.g., the dollar–euro exchange rate, the competitiveness of agricultural exporters in other countries). Therefore, it is far from clear that restrictive agri-biotech regulation in the European Union is responsible for the observed decline of US corn and soy exports to the European Union. We must a priori be skeptical about statements by policy-makers who simply take the difference between US exports to Europe at their peak and their bottom and proclaim this difference to be the cost to the United States of European protectionism.[12]

While it is virtually impossible to isolate from other influences the effect of EU regulation on US corn and soy exports, the available evidence suggest that US corn exports have indeed been driven down by the European Union's strict approval and labeling requirements. Several GE corn varieties approved by US regulators have not been approved in the European Union—as of December 2002, 17 corn varieties had been approved in the United States, only 5 in the European Union. Because most of the US grain handling system operates with unsegregated bulk commodities, many US producers have forgone exports to Europe instead of segregating for what is a relatively small export market. As noted above, it is difficult to determine exactly what US corn exports to the European Union would have been had the European Union adopted the same regulations as the United States, holding all other variables constant. Nonetheless, costs to US corn exporters (in terms of lost export opportunities) in the order of 200–400 million USD per year are plausible.

The decline of US soy exports to Europe is harder to trace back to EU regulation. US GE soy production relies largely on one variety, Roundup Ready soybeans. This GE variety has also been approved in the European Union. Other GE soybean varieties approved in the United States but not the European Union are grown only in small amounts and are processed through segregated crop handling chains. Differences in product approval per se can thus hardly be made responsible for declining US soy exports to the European Union. It is more likely that hostile consumer reactions and higher production costs because of segregation and labeling requirements have pushed US soy exports down to some extent. Similar to corn, export losses in the order of several hundred million USD per annum seem plausible. However, precise quantification of this effect is next to impossible because increased competition from South American suppliers of soybeans and the stronger US dollar have also contributed to declining EU soy imports from the United States.[13]

Such measures of export revenue losses should be viewed in a broader perspective. If we assume that the cost to US corn and soy exporters in the year 2001 was 600 million USD (a rather conservative estimate, in my view), this cost would amount to around 10 percent of total US agricultural exports to the European Union in that year.[14] This amount is far from trivial, all the more so because it does not include processed food containing corn and soy ingredients. Exports of such products have almost certainly suffered from EU restrictions as well.[15]

Most worrying for US exporters is the scenario where all US corn and soy exports to the European Union collapsed as a result of increasingly stringent agri-biotech regulation in Europe; notably, traceability requirements for all GE food and feed, mandatory labeling of GE animal feed,[16] and thresholds for labeling below 1 percent. In 2001, US corn and soy exports to the European Union amounted to more than one-quarter of all US agricultural exports to the European Union. These figures do not include processed foods containing corn and soy ingredients, the amount of which is unknown but probably large.[17]

The scenario of collapsing US corn and soy exports to the European Union is not too far-fetched. Current EU plans, which could be implemented in 2003 or 2004, include stringent labeling and traceability requirements for GE food *and* feed (most US corn and soy exports to the European Union are for feed purposes), with expected tolerance levels for non-GE products of 0.5–1 percent GE content. Compliance with these regulations would require large investments by US producers in segregation and identity preservation. Should EU rules be extended to labeling of products from animals fed on GE feed (e.g., poultry, meat) the impact on US exporters would be even more negative.

In the worst case, US producers will find that the cost of forgoing exports to the European Union is smaller than the cost of restructuring the US crop handling system so as to comply with EU regulations. In addition, US exporters of GE crops approved in the European Union may find that processors, retailers, and consumers there are unwilling to buy (labeled) GE produce. In that case, market-driven product differentiation in the United States will remain slow and differentiation will occur at the international level (readjustment of trade flows) rather than within the US exporting system.[18]

In the best case, US corn and soy exports to the European Union will decline somewhat further but not collapse entirely. In this scenario, production costs of US exporters will rise as a result of stricter EU regulation, making their produce less competitive vis-à-vis products from countries that do not produce GE varieties of the crops concerned. This increase in production costs for US exporters may, however, not wipe out altogether competitive advantages that US producers currently enjoy. Moreover, demand by processors, retailers, and consumers for GE foods and GE feeds in Europe will not decline to zero in this more optimistic scenario.

Whether the pessimistic or somewhat more optimistic scenario will eventually materialize depends to a large degree on how expensive labeling and identity preservation (IP) will be in practice, and on the availability of substitutes for GE products. Estimates of labeling and IP costs vary tremendously. A recent EU estimate puts the costs of identity preservation at 6–17 percent of farm-gate costs, depending on the crop variety and a range of other factors. Other estimates are even higher.[19] Agronomic studies of currently marketed GE crops suggest productivity gains in the order of 0–10 percent (see chapter 2). If these estimates turn out to be correct and if labeling and IP costs would fall predominantly on GE crop producers, US GE corn and soy exports to the European Union may collapse.

This trend could be reversed if productivity of GE crops improved dramatically,[20] labeling and IP costs were reduced, or subsidies for US farmers were increased. In that case the transatlantic problem might be sorted out in the market place. I revisit this point below in the section on market adjustment, and in the concluding chapter. Improvements in productivity are likely but not certain. As to labeling and IP costs: some analysts believe that IP and labeling costs could turn out to be much lower than expected. Indeed, surveys of US farmers and grain handlers show that more than 20 percent of the respondents appear willing to segregate crops if market pressure persists.[21] These producers obviously assume that labeling and IP costs would not eliminate every competitive advantage they may have. However, most US farmers are likely to face a disadvantage vis-à-vis countries that opt entirely for non-GE production. For obvious reasons, it will always be cheaper to operate the entire crop-handling system of a country on a non-GE crop basis than to segregate GE and non-GE crops.[22] In brief, the prospects for US corn and soy exports to Europe are rather bleak.

How US corn and soy exports to Europe will develop also depends on whether the European Union can substitute at similar cost for imports from the United States, should US producers be unwilling to comply with EU agri-biotech regulation. The harder it is to substitute for imports from the United States, the more likely it is that the European Union will make concessions with regard to imports of US GE products.

In the case of corn, where the European Union's self-sufficiency level is almost 100 percent, US exports are unlikely to recover unless productivity gains from GE corn increase dramatically, labeling or IP costs turn out to be far lower than expected, and EU consumer acceptance increases. None of these possibilities is likely to materialize anytime soon. The biggest portion of current EU corn imports consists of corn by-products, such as corn gluten feed or corn germ cake. These products can easily be supplied through somewhat increased EU production or imports from other non-GE corn producer countries.

The case of soy is different (see table 6.1). The European Union's self-sufficiency level is around 10 percent for soybeans, 5 percent for soy meal, and 20 percent for soy oil. Because consumption for food purposes amounts to only around one million tons per year, non-soy or non-GE soy substitutes for food appear easy to find, probably at a rather small premium. Suppliers include Brazil (whose soy production is largely non-GE) and the United States (where segregation is implemented on a small but growing scale). Argentina, in contrast, has no effective segregation system. Because soy producers in Argentina and Brazil depend heavily on the EU market (40–50 percent of their soy production is sold to the European Union), there is considerable room for the European Union to demand effective segregation.

The most important challenge for the European Union lies in securing non-GE soy supplies when new rules on labeling of feed are implemented and if producers of meat and poultry chose to use non-GE feed on a large scale. There is no empirical record on the extent to which other feed

TABLE 6.1
EU imports of soybeans and soymeal (all in soymeal equivalents, soybeans = 79 percent meal)

		1995	1996	1997	1998	1999
Total EU imports	Mio t	25.5	22.2	20.8	24.8	23.5
United States	Mio t	8.5	7.1	7.2	7.0	4.9
	% of total	33.1	32.1	34.7	28.2	20.9
Brazil	Mio t	10.0	8.9	8.6	10.2	9.8
	% of total	39.4	40.2	41.5	41.2	41.5
Argentina	Mio t	5.8	5.2	4.0	6.1	8.0
	% of total	22.8	23.4	19.1	24.6	34.0
Others	Mio t	1.2	0.9	1.0	1.5	0.9
	% of total	4.7	4.2	4.7	6.0	3.6

Source: EU (2000). 1999 was the latest year for which data was available. Estimates for 2001 hold that the European Union imported 16 mio tons of soybeans (mostly from Brazil and the United States) and 17 mio tons of soymeal (mostly from Argentina and the United States). The US share in those imports declined further. In soymeal, the shares of Argentina were 55 percent, Brazil 38 percent and the United States 6 percent. In soybean imports, the shares were 41 percent for Brazil, 41 percent for the United States, and 13 percent for Argentina.

products could substitute for GE soy, nor do we know how demand for non-GE soy would react to price increases. In the past, demand for soy in general has been rather elastic.[23] But we do not know what would happen if demand in the European Union for non-GE soy increased massively. In the short term at least, animal production costs in the European Union would probably rise slightly if GE and non-GE energy and protein rich feedstuffs were segregated and farmers had to replace some soy imports with more expensive domestic production of rapeseed meal, barley, wheat, and other products. This means that the outlook for US GE soy exports to the European Union is somewhat better than for GE corn because it appears harder for the European Union to find substitutes for GE soy at similar cost.

The evidence discussed here suggests that European farmers have not benefited from restrictive agri-biotech regulation in the European Union, and that frequently voiced claims about the protectionist nature of the European Union's agri-biotech regulation are unfounded. While corn and soy imports from the United States have declined, imports of these products from other countries have risen. So have total EU imports of corn and soy. EU farmers using soy-based protein feed may even experience higher production costs as a result of the European Union's agri-biotech regulation.

Costs imposed on US farmers by the European Union's reluctance to approve new GE crop varieties are even more difficult to estimate than the effects on export revenue from existing GE crops. The same holds for the impact on US agri-biotech firms of the European Union's moratorium on new GE crop approvals and its ban on GE crop cultivation. More and more GE crop varieties are being approved in the United States, but no new GE crop varieties have been approved by the European Union since 1998.[24] This deprives US farmers of opportunities to export to Europe GE products in which they might have a competitive edge. It may also slow down the adoption of new GE-varieties in the United States (e.g. new GE soybean varieties) because of uncertainties over their export potential. There is evidence, for example, that US producers have been reluctant to adopt new GE soy and corn varieties as these varieties have not been approved by the European Union or other countries. Similar effects can be observed in other countries, for example, Argentinian farmers' reluctance to plant RR corn in the absence of EU approval of this variety.

Opposition to agricultural biotechnology has also motivated agri-biotech firms to slow down the marketing of new products. For example, in October 1999 Monsanto declared that it would not commercialize the so-called terminator gene, a controversial technique to make seeds sterile. Commercialization of GE wheat and rice has also been held back.[25]

Finally, US fears of a spillover effect from Europe to other countries appear warranted. In 2001, the world market for US corn was predominantly outside Europe. The largest part of US corn exports (around 3 out of a total of 4.5 billion USD) went to Japan, Mexico, Taiwan, Egypt, and Korea. Several key countries in these markets, including Japan and Korea, have introduced mandatory labeling. Other export destinations are also planning to do so. Most of these countries do not permit cultivation of GE corn. For comparison, the EU share in US soy exports is much larger. China, Mexico, Japan, the Netherlands, and Taiwan consumed around 3.3 of the total 5.4 billion dollars US soybean exports.

Whether and to what extent a spillover of restrictions from Europe to other countries will occur is far from clear (see chapter 3). In any event, US exporters received a taste of what might happen when the StarLink problem arose in 2000. In that episode, Japan cut its US corn purchases by 50 percent and Korea, the second largest US corn export market, temporarily banned imports of US corn entirely. In other cases, China imposed restrictions on imports of US GE soy, India froze US shipments of corn and soy, and Zambia turned away US corn.

Effects on National Economic Welfare

Recent work by economists has assessed the effects of regulatory differences with the help of a general equilibrium model of the world economy, the so-called Global Trade Analysis Project (GTAP) model. This model captures linkages between all product markets within countries and regions, and between them via bilateral trade flows.[26]

The work by Anderson and Nielsen,[27] which is referred to in most detail here, reflects the global economy and trade flows of 1995 and is aggregated to 16 regions and 17 primary agricultural sectors and related processing industries. The two authors ran the GTAP model for three scenarios: (1) selected regions[28] adopt GE corn and soybeans with an assumed productivity growth of 5 percent,[29] Western Europe allows imports but not domestic production of GE corn and soybeans; (2) selected regions adopt GE corn and soybeans while Western Europe bans imports of these GE products; (3) selected regions adopt GE corn and soybeans, Western Europe does not ban imports of these GE products, but consumer preferences in some Western European countries shift against GE corn and soybeans.[30]

In this assessment, two-thirds of the estimated global welfare gain of around 10 billion USD per annum in scenario 1 would be eliminated if Western Europe chose to ban imports of GE corn and soy. This loss would fall largely on Western Europe itself (assuming that European consumers are indifferent to GE food), and to a minor extent on North and Latin American exporters of GE crops.

Table 6.2 summarizes key results for the three scenarios. It suggests that North America benefits substantially from the adoption of GE corn and soybeans, whether or not Western Europe allows or bans imports of such GE crops. These benefits flow primarily from the technological change effect (productivity gains). Western Europe, which is assumed to ban domestic GE crop production in all three scenarios, benefits most from scenario 1, where it allows GE crop imports, followed by scenario 3, where imports are permitted but there is a partial shift of consumer preferences against GE products. This estimate by Anderson and Nielsen suggests substantial economic losses for Western Europe in scenario 2 (ban on domestic production and imports of GE crops in Western Europe) as compared to scenario 1. These costs of around 6.3 billion USD per annum, or 15 USD per capita and year, result primarily from allocative efficiency problems; that is, the need to replace imports of GE crops by more expensive and less cost-efficient domestic production of non-GE crops, particularly in oilseeds. Conversely, Western Europe's benefits in scenario 1 result only to a small extent from cheaper imports, but primarily from more competition from abroad that moves domestic resources away from highly subsidized sectors of EU agriculture.

If US decisions on whether or not to escalate the biotech trade dispute with the European Union were solely driven by national welfare considerations, and if the above estimates were indeed accurate and accepted as such by US policy-makers, the probability of a transatlantic trade war

TABLE 6.2
Economic welfare effects of adopting GE corn and soybeans (US$ million per annum)

	Scenario 1: EU allows imports		Scenario 2: EU bans imports		Scenario 3: EU imports decline	
	North America	Western Europe	North America	Western Europe	North America	Western Europe
Total welfare effect	2624	2010	2299	−4334	2554	715
Allocative efficiency effect	−137	1755	27	−4601	−100	393
Terms of trade effect	−1008	253	−1372	257	−1092	319
Technological change effect	3746	0	3641	0	3726	0

Source: Anderson and Nielsen (2000).

might appear low. According to the above estimates, a Western European ban on GE crop imports costs North America around 300 million USD per annum, a small amount in the overall picture (around one USD per capita and year). The biggest loser appears to be Western Europe itself. In view of total agricultural subsidies in Western Europe (more than 17,000 USD per farmer and year), losses of 15 USD per capita and year in Europe are substantial but not dramatic.

Yet, from the lengthy and acrimonious transatlantic trade dispute over bovine growth hormones, we know that even small economic effects of regulation can give rise to trade conflicts. In that dispute, export losses of US producers amounted to only around 120 million USD per annum.[31] With estimated costs of several hundred million USD per annum at present and the prospect of rapidly increasing costs[32] the probability of a transatlantic trade war over agri-biotech regulation appears higher in this perspective.

Obviously there is no straightforward correlation between the size of economic effects of trade-restricting regulation and the likelihood of trade wars.[33] This relationship is, among other things, contingent on how the costs and benefits of the status quo and of escalation are distributed. Studies on trade policy and protectionism[34] have shown that escalation is more likely to the extent that economic losses in (potential) plaintiff countries under the status quo (and thus the benefits of escalation) are concentrated on politically influential groups and the costs of escalation (in the plaintiff country) are dispersed.

This is clearly the case in the agri-biotech sector. As shown in chapters 4 and 5 and in this chapter (see section on export revenues), economic losses under the status quo fall primarily on export-oriented US farmers and input suppliers. They are well organized and politically influential. The costs of escalation, on the other hand, would be widely dispersed. They would be borne by all those affected by the European Union's countermeasures, which are likely to follow US punitive economic actions against the European Union. Costs of escalation would also include a reduction in gains from future agri-biotech applications because a trade war is likely to slow down R&D as well as the adoption of new GE varieties. Further costs involve a dampening effect on WTO efforts to liberalize global agricultural markets. The group of economic actors incurring the costs of a trade war is therefore much larger, implying that the cost per actor will be very small. With this cost-benefit distribution it is likely that export-oriented GE crop farmers and input suppliers will be more successful in lobbying the US government to escalate the latent trade dispute than societal groups in the United States that are opposed to escalation.

Other results produced by the GTAP model support in broader terms what we have learned from the analysis of export revenues and the analysis of the policy process in the United States (chapters 4 and 5). They suggest that the effects of European agri-biotech policy on domestic production, exports, and imports are substantial. While the effects on overall North American welfare are small (as shown above), the impact on US agricultural producers is far from trivial. To take two extreme examples: oil seed production in the United States grows by 3.6 percent if Western Europe permits GE crop imports, but declines by 10.2 percent if Western Europe bans such imports. North American coarse grain exports grow by 8.5 percent in scenario 1, but only by 0.3 percent in scenario 2. If these estimates bear any relationship to the real world, export-oriented US producers of GE crops have a powerful economic incentive to lobby for laxer agri-biotech regulations in Western Europe.

Finally, regulatory restrictions in Europe are likely to have repercussions beyond North America, notably, with regard to developing countries. While Western Europe may easily be able to afford welfare losses in the order of a few billion USD (incomes are high and food is abundant), many developing countries depend on agricultural productivity gains that increase real income and lower the price of basic foods and/or boost their nutritional value.

In the absence of reliable data, I again rely on estimates from the GTAP work by Anderson and Nielsen. In the case of Africa, for example, these estimates suggest that countries in sub-Saharan Africa not adopting GE technology might benefit from a European ban on GE crop imports (scenario 2). These benefits emanate primarily from lower import prices and better terms of trade. They depend, however, on whether these countries could comply with European regulations at low cost, which would enable them to export non-GE products to Europe. Compliance costs are not included in the model.

The estimates discussed here are no more than sophisticated guesses. And some of the assumptions in the model are rather adventurous. For example, the model assumes that the adoption of agri-biotechnology results in a uniform 5 percent productivity growth in all countries adopting the technology. In light of the agronomic evidence on corn and soybeans shown in chapter 2 this assumption is probably too optimistic. Use of the technology is assumed to produce no environmental or public health externalities. Particularly with regard to environmental effects (e.g., liability claims by organic farmers against GE crop producers because of cross-pollination), this assumption may again be too optimistic. Neither technology fees to seed suppliers nor the costs of segregation and labeling are included. As noted in chapter 2, such costs are considerable and may eliminate agronomic productivity gains. The implementation of Western Europe's policy of banning GE crop imports in scenario 2 is assumed to be cost free—again a rather implausible assumption.

Perhaps the most questionable assumption is that consumers are indifferent to GE food in scenarios 1 and 2. The analysis of European agri-biotech policy in chapters 3–5 casts strong doubts on this assumption. If consumers valued non-GE food, this could more than offset the welfare loss in scenario 2. Surveys of consumers' willingness to pay premiums for non-GE food have indeed shown that European consumers, in contrast to US consumers, are willing to pay substantial premiums. In contrast to the results just reported, more restrictive policies in the European Union may thus be economically efficient. Finally, the above estimates center on two crops only, concentrate on quantitative (input traits) but not qualitative aspects of GE products, and they ignore longer-term effects of alternative EU policies on agri-biotech R&D as well as technological spill-overs, notably in developing countries.

Despite all these shortcomings, the above estimates suggest at a minimum that differences across nations in agri-biotech regulation can have substantial economic effects both on regulating states and on their trading partners. If the assumptions in the model were modified in line with the above criticism, we would probably see much lower welfare gains in the United States and larger effects of EU regulations on US welfare. Moreover, welfare losses in Europe would probably be much smaller than in the Nielsen and Anderson estimates. Finally, the above estimates apply only to GE corn and soybeans. If GE varieties of other heavily traded commodities, such as wheat or rice, were adopted and produced in large quantities, it is likely that the welfare implications of Western Europe's regulatory restrictions on GE crop exporters and biotech firms would rapidly grow from a few hundred millions to billions of USD per annum

In summary, the analysis of economic welfare implications supports the findings for export revenues. The European Union's regulatory restrictions impose costs on North American producers in the order of several hundred million USD per year. These costs could grow substantially in the years ahead if regulatory polarization persists. The history of trade policy shows, however, that cost-benefit implications for specific industries in a given country, rather than for overall national or global welfare, tend to shape policy-decisions. GE crop exporters in the United States are unlikely to care much about whether European welfare will suffer ten times as much as US welfare from regulatory polarization. As long as they expect concentrated benefits of US trade action against the European Union and diffuse costs of such action, they have a strong economic incentive to fight against market access restrictions in the European Union. The aggressive political rhetoric one encounters in the transatlantic debate over differences in agri-biotech regulations is clearly more than just rhetoric. The regulatory gap between agri-biotech adopting and agri-biotech restricting countries is growing, and so are the economic implications and the likelihood of trade conflict.

VOLUNTARY POLICY OPTIONS

Global market forces notwithstanding, national diversity remains substantial, particularly with regard to environmental, health and safety regulations, as well as countless technical standards.[35] As countries have become more and more involved in regional and global trading systems this diversity has been felt to an increasing extent. In many areas, regulatory diversity is more a nuisance than a problem (e.g., differences in TV, video, mobile telephone, and electric power supply systems). But in some areas, particularly those where diversity has had larger-scale negative effects on trade, international disputes have arisen. In this and the next section I examine a set of generic policy tools that has been used to accommodate, reduce, or eliminate international diversity in many policy areas, including agri-biotech regulation. This section concentrates on voluntary approaches (mutual recognition, compensation, harmonization, and unilateral regulatory and market adjustment). The next section examines coercive policies (third party arbitration).[36] The focus is on explaining the effectiveness of each of these approaches in coping with regulatory polarization in the agri-biotech arena.

Mutual Recognition

The most widely used policy tool for coping with international regulatory diversity is explicit agreement among a set of countries to recognize each others regulations. That is, each country in such a relationship agrees to grant market access to goods lawfully produced and marketed in any of the other countries. This approach is very common in the European Union, where it has become one of the principal vehicles for implementing the European Union's internal market program.

Mutual recognition is appealing for at least two reasons. First, in many cases it has been easier to negotiate and implement than harmonization of each and every technical standard; the states involved inform each other of their respective regulations; each state decides on whether it can tolerate products in its own market that comply with regulations in the producer country (even if those regulations are different from its own); the parties then establish rules for adjusting the system should regulations in the participating states change. The second advantage of mutual recognition is that it may enhance economic efficiency. It allows for (at least limited) competition among national regulatory models. It thus promotes convergence towards regulatory models that consumers and producers prefer.

The critics of mutual recognition claim that it tends to produce downward convergence of regulations, in the worst case a "race to the bottom." Particularly worrisome, in the view of these critics, is downward convergence in sensitive policy areas, such as social regulation (e.g., consumer and environmental protection). Political scientists have shown that in some cases the stringency of regulations has indeed decreased under conditions of regulatory competition. The "flags of convenience" problem in international maritime transport belongs to the most (infamous) examples. In other cases, mutual recognition and associated competition among regulatory models have, on average, increased the stringency of regulations in a given set of countries. I will revisit this point below by looking at "trading up" processes.

Applied to agri-biotechnology, mutual recognition would mean that a particular set of countries (e.g., the United States and the European Union, all OECD countries, all WTO member states) agree to recognize each others' GE product regulations. The United States, for example, would agree to allow imports of non-GE products and GE products produced and marketed in the European Union according to EU regulations. The European Union would accept imports of American non-GE and GE products produced and marketed according to US regulations.

Consumers on both sides of the Atlantic could then decide for themselves whether they wish to consume GE or non-GE food produced under a particular regulatory system. This would require mandatory labeling in a form that enables consumers to make an informed choice, notably with regard to GE/non-GE food and the country of origin. As shown in chapters 3–5, neither US nor EU consumers are currently free and able to choose. In the absence of mandatory labeling American consumers are unable to distinguish between GE and non-GE food. European consumers who might wish to purchase GE food will not find such food in their shops.

This argument uses consumer preferences as the standard against which to measure the economic efficiency of a regulatory system. That is, if consumers are free and able to choose among GE and non-GE products, competition among regulatory systems produces efficient outcomes (from a consumer viewpoint). In terms of the Pareto criterion, no consumer is made worse off and at least some are made better off in such a system—this requires that the costs of regulation are lower than the premiums consumers are willing to pay for non-GE food. Opponents of labeling dispute this argument, claiming that labels not based on scientific criteria (e.g., product quality in terms of health or nutritional value) are misleading. Labeling, in their view, would slow down technological progress that would otherwise make all consumers better off.

However, if an international system of mutual recognition in combination with effective labeling were established, national regulations would, over time, presumably adjust in line with the dictates of supply and demand. For example, if European consumers were unconcerned about GE foods and laxer US regulations and productivity gains from agricultural biotechnology made GE food imports from the United States cheaper (and possibly also qualitatively better), Europeans would consume growing amounts of US-produced GE food. After some time, EU farmers would probably start to lobby for a relaxation of agri-biotech regulation in the European Union in order to also enjoy the productivity gains experienced by their US competitors. European approval regulation might then converge towards the US model. Conversely, if demand in the United States for (labeled) non-GE food increased and Americans consumed growing amounts of imported products of that nature, US producers would probably lobby the government to adjust regulations towards the European model, so that they could signal credibly to consumers that US products were "just as safe" as imported European products.

In other words, regulatory and market outcomes that would eventually emerge from a system of mutual recognition with internationally harmonized labeling are, in principle, open. Such a system could set in motion a process of deregulation, that is, a movement towards the current US model of GE food regulation. Or it could result in movement towards the European model of regulation.

Establishing a good working system of mutual recognition in the agri-biotech area is a monumental task. It would require sweeping policy changes in countries that have enacted restrictive agri-biotech regulation. The European Union, for example, would have to grant market access to GE crops and GE foods approved in the United States but not in the European Union. The analysis of EU regulation in chapters 3–5 suggests that such policy change would be extremely difficult to achieve.

European consumer and environmental groups, as well as many policy-makers supporting strict regulation, would certainly put up heavy resistance. Many of these agri-biotech critics claim that health and environmental risks cannot and must not be subordinated to consumer sovereignty (the right of consumers to choose freely between GE and non-GE products). In their view, allowing GE product imports while banning domestic GE crop production would also undermine existing EU regulations. From their perspective, it would be nonsensical and even dangerous.

Farmers would oppose mutual recognition because agri-biotech regulation applying to domestic EU production but not to imported goods might put them at a competitive disadvantage should GE crops be productivity enhancing. They would also oppose such policy change because imports of GE products might negatively affect consumer confidence in the safety of the EU food supply.

European and national policy-makers in EU countries would find it very difficult to explain and legitimize mutual recognition to the public under such circumstances. Indeed, they would have to explain why severe restrictions on domestic GE crop production, justified by the precautionary principle for public health and environmental reasons, are necessary, while all GE products approved in the United States could be freely sold in the European Union. There is a high risk that such policy changes would destroy the existing fragile consensus on agri-biotech policy in the European Union and lead to a proliferation of unilaterally imposed national restrictions that exceed EU standards.

Furthermore, as noted above, a good working international system of mutual recognition in the agri-biotech area would require mandatory labeling. The labels could state, for example: "This product contains the following genetically engineered ingredients produced in country x and approved under US {EU} law y." Only then could consumers freely choose among GE and non-GE products, and only then could market forces decide on the regulatory model that is, from a consumer perspective, preferable. In addition, to be even remotely acceptable to Europeans, a system of mutual recognition would have to operate on the basis of mandatory labeling.

Regulators and many producers in countries with lax agri-biotech regulation (notably the United States) are also likely to oppose mutual recognition on the basis of harmonized labeling standards. The ideal policy from their viewpoint would be mutual recognition without labeling. Such a policy would tear down import restrictions imposed by countries with stricter agri-biotech regulation. It would allow GE food and feed producers to more fully exploit productivity gains (to the extent they exist). And it would not allow consumers to discriminate against GE products either in terms of avoiding such products or paying a premium for non-GE products.

From the perspective of regulators and producers in countries with lax agri-biotech regulations, mutual recognition with internationally harmonized labeling might offset possible productivity gains from GE products due to labeling costs, negative premiums for GE products, and consumer aversion. Moreover, such a system would, in the medium to long term, probably lead to mandatory labeling in the United States as well. US regulators would find it too difficult to explain to the public why enabling consumers to freely chose among GE and non-GE products is necessary at the international but not at the domestic level. Surveys of US consumer preferences show that when GE/non-GE labels are put on products, consumers tend to opt for non-GE products.

In other words, a formal system of mutual recognition with internationally harmonized labeling would undermine the legitimacy of both the current EU and US regulatory systems for agricultural biotechnology.[37] It is difficult to see how such a system could be made acceptable to both sides.

Compensation

This policy option is comparable to an out-of-court settlement where the party whose behavior imposes costs on another party agrees to pay a specific amount to the latter in order to avoid an escalation of the conflict (including a formal legal case in court). Although this solution is not entirely free of coercion, it is voluntary to the extent that the accused country must willfully agree to provide compensation. Voluntary compensation in the narrow sense of the term (straight cash payment) is rarely used in international trade relations. Less formal and thereby less visible forms of compensation are more common (e.g., tariff reductions in another than the disputed trade area).

As to the transatlantic dispute over agri-biotech regulation, the European Union could, for example, offer to pay compensation to US farmers according to an agreed formula for calculating export losses resulting from EU restrictions. It could also offer a reduction of trade restrictions (e.g., tariffs) in other areas (e.g., steel, cars, wine). Such measures have repeatedly been proposed as solutions to the transatlantic conflict over growth hormones.[38]

Such a solution will probably not be feasible in the agri-biotech case for several reasons. It is hard to see how policy-makers in the European Union could successfully ask European taxpayers to compensate US farmers (and perhaps also US biotech firms) in the order of hundreds of millions of dollars for EU regulations that most Europeans regard as fundamentally legitimate and justified.

Even if EU policy-makers were prepared to pay compensation, they would run into financial difficulties. The European Union's agricultural budget, from which such compensation would presumably have to come, is already overstretched. This constraint will grow as the European Union expands to include recipients of agricultural subsidies in Central and Eastern Europe. Individual EU members are unlikely to fill the financial gap if current opposition among net contributors to increasing the EU budget is any sign.

The above analysis has shown that the cost imposed by EU regulation on the United States currently amounts to several hundred million USD, but could increase to several billion USD. Political opposition to compensation will grow with the amount of compensation to be provided.

The extent of damage suffered by the United States is very difficult to assess. The amount of compensation could, in principle, be calculated in terms of the value of products that would, in a given time period, have been exported by the United States to the European Union had the European Union not imposed restrictive agri-biotech regulation, holding all other influences constant. From a technical viewpoint, such calculation can never be precise. Politics consists of compromises and countries may eventually agree on a formula. However, uncertainty over the precise amount of damage to US exporters and biotech firms would contribute to undermining the legitimacy of such a solution.

Finally, the European Union would probably encounter great difficulties in mobilizing political support for compensation in the form of reducing trade barriers against other US agricultural or non-agricultural products. Such a solution would also fail to satisfy agri-biotech adverse farmers and consumers in the European Union and agri-biotech firms and farmers in the United States.

Harmonization

Harmonization of regulations, another voluntary policy option, is very common in regional and global trading systems. In essence, the European Union's internal market relies on a system where most obstacles to intra-EU trade and investment that cannot be removed through mutual recognition are removed through harmonization. When all countries trading with each other in a given good apply the same regulations to that good, trade flows are obviously not distorted by differences in regulation. A given good can thus be freely traded in a market where prices are determined exclusively by supply and demand. The European Union has harmonized approval and labeling regulations for agricultural biotechnology for precisely these reasons.

In principle, the negative consequences of regulatory polarization for international trade could be mitigated by full harmonization of agri-biotech regulation, or by a hybrid system of harmonized labeling combined with mutual recognition of GE product approvals.[39]

Full international harmonization of approval and labeling regulation is almost beyond imagination. Such a solution would require at a minimum internationally agreed scientific risk assessment and approval procedures, a mutually agreed and regularly updated list of approved GE products (i.e., a centralized approval process), internationally agreed labeling standards, and perhaps even international IP and liability rules. For reasons analyzed in chapters 3–5 it is hard to see how such harmonization at the level of the current US regulatory model could be made acceptable to EU policy-makers, or how such harmonization along current EU lines could be made acceptable to US regulators.

The chances of achieving the hybrid model are somewhat better. A report published in 2000 by the European Union–US Consultative Forum on Biotechnology contains ideas that could be developed in the direction of a hybrid model of mutual recognition and labeling. However, this report has been largely rejected by the Bush administration. I will revisit this issue in the subsequent section and in the concluding chapter.

Several bilateral EU–US initiatives aimed at fostering some degree of harmonization have largely failed, including the Transatlantic Economic Program's Biotechnology Working Group, the United States–EU Senior Level Group, and the European Union–US Biotechnology Consultative Forum. In the same vein, the OECD's Task Force for the Safety of Novel Foods and Feeds, the OECD's Working Group on Harmonization of Regulatory Oversight in Biotechnology, and various informal attempts in the UN Food and Agricultural Organization (FAO), the World Health Organization (WHO), the UN Environment Program, and elsewhere have failed to diffuse the brewing trade conflict. The WTO, which is geared primarily to removing tariff and non-tariff barriers to trade and has no experience in harmonizing environmental and public health standards, has not been able to fill the gap.[40]

The two most ambitious multilateral harmonization efforts in this policy area have also been deadlocked and are likely to remain so for the next few years; those in the CODEX Alimentarius Commission, and those in the context of the UN Convention on Biodiversity.

CODEX, a subsidiary of the UN Food and Agricultural Organization

(FAO) and the World Health Organization (WHO), has for several years tried to harmonize approval and labeling regulations for agricultural GE products.[41] The CODEX Commission meets every two years and operates several committees between its biannual sessions. CODEX standards, guidelines and recommendations are voluntary, that is, not legally binding commitments under international law. But since 1994 the WTO has recognized CODEX standards as reference points in international trade disputes.[42] Analysts have noted that this has made proposed CODEX standards more contentious and has slowed down the establishment of new standards.[43]

In June 1999, the CODEX Commission established an ad hoc intergovernmental task force to work out standards for GE foods, with a focus on risk assessment. This task force is to submit a report in mid-2003. The ongoing transatlantic dispute makes it very unlikely, however, that it will come up with clearly defined and operational principles for risk analysis and guidelines for conducting safety assessments, as well as recommendations on the implications for labeling and traceability.[44]

Agri-biotech proponents and countries with laxer regulation have proposed that testing be based exclusively on the concept of "substantial equivalence," a concept developed and propagated by the WHO. With this method, scientists determine whether and in what respect a GE product differs from its conventional counterpart. This information is used to judge the safety of the GE product. More testing is recommended for non-equivalent GE products. Thus far, there is no agreement on whether substantial equivalence should be the backbone of a harmonized safety testing system. Nor is there agreement on specific testing procedures, additional standards for approval, and risk-management procedures.

Agri-biotech critics and countries with stricter regulation fear that a CODEX endorsement of the substantial equivalence approach would make strict labeling (and also approval) regulation vulnerable to challenges in the WTO. Particularly vulnerable in this regard would be regulation that mandates labeling of *all* GE products (including those that are substantially equivalent but labeled because of non-safety concerns[45]). The WTO uses CODEX standards as a benchmark in its dispute settlement procedure. The critics are thus worried that the WTO would not protect national (or, in the EU case, regional) standards that exceed global (CODEX) standards should a formal WTO dispute arise. In addition, they claim that substantial equivalence alone would promote rapid commercialization of GE products without adequate testing for unintended side-effects and long-term effects.[46]

Another CODEX body, the CODEX Food Labeling Committee, has sought to develop international guidelines for countries that introduce mandatory labeling of GE products. No progress has been made for several years because of opposing EU and US views. The United States has proposed CODEX guidelines that would permit mandatory labeling only if GE foods differ significantly from their conventional equivalents in terms of composition, nutritional value, or intended use. This position reflects current FDA policy. The European Union has proposed to include an option for mandatory labeling of other GE products as well. It has also proposed to include traceability requirements. The United States has rejected such proposals.

The Biosafety (Cartagena) Protocol to the 1992 UN Biodiversity Convention was signed in January 2000 and will enter into force in September 2003. It is to govern transboundary movements, handling, transit, and use of living GE organisms that may have adverse effects on biological diversity.[47] Such organisms include, for example, seeds for planting, fish for release, or microorganisms for bioremediation. The Protocol addresses primarily environmental effects of trade in GE products, but also takes into account public health aspects. It does not apply to pharmaceutical GE products and the contained use of GE organisms.

Implementation of the Protocol is to be facilitated by an internet-based clearing house that will assist in the exchange of scientific, technical, environmental, and legal information on living GE organisms. Under an advance informed agreement (AIA) procedure, exporters of living GE organisms must seek the consent of importers before first shipment of such organisms. Exempt from the AIA procedure are bulk shipments of living GE commodities, such as soybeans and corn, that are intended for food, feed, or processing. But these must be documented. Documents must state that the shipment may contain GE organisms that are not intended for intentional release into the environment. Importers must notify domestic approvals to the clearing house. The agreement establishes a procedure for working out more detailed provisions for the identification of GE commodities in international trade. The European Union has proposed the inclusion of traceability rules in the Protocol's pending rules for documentation of bulk commodity grain shipments. As of May 2003, no agreement had been reached. The Protocol also promises help to developing countries in establishing effective regulatory systems for biotechnology.

The Biosafety Protocol is unlikely to mitigate the international trade implications of regulatory polarization. The United States is neither a party to the UN Biodiversity Convention (a prerequisite for joining the Biosafety Protocol), nor does it intend to ratify the former (and, for that matter, also the Protocol) in the foreseeable future. In contrast, the European Union has ratified the Convention and the Protocol and has already passed implementing legislation.

The so-called Miami group (including the United States, Argentina, Australia, Canada, Chile, and Uruguay) had blocked the first attempt in February 1999 to conclude a Biosafety Protocol because it opposed inclusion of GE bulk commodities (such as soybeans and corn) in the agreement. The agreement reached in 2000 thus contains "softened" clauses on bulk commodities that are unlikely to become operable anytime soon. Bulk commodities will only be subject to the internet-based clearing house process, and not the AIA procedure. The latter will only apply to seed stocks. Despite this watering down of contentious clauses, the members of the Miami group are unlikely to ratify the Protocol in the near future. They also remain fundamentally opposed to other provisions of the agreement, such as those that allow countries to restrict or ban imports of GE products on the basis of the precautionary principle. Indeed, the Protocol does not specify in detail the role and definition of the precautionary principle in risk assessment. It remains unclear, therefore, how far that principle could be "stretched" by countries restricting imports of GE products.[48] Many analysts believe that the Biosafety Protocol may promote persisting diversity in political and market responses to agricultural biotechnology, thus reinforcing a trend towards a two-tier market with segregated and labeled non-GE and GE products. Whether the Protocol as such will promote or dampen the prospects of GE products remains unclear.

Some observers have speculated that the Biosafety Protocol has made a full-blown transatlantic trade war within the WTO more likely because its precautionary principle encourages the European Union to pursue stringent agri-biotech regulation. Others claim that the Protocol has made a trade war less likely because it legitimizes the European Union's position and thus deters the United States from escalating the dispute.[49] Which of the two effects will eventually dominate is impossible to predict. The following section shows, however, that escalation by the United States of the dispute within the WTO system is unlikely to solve the problems associated with regulatory polarization.

Unilateral "Trading Up": Regulatory and Market Adjustment

Mutual recognition, compensation, and harmonization, as discussed above, are essentially bi- or multilateral in nature, that is, they require explicit agreement among a given set of countries. Completing this review of voluntary approaches I now look at two forms of "trading up," both of which involve unilateral efforts, in our case by the United States, to diffuse trade tensions. Trading up means that the United States formally adjusts its domestic regulation, or that US producers adjust their production methods and product qualities in the absence of new domestic regulation, so that US products become acceptable to trading partners, notably, the European Union.[50]

To what extent has the United States engaged in trading up? To what extent have such efforts diffused trade tensions with the European Union? What is the potential for additional unilateral US measures to diffuse trade tensions?

As noted in chapters 3–5 formal regulatory adjustment in the United States has been minimal. And it is unclear to what extent observable adjustment has been motivated by domestic or by international trade considerations. At the federal level, the USDA, EPA, and FDA have engaged in reassessments of their respective regulations and policies. These reassessments and subsequent policy reforms have slightly increased transparency, particularly in the approval process. They have led to additional risk assessment and mandatory notification (but not approval requirements) prior to commercialization. And they have resulted in guidelines for voluntary labeling of GE foods.

In an overall perspective these adjustments have been marginal. All attempts at further reaching regulatory reforms, most of which were made through law proposals submitted in the US Congress, have been unsuccessful. With a view to the fact that most of these law proposals were sponsored by Democrats and given the Bush Administration's ideological hostility to new regulation it is highly unlikely that any of these initiatives will succeed in the next few years. Efforts to initiate regulatory reform at the state level have ultimately been unsuccessful as well.[51] State legislative initiatives and referenda have focused on mandatory labeling, mandatory environmental assessment, moratoria on GE crop cultivation, liability rules, and bans on GE food in public schools.[52] For example, a ballot initiative in Oregon that provided for mandatory labeling was rejected.

While the US regulatory system has not responded in significant ways to increasing regulatory stringency abroad, US exporters have made considerable efforts to accommodate changes in EU and other countries' regulations and consumer preferences. Some US corn processors have set up IP systems that keep GE corn varieties not approved by the European Union out of the export-oriented production chain. US soybean producers have worked with biotech firms and farmers to do the same for GE soybean varieties and have also restricted cultivation of GE soybean varieties not approved by the European Union. The USDA has supported these efforts by facilitating the creation of testing procedures and quality control mechanisms. Commercialization of GE wheat has been held back not least by the US wheat industry's insistence that such GE crops be segregated and subject to an IP system—as in the case of soya, a large part of US wheat production is exported. As to sugar beet, US sugar refiners have asked farmers not to growth GE sugar beets for fear of losing export markets. National commodity associations, the USDA, and the US State Department have established programs through which US farmers are informed more systematically about regulation and consumer preferences in export markets and US grain handlers' and processors' requirements in this regard. US food processors have adjusted in part by eliminating GE ingredients altogether or by restricting their inputs to EU approved GE ingredients. Some US food processors have also shifted parts of their production to the European Union to facilitate compliance with EU regulation.[53]

The analysis in chapters 3–6 suggests that trading up will remain very limited for the years to come. It will occur primarily through unilateral market adjustment. Adjustment by individual farmers, processors, and commodity associations is obviously easier to achieve, both because it is smaller in scale and because these economic actors have a direct and strong incentive to adapt. However, market adjustment in the United States will be constrained by several factors, particularly the fact that US agricultural exports to Europe account for only 10–15 percent of total US agricultural exports. In addition, US agricultural exports as such are rather small compared to domestic consumption. As long as US agri-biotech regulation remains lax and US consumer demand for non-GE foods remains small there will be clear limits to trading up through market adjustment. US producers will continue to have strong incentives to maintain non-segregated and non-IP systems as far as possible and introduce IP systems only under severe pressure. Operating two systems in parallel creates additional costs, particularly vis-à-vis countries that opt fully for non-GE crops. The resulting differences in production costs and the associated implications for international competitiveness will continue to be a source of tension in the world trading system.

We might also see some limited regulatory adjustment, possibly emanating from state-level initiatives driven by a spill-over of consumer campaigns from Europe to the United States. Yet, as noted in chapters 4–5, a variety of factors exert strong constraints on regulatory adjustment, particularly at the federal level. It seems that only a major accident with the technology could move US agri-biotech regulation towards the EU model. From what we know about R&D in this area the probability of an accident of this nature is low.

Market adjustment may thus temporarily mitigate transatlantic trade tensions to some extent. But it will not eliminate them. As the stringency of EU regulation and the gap between GE product approvals in the European Union and United States grows and regulatory laxity in the United States persists, market adjustment will become increasingly expensive for US producers. In particular, it will require large-scale restructuring of the US grain handling system to meet regulatory requirements in export markets. And it may increasingly shift the costs of stricter regulation in Europe from US farmers to agri-biotechnology firms as US farmers restrict crop cultivation to EU approved GE varieties. The US agri-biotech sector is well organized, politically influential, and under massive pressure to recuperate R&D investment in the technology through GE seed sales in the United States and abroad. US exporters, biotech firms, and the US government are thus likely to conclude that the expected costs of escalation are smaller than the costs under the status quo.

COERCION THROUGH THE GLOBAL TRADING SYSTEM

The likelihood of US agri-biotech trade action against the European Union is also influenced by the anticipated effectiveness of coercive policy measures. These include, notably, the (potential) plaintiff's chances of winning a legal case in the WTO's dispute settlement system, and the chances of the defendant backing down before a WTO panel decision (in the "shadow of the law") or after a "guilty" verdict.

Coercion is a common policy tool in international trade relations when problems over regulatory diversity arise. It materializes in many forms and differs in terms of its magnitude and visibility. In principle, any implicit or explicit threat by one state to impose costs of some sort on another state if the latter does not comply with a particular request by the threatening state amounts to coercion. I concentrate only on two forms of coercion that often appear in combination: unilateral punitive measures (often referred to as sanctions), and decisions by an authority above and beyond the states involved in a dispute.

As to the former, the list of possibilities is virtually unlimited. The United States could, for example, threaten the European Union with unilateral imposition of punitive tariffs on wine or cheese imports, or it could escalate one of the many lingering transatlantic trade disputes, for example by launching formal WTO proceedings.

Decisions by an authority above and beyond the states involved can also be regarded as a form of coercion. In the WTO context, which is of principal interest here, dispute settlement panels and the appellate body of the WTO can issue decisions against the will of a defendant country. Once the defendant has exhausted all possibilities of appeal and lost the case, from a legal viewpoint it is obliged to comply with the verdict. As in the domestic arena, however, coercion in a commonly understood sense occurs primarily when the verdict is enforced. In the international arena, including the WTO, enforcement is usually decentralized. That is, the WTO may find a state guilty and may formally approve a specific economic punishment of the culprit. But the execution of the punishment is in the hands of the plaintiff.[54] Typically, the punishment is not designed as a punishment per se, but rather as an incentive for the defendant state to change its regulation in ways that eliminate negative effects of domestic regulation on international trade and restore compliance with international legal commitments. In the growth hormones case, the WTO authorized the United States to impose around 120 million USD per annum in punitive tariffs on imports from the European Union.

The most plausible scenario in the agri-biotech case is that the United States asks the WTO to decide on whether the European Union's agri-biotech regulations are compatible with legal obligations under the WTO agreements. If the European Union was found guilty and the WTO approved a set of economic countermeasures, the United States could then impose these measures on the European Union, hoping that this would cause an adjustment in EU regulations according to US preferences.

In fact, in mid-May 2003 the United States requested formal WTO consultations on what it called an illegal EU moratorium on GE crop approvals. WTO rules hold that if such consultations do not lead to an agreement between plaintiffs and defendants within 60 days the plaintiff may forward the case to a dispute settlement panel. Previous experience shows that the panel process can take 10–18 months, potentially even longer if there are appeals or if an initial legal case is extended – for example, if the United States extended the case from approval regulation to EU labeling and traceability rules. If neither the United States nor the European Union backs down at some point along the way final WTO decisions in this case could be made in late 2004 or early 2005.

In this section I argue that it is far from clear whether the United States would win a WTO case from a legal viewpoint. And even if it did, it is very unlikely that the European Union would back down and change its regulations in line with US requests. The European Union is also unlikely to acquiesce to WTO approved punitive measures by the United States, as it has done in the case of beef hormones. The economic order of magnitude of punitive measures (if they were roughly in line with economic losses of US producers) and popular support for EU regulation will not allow EU policy-makers to accept punishment. If the United States escalated the issue in the WTO, and if a verdict favorable to the US resulted, we would probably see a series of punitive measures and countermeasures. Such considerations are likely to cast a shadow from expected future outcomes back to the present: because WTO rules do not provide clear-cut guidance on who is right or wrong in this case, and because political resistance on the part of the defendant is bound to be strong, the WTO is unlikely to invalidate the European Union's agri-biotech regulations. In principle, this should deter the United States from escalating the dispute. However, I also discuss why the United States may still opt for escalation.

How Much Legal Guidance Do WTO Rules Provide?

The General Agreement on Tariffs and Trade (GATT) was established in 1947 and was developed further in several rounds of global trade talks (most recently the Uruguay Round). In 1994, the World Trade Organization superseded the GATT structure. The GATT/WTO's aim is to liberalize international trade. The key vehicles to that end are the principles of "most favored nation treatment" and "national treatment." The former holds that market access granted by one WTO member state to another WTO member state must be granted to all other WTO members (no discrimination among trading partners). The latter holds that WTO states must afford the same treatment to imported goods and services than to domestically produced goods and services (no discrimination among imported and domestic goods).

WTO countries may still establish domestic regulations that constitute trade barriers (and thus discriminate against imported goods), but only under certain circumstances. Most relevant to the agri-biotech case are Articles XXb and XXg of the GATT/WTO. These allow for such measures if they can be justified for the protection of human, animal, or plant life and health, or for the conservation of exhaustible natural resources. They must also meet some other conditions that are discussed below.

It is easy to see how an agri-biotech dispute can enter the WTO system. Country A establishes strict agri-biotech regulation that negatively affects imports from country B. This regulation is justified under Article XX. Country B claims that this regulation is in fact protectionist, constitutes a non-tariff barrier to trade, is arbitrary, and cannot be justified on environmental or public health grounds.

The procedures in GATT and the WTO for coping with such disputes have become increasingly sophisticated and mandatory.[55] Through the 1960s, the GATT used a system in which panels of 3–5 persons (usually diplomats) were established with the consent of all parties to a dispute. In the 1970s and 1980s, this system was "judicialized," with lawyers and economists replacing diplomats on the panels and a more consistent case law emerging. An important weakness in the system remained: any party to a dispute maintained the right to block the establishment of a panel and the adoption of a panel report. This weakness was removed in 1994.

Under the new WTO system, defendant countries cannot block dispute settlement, which proceeds according to strict time frames. Moreover, the WTO maintains a standing appellate body that is the ultimate arbiter in disputes. It also specifies measures that may be used to enforce panel decisions.

In 2000, the first agri-biotech case entered the WTO system. Thailand challenged an import ban imposed by Egypt on canned Thai tuna. Egypt claimed that this tuna was packaged in GE soybean oil. Thailand argued that there was no legal basis for the ban because of a lack of scientific evidence on health risks posed by GE soybeans and on whether the oil was actually produced from GE soybeans. It also noted that a ban of Thai tuna alone was discriminatory. After consultations between the two countries, the case was withdrawn. The Thai–Egypt case should not be interpreted as a sign that the European Union would lose a WTO case on agri-biotech regulation. In contrast to the European Union's regulations, Egypt's import ban was poorly justified and clearly in breach of the WTO's non-discrimination rules. However, some analysts of the global trading system assumed that it was only a matter of time before a new and potentially more controversial agri-biotech case would enter the WTO system.[56]

As noted above, the United States launched such a case in mid-May 2003, just as this book went to press. Supported by Canada and Argentina, it attacked the European Union's agri-biotech regulation on two fronts. First, it claimed that the European Union's 1998 moratorium on approvals of new GE crops was illegal under WTO rules. It also listed a range of new GE crops held up in national and EU-level approval processes. Second, it claimed that the refusal of EU approved GE crops in Austria, France, Germany, Greece, Italy and Luxembourg was illegal. To the surprise of many observers, the United States did not, at least at this point in time, attack the European Union's labeling and traceability rules. Most analysts assume that even if the United States succeeded in coercing the European Union into restarting the approval process labeling and traceability rules would still keep GE crops out of the EU market because of negative consumer reactions and high compliance costs.

While most economists' predictions of whether the US government will or will not escalate the dispute into a full blown trade war are based on the analysis of economic costs and benefits,[57] lawyers' predictions have been informed mainly by legal assessments of whether the United States will or will not win such a dispute. In this and the next section I argue that legal assessment alone is insufficient for predicting the outcome of a WTO case on agri-biotechnology. The reasons are, first, that it is far from clear whether the United States will win the legal case, and second, WTO bodies are likely to behave strategically in this situation. The first aspect is discussed in this section, the second one in the next.

Those concluding that the United States would win (mainly the proponents of legal action) claim that agri-biotech regulation more stringent than that of the United States violates the WTO Agreement on Technical Barriers to Trade (TBT Agreement) and the WTO Agreement on Sanitary and Phytosanitary Measures (SPS Agreement).[58]

The TBT agreement was signed in 1979. Its scope was extended in the Uruguay Round (1986–94). All WTO members are bound by its provisions. The agreement applies to, among other things, all technical regulations in the agro-food sector, except those concerning animal, plant, and human life and health. These are governed by the SPS agreement. Important in our case, the TBT agreement applies to all regulations and standards for packaging, marking, and labeling of agricultural products. The agreement rests on three general principles: (a) regulations must not discriminate unjustifiably between domestic and foreign products; (b) regulations must fulfill a legitimate purpose and achieve this purpose in a way that minimizes restrictions on trade; (c) states are encouraged to subscribe to international standards and compliance with such standards is viewed favorably. The TBT Committee, which is open to all WTO member states (but not firms or NGOs), is the clearing house for notifications by countries that introduce new regulations that depart from international standards (to the extent they exist). Most problems arising from such regulations are usually solved at the TBT Committee's biannual meetings.[59] The use of WTO dispute settlement panels remains the exception.

The proponents of legal action argue that, with regard to the TBT Agreement, the European Union's agri-biotech regulations, particularly those on labeling, fail the test on at least three accounts: (a) they cannot be justified in terms of preventing deception of consumers or protecting public health (i.e., there is no legitimate purpose); (b) voluntary labeling would achieve the same objective (satisfy consumer demand for more information); and (c) they are not consistent in terms of stringency, neither internally across different GE food or feed products, nor across agricultural and medical biotechnology.[60]

The proponents of legal action also claim that the European Union's regulations violate the SPS Agreement. This agreement governs food safety and animal and plant health standards. The SPS Agreement allows countries to set their own standards as long as these are based on scientific evidence and justification, are necessary to protect human, animal, or plant life, or health,[61] and do not arbitrarily or unjustifiably discriminate between countries where identical or similar conditions prevail. Like the TBT Agreement, the SPS Agreement also encourages the use of international standards, where they exist. Domestic regulations in line with international standards are, quasi automatically, regarded as compatible with legal commitments under the WTO. If national standards exceed international ones, they must be based on scientific risk assessment. They must not be discriminatory or create disguised trade barriers through different levels of SPS protection in comparable situations. Stricter standards may be established if they are temporary and there is a process to provide the missing information in a timely manner—this provision can be interpreted as allowing for the application of the precautionary principle. Finally, the measure used must not be more trade restrictive than necessary for reaching the SPS protection a country envisages.[62] The SPS Committee, which is open to all WTO member states, provides a forum for exchanging information and solving problems through consultation and negotiation.[63] If a problem cannot be solved at that level, countries may use the WTO's dispute settlement procedure.[64]

Those favoring an escalation of the transatlantic trade dispute claim that the European Union's agri-biotech regulations violate most of the provisions of the SPS Agreement. In their view, the European Union's approval and labeling standards cannot be justified with the available scientific evidence. Voluntary labeling and less onerous approval rules would achieve the same purpose in terms of protecting public health and the environment. Moreover, in the view of agri-biotech proponents the European Union's regulations discriminate against countries exporting GE products.

Those claiming that the United States would not win a WTO dispute over the European Union's agri-biotech policy point out that the TBT rather than the SPS agreement would have to be applied, particularly in a challenge of mandatory labeling. They argue that mandatory labeling of GE products is a technical standard justified mainly by consumers' right to know as well as ethical and religious considerations rather than food safety aspects. Consumer surveys in fact show that EU consumers are more concerned about GE food on moral than on health risk grounds.[65] Legal reviews show that upholding mandatory labeling would be easier under the TBT than the SPS Agreement because the role of science as an arbiter is stronger under the SPS than the TBT agreement.[66] In other words, legal uncertainties arise already with regard to which of the two agreements is primarily applicable. This uncertainty may have played a role in the US decision to launch its first attack against the European Union's approval rather than its labeling and traceability rules.

As shown in table 6.3, supporters of mandatory labeling could resort to a range of arguments in defense of existing EU regulations. Similarly, the European Union's defense of its approval rules is likely to focus on several arguments, namely, that:

TABLE 6.3
Legal challenges and defenses under the TBT and SPS Agreements

Challengers	Defenders
TBT Agreement	
Mandatory labeling is discriminatory and more trade restrictive than necessary; it treats like (or substantially equivalent, in terms of composition, flavor, and texture) products differently	Substantial equivalence is too narrow a concept to distinguish GE and non-GE products; it is not an international standard (in CODEX or elsewhere);[a] applying common WTO standards such as consumer tastes and habits, physical properties, end uses, and possible long-term side effects shows that GE and non-GE products are different; regulations are applied to all domestic and foreign producers
Mandatory labeling is more trade restrictive than necessary because it has no legitimate objective in protecting human health or safety, animal or plant life or health, or the environment	There is no authoritative interpretation of these terms under the TBT Agreement and they should thus be handled liberally; mandatory labeling is an effective means of achieving the objectives of increasing consumer awareness and their right to know what is in their food; voluntary labeling would not achieve that objective; there are no CODEX standards the exceeding of which defendants must justify; the Biosafety Convention (BSC) supports the precautionary principle on which mandatory labeling is in part based;[b] WTO rules do not have priority over BSC rules
SPS Agreement	
There is no rational relationship between risk assessment and mandatory labeling; scientific risk assessments show that there is no safety problem with GE food	The main justifications for mandatory labeling are non-food-safety related and "pure science" should thus not be the arbiter; other justifications draw on the precautionary principle since the long-term effects of GE products are unknown
Mandatory labeling involves arbitrary and unjustifiable discrimination	Same as arguments against mandatory labeling under the TBT Agreement (see above)

[a] Proposals to use substantial equivalence in CODEX standards for safety testing of GE products are heavily contested. Because neither CODEX nor Biosafety Protocol standards are widely accepted it is unlikely that the WTO would use them as the backbone of a controversial decision.

[b] For an expression of fear that new CODEX and Biosafety Protocol rules could bolster biotech adverse countries' position, see Paarlberg (2000b, 2001c).

1   the same regulations are applied to EU and non-EU producers, that is, these regulations are non-discriminatory;
2   there is no formal moratorium in the European Union but only a slowdown in approvals that is temporary and, in view of existing scientific uncertainties about risks as well as problems such as the Starlink and ProdiGene cases, based on the precautionary principle;
3   those few international standards that exist, notably, the Biosafety Protocol's provisions on the precautionary principle, provide sufficient legal cover for the Union's policy;
4   EU food safety rules are broadly consistent across different areas (notably, biotech and non-biotech food) in that they are all building on the precautionary principle and scientific risk assessment.

In view of these challenges and defenses it appears all but certain that the United States would win the legal case. This conclusion is consistent with outcomes in the three SPS food safety cases that have so far gone all the way through the WTO dispute settlement procedure: the transatlantic dispute over bovine growth hormones (see also below), a dispute between Canada and Australia over the latter's ban on imports of fresh or frozen salmon, and a dispute between the United States and Japan over the latter's testing requirements for imported fruits and nuts.[67] In all three cases national regulations were at least in part invalidated by the WTO (i.e., the challengers of stricter regulation prevailed). Paradoxically, however, the evidence on these three cases suggests that the United States would not win an agri-biotech case in the WTO.

   In an analysis of the three cases, Victor (2000) shows that the SPS requirement to establish a "rational" (i.e., science-based) relationship between risk assessment and regulation was interpreted in flexible ways. He claims that this requirement and the application of international (notably, CODEX) standards in dispute settlement have not significantly affected the levels of SPS protection.[68] In the only case where the WTO made extensive use of international standards, the one on bovine growth hormones, the Dispute Panel interpreted the SPS Agreement as requiring conformity of national with international (in this case CODEX) standards. But the WTO's Appellate Body rejected this interpretation. Flexibility of national (or EU) regulators in the agri-biotech case, where there are no international standards accepted by the United States *and* the European Union,[69] is likely to be even higher. The Appellate Body of the WTO has also interpreted the "rational relationship" and the requirement for risk assessment in an elastic manner, providing much room for agri-biotech adverse nations to justify restrictive regulation.[70]

   In other words, CODEX and other international standards have probably had an effect on procedures and related justifications in setting national (or EU) SPS standards, but not on protection levels.[71] Even with regard to procedures and justifications, this effect has been rather opaque. It remains unclear to what extent the WTO would tolerate formally provisional but de facto definitive regulations justified by the precautionary principle and a never ending process of scientific risk assessment. Moreover, it remains unclear to what extent the WTO would be willing to tolerate justifications based on ethical, religious, or economic concerns.[72] In any event, we are likely to see increasing use of the precautionary principle as countries seek to justify regulations that are based on insufficient risk assessments or are driven by social rather than scientific motivations. Current justifications by the European Union of its agri-biotech regulations hold that these regulations are designed to enhance consumer safety and social acceptance of GE food, to enable consumers to make informed choices, and to keep track of environmental and health effects. It also argues that these rules are applied evenly to all domestic and foreign producers.

The evidence on past SPS cases suggests more generally that invalidation of national regulations is unlikely (a) if the latter do not clearly discriminate against particular countries, (b) if they are conceptualized as temporary and following the precautionary principle, (c) if very similar or identical regulations are applied in comparable situations, (d) if scientific risk assessments are carried out, (e) if regulations are not obviously protectionist (e.g., if it is hard to show that they benefit domestic producers at the expense of foreign producers), and (f) if it is hard to demonstrate that other, less trade restrictive, measures could have achieved acceptable levels of risk at the same or lower cost. These conditions are quite easy to meet in EU regulation of agricultural biotechnology.

In brief, the WTO has established detailed rules and procedures that may be resorted to in order to distinguish legitimate from illegitimate (protectionist) regulations. However, the applicable WTO agreements (the TBT and SPS Agreements, and their legal interpretation in past disputes) do not provide clear guidance with regard to the European Union's agri-biotech regulations. The European Union will be able to mount a range of substantial and legally plausible arguments in its defense. The next section expands on this point, and on why the problem would not be solved even if the United States won a WTO case against the European Union.

Why the United States Is Unlikely to Win an Agri-Biotech Case in the WTO

In this section I argue that insufficient legal guidance in the agri-biotech case must be viewed in combination with the fact that the European

Union would probably not back down when facing an adverse WTO verdict. In the presence of these two conditions and others discussed here, the WTO is unlikely to invalidate the European Union's agri-biotech regulations. In the unlikely event it still did, the political and economic fallout from such a verdict would exceed by far any gains the United States might experience.

Studies on environment and consumer health cases in domestic, European, and global judicial systems show that courts usually behave as strategic actors that attempt to strike a balance between legal consistency and political support. If courts rule too often and in costly ways against politically influential actors, they risk undermining their long-term viability. In the worst case, influential losers may try to abolish a court. They may not comply with its verdicts. Or they may initiate political reforms that weaken the court's influence. If courts bow too much to political pressure, they risk losing their legitimacy as independent and impartial arbiters.

Kelemen, Garrett and Smith, and others[73] have sought to explain WTO dispute outcomes in such terms. Drawing and expanding on that work I argue that the likelihood of the WTO upholding the defendant's regulation is higher when:

1　legal rules do not provide clear-cut guidance as to whether the defendant's regulations are legitimate or not;
2　the defendant is economically powerful and unlikely to comply with an adverse verdict;
3　the defendant is, implicitly or explicitly, supported by other influential WTO countries;
4　important global trade talks are under way;
5　a recent and comparable case ended with substantial political backlash.

This explanatory framework helps in predicting what the outcome would be in a WTO case on agricultural biotechnology.[74] The available evidence for all five conditions suggests that an invalidation of the European Union's agri-biotech regulations is unlikely. If this framework provides any guidance, the United States would lose a WTO case over agricultural biotechnology if it escalated the case through the full dispute settlement process. Let us look at each of the five conditions in more detail.

The above section has provided evidence on the first condition. It shows that WTO rules offer only very limited guidance as to whether or not the European Union's regulations are (according to WTO laws) legal. In this section I show that the European Union is very unlikely to back down in the event of an adverse WTO verdict. This position of the European Union would at least tacitly be supported by several other countries. Moreover, ongoing efforts to liberalize global agricultural trade and the recent WTO case on growth hormones reduce the likelihood of a verdict that is favorable to the United States.

First, the analysis in chapters 3–5 of regulatory policy in the European Union suggests that the latter would not make the concessions requested by the plaintiff, either before a WTO verdict (in the "shadow of the law") or after. It goes almost without saying that the European Union is crucial to the viability of the WTO system because the Union is the world's second largest economy and the world's biggest trader. Moreover, the European Union and the United States are engaged in the world's largest bilateral trading relationship.

Regulatory authorities and governments of the European Union and its member states are under severe pressure from environmental and consumer groups. Many of these groups regard labeling as only an intermediate step on the way to more restrictions on the technology. In their view, labeling solves problems of information asymmetry, but does not accommodate consumer demands for risk shielding.

Similarly, labeling does not solve European farmers' problems of agricultural surpluses, market disruptions caused by food safety crises, and the prospect of growing competition from new generations of GE products imported from the United States and elsewhere. Consequently, farmer preferences are likely to move from mandatory labeling to more restrictions on GE crops rather than from mandatory to voluntary labeling. Because of substantial consumer concerns over GE products and anti-agri-biotech campaigns by NGOs, support by processors and retailers for a relaxation of agri-biotech regulations is very unlikely.[75]

Invalidation by the WTO of the European Union's agri-biotech regulations would also raise a political storm among critics of globalization (potentially a much larger group of voters than agri-biotech critics alone). These critics have for years expressed fears that "faceless international bureaucrats" could strike down important domestic consumer and environmental regulations in the name of free trade.

When deciding, WTO panel or appellate body members would presumably also seek to estimate the damage to the WTO and its dispute settlement system that might result if the United States lost the case. Evidence from other GATT/WTO disputes shows that in most of the highly contentious cases plaintiffs find it easier to lose a case than defendants. We may thus assume that the political fallout for the WTO would be smaller if the United States lost the case than if the European Union lost the case. Plaintiffs who lose do not have to go back home and change domestic regulations to comply with a verdict. They can simply argue that they tried to defend the rights of domestic producers and lost the case, and they can blame the WTO and the defendant. Defendants who lose are likely to face much higher costs because compliance with a WTO verdict usually means eliminating or changing domestic regulations that are supported by important constituencies. In brief, if the United States lost the case, the status quo would persist. In contrast, many observers expect that the European Union would, in the extreme, simply ignore a verdict that would demand the elimination of mandatory labeling and a relaxation of approval regulation.

Second, as shown in chapter 3, several other important economies have adopted mandatory labeling and stricter than US approval standards for GE foods. Should the European Union's agri-biotech regulations be invalidated by the WTO, theirs might be next in line. Countries such as Japan (the world's third largest economy) are thus likely to at least tacitly support the European Union's position. In Japan strong consumer support for strict agri-biotech regulation, potentially growing support by farmers for more stringent regulation, weak support by the biotech industry for a relaxation of existing regulations, and differences among processors and retailers make it unlikely that Japan will revert to laxer agri-biotech rules. If Japanese agri-biotech policy moved away from the status quo, it is likely to be towards the European rather than the US regulatory model. The European Union is also likely to receive support from many developing countries which are concerned about wider issues, such as biodiversity problems associated with agri-biotech applications and property rights on genetic resources. US efforts to build a pro-agri-biotech coalition in the TBT and SPS Committees, the WTO and CODEX have largely failed. The pro-agri-biotech coalition remains limited largely to the United States, Canada, and Argentina.[76]

The case of Egypt illustrates the limits of the US-led coalition. Following open threats by the US government that it would slow down or even cancel ongoing bilateral free trade negotiations unless Egypt supported US biotech food policy, Egypt first signaled that it would join the US request for WTO proceedings on the legality of EU agri-biotech regulations. Then it backed off, probably in view of its economic dependence on the European Union. In more general terms, Egypt's behavior illustrates a trend where the European regulatory model appears to be gaining ground in many developing and industrialized countries. As a result, the European Union has also won more political and commercial influence in this realm. This development is bound to make it much harder for the United States to obtain a favorable verdict from the WTO and, if it obtains such a verdict, to obtain the requested concessions from the European Union and other countries with similar regulation.

Third, due to a long history of protectionism, liberalizing global agricultural markets is perhaps the most contentious area of WTO activity. The Uruguay Round, concluded in 1993, resulted in only modest progress. Many industrialized and developing countries have thus been pushing for further liberalization in the recently initiated Doha round.[77] So far, these efforts have not had much success. An escalation of the transatlantic agri-biotech dispute would certainly not be conducive to progress in this area.

Fourth, the political fallout from the transatlantic trade dispute over growth hormones in beef production is likely to deter WTO decision-makers from invalidating the European Union's agri-biotech regulations. It is worthwhile to look at this case in some detail.[78]

Through decisions taken in 1981, 1988, and 1996, the European Union banned the import of meat from farm animals treated for the purpose of growth promotion with natural or synthetic hormones. While the European Union legitimized its ban with reference to possible health risks the United States accused the European Union of using this regulation to keep US beef out of the EU market. The United States challenged the European ban under the old GATT's TBT agreement. Because the TBT agreement was, at that time, voluntary and the dispute settlement procedure was not mandatory, the European Community (as it was then called) was able to veto the establishment of a panel. The conflict became symbolic of an example of the GATT's inability to prevent growing non-tariff barriers to trade. The dispute settlement process was strengthened during the Uruguay Round, not least with this case in mind.

Once stricter procedures were in place, the United States successfully demanded the establishment of a panel and obtained a favorable verdict. This time, the United States had challenged the European Union's ban primarily under the new SPS Agreement (see above). The WTO dispute panel ruled against the European Union on three accounts.

It declared the European Union's ban illegal because five of the six growth hormones the European Union had prohibited were covered by more permissive international standards. In 1995, the CODEX Commission had adopted such standards by a narrow majority. This WTO ruling was later overturned by the Appellate Body, suggesting that domestic rules should be based on but not necessarily conform to international standards.

The WTO panel ruled that the European Union's measures were not based on adequate risk assessment as required by the SPS Agreement. The Appellate body somewhat widened the interpretation of what an appropriate risk assessment was (the panel had focused exclusively on "hard" scientific evidence of health risks). However, both bodies found that the European Union had not systematically assessed the risks on the basis of which it had justified its import ban on hormone-treated beef. Assessments of health risks under conditions of good practice use of growth hormones, carried out by European Union and other bodies, had not demonstrated any health risks. The risk of misuse of growth hormones, invoked by the European Union, had not been assessed at all. Neither had the sixth hormone (MAG) that the European Union had banned. The EU ban thus failed the test of a "rational relationship" between regulation and risk assessment.

Moreover, the panel invalidated the European Union's regulation because it provided for different levels of protection in comparable situations that could not be justified by the European Union. The European Union had allowed the use of two other hormones (carbadox and olaquindox) for pigs. The Appellate Body overturned this ruling, arguing that the plaintiffs did not provide sufficient evidence that the mentioned differences were arbitrary and unjustified and thus harmful to trade. In the end, the United States won the legal case because of the European Union's failure to carry out adequate risk assessment.

This legal outcome has not solved the problem. Due to strong political support for the ban, the European Union has not made any concessions. The United States has responded by imposing punitive measures in the order of 120 million USD per year on EU countries. The European Union has thus far refrained from re-opening the case in the WTO or unilaterally imposing countermeasures against the United States—probably because the cost of US measures to the European Union is rather small. While the amounts of money involved are minor, many analysts view the still festering growth hormones dispute as detrimental to the functioning of the WTO's dispute settlement system.

The outcome in the growth hormones case is likely to deter WTO decision-makers from invalidating sensitive EU regulations in another, comparable, case. The WTO ruling on growth hormones suggests that more systematic risk assessment by the European Union of agri-biotech applications combined with justification of regulation in terms of the precautionary principle would position the European Union rather close to existing SPS and TBT rules. In terms of the explanation presented above, it would thus mitigate the pressure on WTO decision-makers to lean on the side of legal consistency at the expense of political support. Under these conditions, strong signals by the European Union that it would not back down in the event of an adverse ruling are likely to push WTO decision-makers toward a ruling shaped by considerations of political support.[79]

Towards a Full Blown Trade War?

The above analysis suggests that, if the United States escalated the trans-atlantic agri-biotech trade conflict all the way through the WTO dispute settlement system, it would not obtain a favorable verdict. It also suggests that, even if the dispute settlement procedure produced the verdict favored by the United States (possibly in late 2004 or early 2005), the European Union would not make concessions.[80] In the best case, the European Union would simply "swallow" economic punishment by the United States, possibly in the order of 300 million USD or more per year. In the worst case, it would retaliate by imposing all sorts of economic costs on the United States in other areas, for example, in the form of escalating other trade disputes. The WTO system and the long-term prospects of the technology would be negatively affected in either case.

In the first case (upholding of the European Union's regulations), other countries would be encouraged to impose more restrictive agri-biotech regulations, knowing that the WTO would protect them. Particularly in countries exporting agricultural products to the European Union adoption of the technology would slow down. In addition, support by important US political constituencies for the WTO would suffer, with obvious implications for ongoing trade talks, notably, the Doha round whose conclusion is scheduled for 2005.

In the second case (invalidation of the European Union's regulations), political support for the WTO among important European Union constituencies could decline dramatically. Against the background of already strong opposition against further liberalization of agricultural trade, further trade talks in this area would almost certainly collapse. Moreover, the WTO's dispute settlement system would be heavily taxed by another food safety case that produced a legal but not a de facto solution. Trust in that system would suffer on all sides.

In view of these considerations one might think that US policy-makers acting in the interest of their country as a whole will not escalate the conflict. Neither should one expect agri-biotech firms and US farmers and processors to push the US government towards escalation. But it remains uncertain how much weight the US government and the private sector will attribute to such arguments and to several contextual factors.

Quantitative evidence on the totality of trade disputes in the GATT/WTO system shows that governments quite often initiate formal trade disputes but do not win the case.[81] This suggests that the expected effectiveness of coercion through the global trading system (the third of the three conditions outlined at the beginning of this chapter) may frequently be overridden by other considerations when countries decide on whether or not to escalate a dispute in the WTO.

Escalation by one country in one trade area may serve as a strategy to deter another country from escalating a trade conflict in another trade area, to motivate another country to make concessions in another trade dispute, or to deter other countries from establishing more restrictions in the disputed area. For example, the United States may decide to escalate the agri-biotech dispute to deter the European Union from escalating disputes over US export subsidies and anti-dumping measures in the steel sector. It might do so to obtain concessions by the European Union with regard to regulations on bovine growth hormones. It might also do so to deter the European Union and other countries from establishing more restrictions on agri-biotechnology. Conversely, holding back in one trade area may serve to motivate another country not to escalate a dispute in another trade area.[82] For example, the United States could hold back on agri-biotechnology, hoping that the European Union will, in exchange, hold back in the export subsidies and steel cases. The European Union could hold back on steel and export subsidies (where EU claims were approved by the WTO) in exchange for US tolerance of EU agri-biotech regulation. In some (albeit rare) cases, governments may even decide to escalate a non-winnable dispute in order to fight protectionist interests in their own countries.

Escalation may also occur because potential plaintiffs conclude that winning political support from crucial constituencies by escalating a trade dispute is more important than actually winning the case. Such action promises short-term gains—the political science literature demonstrates that politicians' time horizons are usually short. WTO proceedings, on the other hand, often take years and adverse outcomes at some point in the future may be blamed on the WTO and the defendant country.

The costs of escalation to the plaintiff country are often diffuse while the benefits for important political constituencies are concentrated and high. The above analysis shows that the costs of EU regulation fall on a small but powerful group of economic actors in the United States. In principle, this small group would benefit from concessions by the European Union, should escalation in the WTO be successful. It thus has a powerful incentive to organize and push the US government towards escalation. The costs of escalation (e.g., punitive economic measures and countermeasures, disruption of further trade talks, slow-down of agri-biotech adoption in other countries), on the other hand, would obviously be much more dispersed. The incentive for those negatively affected by escalation to organize and lobby the government not to escalate is much smaller.

Some of those potential driving forces are clearly reflected in what analysts tend to regard as the principal reasons for the May 2003 decision by the Bush Administration to escalate the dispute.

First, only a few days before the US decision was made public (May 13, 2003) the European Union had threatened to impose four billion USD in WTO approved trade sanctions against the United States in the dispute over US export subsidies (Foreign Sales Corporations). Escalating the agri-biotech dispute might serve to deter the European Union from carrying out its threat.

Second, the refusal of US food aid by several African countries in 2002 (some of that food contained GE crops) alerted the United States to the possibility that more and more developing countries could be following the EU regulatory model for agri-biotechnology. Both the United States and the European Union have, in recent years, competed to sign free trade agreements with developing countries. Those agreements, some of which also cover non-tariff barriers to trade, such as environmental and consumer risk regulation, may have the effect of locking in either the US or the EU model of agri-biotech regulation in large parts of the developing world. Escalating the dispute in the WTO might deter developing countries (including, for example, China, India, and Brazil) from emulating the European Union's agri-biotech regulation. Some observers argue that the WTO case on growth hormones, which was won by the United States, seems to have had such an effect, even though the European Union, the principal defendant, has not complied with the verdict. In other words, current political rhetoric claiming that the European Union's agri-biotech regulations are contributing to starvation in Africa may be masking more self-serving motivations, such as the desire to open developing countries' markets for US biotech products.

Third, escalating the agri-biotech case might serve to deter the European Union from installing more stringent environmental and consumer risk regulations in other areas, most notably, testing and approval of chemicals and recycling of electronic goods. US firms and regulators have, in recent years, become increasingly nervous about ever stricter EU regulation in these two and also in other areas. While this regulation does not openly discriminate US firms, it may favor EU based firms because the latter are allegedly able to cope more effectively with this regulatory environment.[83]

Fourth, several members of Congress from the US Farm Belt, most notably the chairman of the Senate Finance Committee, Chuck Grassley (a Republican from Iowa), aggressively lobbied the White House to escalate the dispute. Given Grassley's crucial role in obtaining congressional approval for the Administration's plan for tax cuts, and with elections coming up in 2004, escalating the agri-biotech dispute promised to win votes from the Farm Belt.

Fifth, Monsanto and other US biotech firms that have close ties to the Bush administration are planning to market GE wheat and rice in the next few years. In their view, escalating the dispute might help either in opening directly the EU market to these products. Or it might help in forcing the European Union to negotiate international rules with the United States that would facilitate market access of GE products.

Sixth, there were signs that the US administration had given up hope in achieving a substantial liberalization of global agricultural markets in the ongoing Doha round, which is supposed to be concluded in 2005. The US Administration may thus have come to the conclusion that the opportunity costs involved in escalating the dispute—in terms of a breakdown of global trade talks—would be small.

Finally, in January 2003 the US Administration had appeared ready to escalate the agri-biotech dispute, but then held back while it was hoping to convince Europeans to join the US war against Iraq. Completion of large-scale military operations in Iraq and continued US anger at German and French opposition to the war opened a new window of opportunity for escalating the lingering trade dispute.

CONCLUSION

The analysis in this chapter has shown that the United States and the European Union are on a collision course in the agri-biotech area. I started out by claiming that the United States is more likely to escalate the conflict if: (a) its economic losses resulting from EU agri-biotech restrictions are high and concentrated on politically influential economic actors; (b) non-coercive policy measures for resolving the problem are ineffective; and (c) the prospects of winning the case through the WTO are good.

The review of agricultural trade data and estimates from a global trade model show that the costs imposed by EU regulation on the United States are modest but growing. They also show that these costs fall on concentrated and politically influential groups in the United States, primarily biotech firms and large export-oriented farmers. These economic actors have a powerful (short-term) incentive to push the US government towards escalation. The analysis also shows that non-coercive measures (mutual recognition, compensation, harmonization, unilateral regulatory and market adjustments) are unlikely to solve the problem. The evidence for the third factor is ambiguous. On the one hand, it suggests that the United States would not win a legal agri-biotech case in the WTO. Even if it did, the European Union would not make concessions. This should discourage the United States from escalating the conflict. On the other hand, evidence from other trade disputes suggests that prospective ineffectiveness of the WTO mechanism (from the plaintiff's perspective) may not deter the United States from escalation. The reason is that escalation often produces short-term and concentrated benefits in the plaintiff country, but longer-term and diffuse costs. The chapter has also pointed to several contextual conditions that may promote escalation.

By setting in motion the WTO's dispute settlement procedure in mid-May 2003, the United States took an important step towards escalation. When this book went to press three scenarios appeared possible.

First, the European Union lifts the moratorium on approvals, possibly in late 2003 or in 2004. The US Administration seizes the opportunity to score domestic political points in the 2004 election year by claiming that its trade action helped in re-starting the EU approval process—whereas, in reality, the European Union was planning to restart the approval process anyway. The case is withdrawn from the WTO.

Second, the European Union lifts the moratorium, but the United States extends the dispute to labeling and traceability issues. It escalates the dispute all the way to a formal WTO decision and—if it obtains a favorable verdict—implements punitive economic measures.

Third, the European Union does not lift the moratorium and the United States continues to escalate the dispute.

As of May 2003, the probability of scenarios two or three appeared much higher than the probability of scenario one. Though the US legal case had not yet been presented in detail, the accusation by the United States focused primarily on the EU moratorium on approvals. However, the United States faces a problem of "moving goal posts." EU approval regulation is only one element in the European regulatory system that is preventing market entry of GE crops, and it may not even be the most important element. Labeling rules, traceability requirements, liability issues, and rules on how to manage co-existence of GE crops and organic and conventional crops are at least as important in terms of constituting obstacles to market entry. These regulations impose costs on GE crop producers and biotech firms and also reduce consumer demand for GE products. For example, a recent USDA study suggests that even US consumers, who are less worried about GE food than European consumers, on average discount labeled GE products by 14 per cent.[84] If the United States really wants to succeed in forcing open the European market to currently produced GE crops it will have to challenge the European Union's labeling and traceability rules. Even if the United States won the WTO case on approval rules and the European Union restarted its approval process, this would not help GE crop exporters and biotech firms in the United States: European consumers would not rush to buy labeled GE products imported from the United States, and EU farmers would not rush to cultivate GE crops. Winning legal cases on labeling and traceability regulations will be much more difficult and time consuming than winning the legal case on approval rules.

Moreover, EU countries have not yet come to full agreement among themselves on several key elements of agri-biotech regulation that are widely assumed to be prerequisites for restarting the approval process. Even those pieces of legislation that have been passed at the EU level have been implemented with long delays in EU member countries. For example, in May 2003, only three out of fifteen EU countries had passed implementing legislation for the new approval and environmental release directive, which had entered into effect in October 2002. The WTO dispute may motivate EU countries to postpone the resolution of internal EU differences even further until the problem in the WTO is resolved—that could easily take one to two years. This postponement, in turn, could motivate the United States to continue escalation.

Finally, many recent statements by US policy-makers suggest that the US case against European agri-biotech regulation may target not only this regulation per se. They suggest that the real target are *all* European environmental and consumer risk regulations based on the precautionary principle rather than on what US regulators call "sound science".[85] If this assessment is at least partly correct, and I believe it is, the biotech dispute may well be the tip of the iceberg. There is a high risk that the biotech trade conflict could turn into a larger and more fundamental conflict over appropriate regulatory models for environmental and consumer risks. The final chapter of this book explores possibilities for avoiding what could turn out to be a lengthy and costly transatlantic trade dispute.

CHAPTER SEVEN

Coping with Diversity

THE PRECEDING parts of this book, which are summarized in chapter 1, have shown how and why differences across countries in public opinion, interest group politics, and institutional structures have led to strong and growing differences across nations in regulatory constraints on food biotechnology. EU countries have imposed severe restrictions on agri-biotechnology, whereas the United States has opened its market to most food biotech applications. Other countries have either aligned with one or the other of the world's two largest economies, or they have been struggling to find some middle ground.

This regulatory polarization has led to increasing tensions in the global trading system, particularly between the European Union and the United States. As shown in chapter 6, cooperative and unilateral policy tools for coping with trade tensions of this nature have not been effective in the food biotech case. I also explained why these policy tools have not been effective, and that they are unlikely to be effective in the years to come. This analysis led to the conclusion that the risk of escalation into full-blown trade conflict is high.

Regulatory polarization and trade conflict cast a dark shadow over the prospects of agri-biotechnology, primarily by exacerbating domestic controversies over the technology, fragmenting markets, and reducing investment and technology adoption in this area. At stake are a potential global market of 100–500 billion USD per year, and possibilities for increasing food security in developing countries.

In this final chapter I outline suggestions for policy reforms that could help to avoid the seemingly unavoidable trajectory from regulatory polar-ization to trade conflict to stagnation or even decline of food biotechnol-ogy. I begin by arguing that currently prevailing public and private sector policies do not add up to an effective strategy for creating a global market for the technology.[1] In the absence of substantial policy reforms, persis-tent polarization and trade conflict will continue to wreak havoc on the technology's current and potential markets.

The suggestions outlined below focus on establishing strong regulatory authorities, market-driven product differentiation based on mandatory labeling of GE products, and support for developing countries. These measures would help in striking a sensible balance between public safety concerns and private economic freedom. And they would equip food biotechnology with a fair chance to prove its environmental, health, humanitarian, and economic benefits in the long run.

UNPOPULAR CHOICES

The policy-reforms proposed below would create some additional costs for producers and consumers. Hence they will probably not receive an overly warm welcome, particularly from agri-biotech firms, GE crop farmers, and pro-biotech processors and retailers, and also from all those who advocate regulatory decisions based solely on existing scientific evidence of health and environmental risks. Some of the proposals will also cut against policies favored by opponents of the technology. But before lashing out at these proposals, proponents and critics of agricultural biotechnology may first wish to reconsider the alternatives.

The most popular strategies among private and public sector proponents of the technology are to: (a) educate the public about the benefits of agri-biotech applications and highlight forthcoming benefits of agri-biotechnology; (b) use international legal procedures and economic and political pressure to pry open markets in agri-biotech adverse countries; (c) accommodate consumer demand for non-GE products through market-driven product differentiation that involves segregation and voluntary labeling.

Critics of the technology concentrate primarily on introducing stricter and more complex regulation of agri-biotech applications.

With the exception of market-driven product differentiation, most of the above strategies will not help much in overcoming the current biotech food crisis.

There is no convincing empirical support for the assumption that people who know more about agricultural biotechnology are, as a consequence, more supportive of that technology. Consumer survey data shows that supporters of agri-biotech applications tend to perceive the technology as useful, morally acceptable, are less concerned about risks, and trust the safety of their food supply. Opponents hold opposite views. Some analyses also show that more engaged and informed male persons with a higher education are slightly more supportive of the technology. But the causal relationships underlying such (statistically weak) correlations are extremely hard to fathom. One of the reasons why knowledge and agri-biotech support correlate only slightly might be that support for or opposition to the technology is driven by all sorts of motivations and values rather than the level of knowledge. It is worth noting that EU consumers, according to many surveys, appear better informed about agricultural biotechnology than US consumers, are not more "technophobic" than US consumers, but are much less supportive of agri-biotech applications.[2]

It is difficult to see, therefore, how even large-scale public relations (or educational) campaigns by agri-biotech supporters from government or the private sector could create and sustain long-term consumer confidence in agricultural GE products. The same holds for promises of ever more spectacular future benefits of the technology. Arguments and evidence based on "pure science" are unlikely to impress opponents of the technology whose interests are driven by ethical or economic (fears of corporate dominance, protectionist aims) considerations or by diffuse fears over new technologies and the safety of the food supply. Indeed, the available evidence cuts against the assumption that the pro-agri-biotech campaigns undertaken thus far have increased consumer support for the technology. Such campaigns and consumer education in general might work somewhat better if they were combined with the marketing of products that had substantial and clearly visible consumer benefits (much lower prices and/or much higher quality). But from what is known about ongoing R&D no such products are likely to enter mass consumer markets in the next few years.

As noted in chapter 1 agri-biotech proponents may be heading for a "legitimacy trap" in this regard. Persistent efforts to legitimize the technology with promises that it will help in feeding the poor and result in products with spectacular consumer benefits are raising public expectations. Creating such expectations leaves the technology very vulnerable to failure (due to regulatory constraints and other reasons) in delivering on these promises in the short to medium term.

Some protagonists in the biotech debate suggest that rapid innovation in genomics could soon reduce or eliminate the controversy over food biotechnology. Robert Goodman, for example, claims that "From a scientific perspective, the public argument about genetically modified organisms ... will soon be a thing of the past. ... The science has moved on and we're now in the genomics era."[3] The genomes of rice and *A. rabidopsis*, that is, the entire set of genetic instructions in these organisms, are now known, and the genomes of other plants are being mapped at an increasing pace. Scientists will thus be able to use the emerging knowledge about the location and functions of genes, particularly genes that shape plant growth and development, to guide plant breeders in their application of traditional and technologically more advanced breeding techniques, including methods that do not rely on recombinant DNA techniques. For example, new crop varieties and food products could be developed by switching on or off individual genes within existing organisms, rather than by transferring genes from one organism to another (as, for example, in the case of Bt corn).

Those who believe that genomics will reduce controversies over food biotechnology argue that these "new era applications" will make the resulting foods look more natural in the eyes of NGOs and consumers and thus increase public acceptance. They claim that demonstrating the usefulness of molecular genetics in conventional and non-conventional crop breeding will diffuse controversies currently focusing exclusively on transgenic crops. They also argue that new crop varieties of this nature might be harder to patent, particularly if produced through a combination of genomics and traditional plant breeding. This would reduce the incentive for commercial agri-biotech firms to invest in R&D in this area. It would deprive biotech critics of the argument that the technology is benefiting mostly large Western firms. And it would make diffusion of the technology to poorer parts of the world easier.[4]

For the time being, such claims remain largely in the realm of speculation, notably, with regard to the effects on consumer perceptions and corporate dominance of the food chain (patenting). As noted in a recent AgBiotech InfoNet contribution, "The relative roles, capabilities, and tools of transgene-based versus 'New era' applications will be the focus of much discussion in the years ahead, since most ag biotech skeptics are either generally to fully supportive of 'New era' applications like marker-assisted breeding."[5] Whether increasing use of genomics in plant breeding will ultimately promote traditional forms of breeding at the expense of transgenic crops, or vice versa, is highly uncertain. And so are consumer reactions to new food products of this nature. In other words, relying on a scenario in which genomics opens global markets for agri-biotechnology would be highly speculative and possibly an illusion.

As shown in chapter 6 attempts to coerce agri-biotech adverse polities into opening their markets to this technology are bound to fail. International legal mechanisms, notably the WTO, are unlikely to produce verdicts that are favorable to agri-biotech interests. If stricter regulations were upheld by the WTO in a formal trade dispute, this may encourage the European Union to adopt even stricter regulation. It may also encourage other countries to emulate the EU regulatory model. Even if agri-biotech regulations in the European Union and elsewhere were invalidated by the WTO, which is unlikely, this would not solve the problem. Such verdicts would probably not be implemented by the defendants. They would lock in current regulatory differences and close still existing windows of opportunity for global regulatory reforms: policy-makers in the European Union and other countries would find it impossible to back down in view of the unavoidable public outcry over attempts by the US government and US multinational firms to "force-feed" GE food to their citizens. WTO verdicts would thus not benefit GE crop farmers. They would burden the WTO with an impossible task. They would, by amplifying already existing turmoil in global markets for agricultural GE products, be detrimental to further private and public investment in the technology.[6]

Market-driven product differentiation can help in diffusing international trade tensions and mitigating other negative consequences of regulatory polarization. But to be effective it must be supported more actively and systematically by the public and private sector. I will expand on this point below.

Finally, ever stricter and more complex and costly regulation that is increasingly divorced from scientific evidence of health and environmental risks may satisfy radical opponents of the technology. But it will probably fail to respond to the concerns of moderate critics and proponents of agri-biotechnology who seek to promote applications of the technology that are safe and beneficial from a human health and environmental viewpoint. Such regulation risks creating a vicious circle that may in fact undermine consumer confidence, trust in regulatory authorities, and public acceptance of agri-biotechnology: complex and costly regulation risks being followed by implementation failures, further decline of public trust in food safety and regulators, even more complex regulation in response, rapidly growing market concentration as firms try to cope with uncertainty and implementation costs through vertical integration, and so on.

The most serious problems of this nature in the richer part of the world are those in the European Union. In fact, the European Union faces a "trilemma", as summarized in figure 7.1. In this trilemma, EU regulators can obtain favorable outcomes only on two out of three dimensions. They can maintain the European Union's system of decentralized, network-like regulation, where individual EU states maintain considerable autonomy in setting and implementing standards, and where the European Food

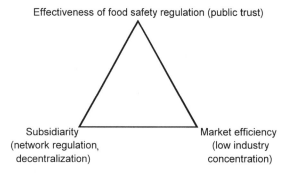

Figure 7.1   The European Union's food safety trilemma.

Safety Authority remains weak. They can, at the same time, also achieve higher levels of food safety and (associated) public trust in the food supply. But these two goals can only be achieved at the expense of rapidly growing market concentration. The reason is that strict biotech regulation in a network-like (decentralized) regulatory setting favors large and vertically integrated firms. Such firms benefit from scale economies in implementing strict and complex regulation. And they are better able to fill control gaps that arise almost unavoidably in such regulatory systems. Hence they are also better able to cope with problems of liability and incomplete insurance coverage. In the long run, such a system promotes dominance by large multinational food firms of regulatory processes and schemes of industrial self-regulation.

Many biotech analysts tend to see the future of second- and third-generation GE food products in niche-markets, and not in mass commodity markets. Indeed, as I will argue below, market-driven product differentiation should be made a key element in global strategies for coping with regulatory polarization and its negative effects. However, to establish and sustain efficient market-driven product differentiation, substantial reforms in the European Union's regulatory system will be required. At present, the European Union's agri-biotech policy is driven far more by ad hoc demands and food safety scandals than by a long-term strategy. EU regulators have thus far been unable to cope effectively with the aforementioned trilemma.

Decentralized network regulation prevails in the European Union and looks likely to prevail for the years to come. Public trust in the food supply and in food biotechnology in particular is low. Market concentration is growing (and so is self-regulation in the food industry).[7] But this trend cannot fully compensate for heterogeneity and implementation failures in the EU regulatory system. Liability rules for agri-biotechnology and its applications are in their infancy while insurance coverage for biotechnology is being reduced. This trend looks set to continue. If it does, ever more complex biotech regulation will impose a growing burden on the food sector (both on firms adopting and firms not adopting the technology, and on consumers). Firms and consumers will be deprived of future biotech applications that may be more beneficial than first generation GE products. And we are likely to see more implementation failures and persistently low public trust in regulators and the food supply.

This leaves us with unpopular choices. I submit that the reforms proposed below are the price to pay for long-term consumer confidence and investment in the technology. The cost of persisting regulatory polarization, trade tensions, and turmoil in markets for agri-biotech products—the most likely scenario in the absence of regulatory reforms along the lines suggested here—is much higher.

POLICY REFORMS

The starting point for policy reforms should be the development of a common understanding of what the biggest obstacles on the demand side of the technology are. The analysis in this book suggests that those obstacles are: (a) low consumer trust in the safety of the food supply in key markets, notably the European Union; (b) public concerns about the long-term health and environmental effects of agricultural biotechnology; (c) problems of moral acceptability and fears of corporate dominance of the food supply; and (d) insufficient consumer benefits from GE products currently on the market.

Policy reforms along three lines could help in mitigating these problems: strengthening regulatory authorities, market-driven product differentiation, and support for developing countries.

Strengthening National and Supranational Regulatory Authorities

All jurisdictions producing and/or importing agricultural GE products, above all the European Union, should establish politically independent and science-oriented regulatory authorities with substantial regulatory powers, possibly along the lines of the US FDA. National (and in the European Union also supranational) authorities are the backbone of public trust in the food supply. The US FDA has been widely criticized by agri-biotech critics for its close ties with the biotech industry, its deficiencies in involving non-industry interest groups, and its lax regulation of agri-biotechnology based exclusively on the principle of substantial equivalence. Yet, in terms of its institutional features (strong and centralized authority) and its largely positive record in food safety matters, the FDA still is a role model for reforms in other countries.

Take the European Union as an example of deficiencies in this regard. Because agricultural products can flow freely within the entire European Union, the scope of regulatory control should, ideally, match the scope of the respective market. In reality, we observe persistent fragmentation of regulatory authority in the food safety area. In some policy areas, such as taxation, some degree of competition among jurisdictions may be economically sensible. Not so with regard to food safety. As the European Union's food markets become ever more integrated, public trust in the food supply becomes ever more indivisible: implementation failures in one EU country affect food safety and public trust in other EU countries to a growing extent.

The above analysis of the European Union's food policy trilemma suggests that centralization of regulatory control is likely to be the most effective means for restoring food safety and public trust while limiting market concentration under conditions of complex and strict regulation and market-driven product differentiation. Interestingly, the most recent Eurobarometer survey shows that, as far as biotechnology regulation is concerned, the EU public has more confidence in the EU Commission than in national authorities.[8]

The European Food Safety Authority (EFSA), established in 2002, is a small but relevant step in the right direction. But it is far from sufficient. The same holds for proposals to equip the EU Commission and the EFSA with more decision-making power with regard to risk assessment and approval of GE products. As of now, the EFSA is poorly equipped in terms of resources—for comparison, the US FDA has a staff of 9000 and an annual budget of 1.7 billion USD, still with many complaints about lack of resources. The EFSA, which has a much smaller staff and budget than the FDA, has primarily advisory functions and will have to be equipped with much stronger regulatory powers.[9] Ideally, regulatory reforms should also focus on tightening liability laws.

If successful, such reforms would help very much in reducing general public concerns about food safety, which also reduce public acceptance of agricultural biotechnology. If properly designed, they would also be instrumental in establishing and operating effective approval, identity preservation (IP), and labeling systems that are not biased towards parochial interests of either biotech companies or biotech adverse environmental or consumer groups.

The main alternative to strengthening the EFSA and thus centralizing rule making, supervision, and rule enforcement in the European Union would be to strengthen agency networks at the European level. This would mean increasing the effectiveness (in terms of food safety) and legitimacy (in terms of public participation and accountability) of horizontal linkages among existing food safety authorities in the European Union. Social science research on this issue shows, however, that the network approach may well be inferior to centralized regulation in terms of its transparency, public accountability, and effectiveness.[10]

Market-Driven Product Differentiation

More active government support for market-driven product differentiation, particularly in the United States and in Europe, would go a long way towards diffusing international trade tensions and coping with other negative consequences of regulatory polarization. IP and labeling are key elements in systems of product differentiation. An analysis by Nielsen et al. (2002) shows in fact that world markets can adjust without extreme price differentials of GE and non-GE crops and without extreme changes in patterns of trade and production if the costs of labeling and market segmentation are not too large.

Agri-biotech proponents may view IP systems and labeling as unnecessarily burdensome in the short term and with regard to existing GE crops (in particular, GE soybeans and GE corn). But opposition to IP and labeling and associated business strategies relying on lax regulation, consumer ignorance, and mass commodities are highly risky, as exemplified by Monsanto's poor economic performance since 2000. Experimental evidence on US consumer behavior shows that these might be willing to pay a 10–15 percent premium for non-GE foods, whereas the costs of designing, testing, and monitoring the truthfulness of labels could amount to 5–15 percent of farm-gate prices.[11]

Opposition to IP and labeling also ignores an increasing trend in agricultural markets towards segregation and specialty-products. Establishing effective IP and labeling systems now is likely to be of great benefit to GE crop/food producers who are able to offer products with compelling consumer benefits at some point in the future. IP markets in the United States and elsewhere, including those for soy and corn, have been growing fast and could reach market shares of up to 25 percent in a few years.[12]

Effective IP systems involving traceability of GE products throughout the food chain are indispensable for credibly signaling and controlling the quality of products. They can also help in coping in a low-key and technocratic manner with problems arising from differences across countries in approval of GE products. Notably, effective IP systems would help in removing from the market illegal or controversial (in terms of health and environmental effects) GE products quickly and at low cost, thereby avoiding broader negative effects of such incidents on related food markets and general consumer confidence.

The StarLink controversy in the United States has shown that, in the absence of an IP system, food products containing de facto or allegedly risky GE products are difficult to withdraw from the market. It has also shown that such difficulties can have wider repercussions for international trade in non-GE counterparts of such products. Such problems could grow dramatically if genetically modified animals (e.g., GE fish) were marketed because such species are more mobile than GE crops. Similar problems apply to pharmaceuticals and chemicals produced through GE crops.[13] Effective IP systems would also help in dealing with liability problems should unapproved GE varieties enter the food or feed chain, or should approved GE products turn out to be harmful. Finally, IP systems would be conducive to the long-term monitoring of health and environmental effects of agri-biotechnology.

Markets have to some extent already adjusted to shifts in consumer preferences and regulation. However, the available evidence for the United States, Argentina, and Canada (the largest GE crop producers) shows that many farmers, food processors, and retailers may not be able or willing to act on the aforementioned longer term benefits of IP systems and labeling because of short-term cost implications.[14]

Such disincentives could be reduced through start-up funding by governments. A tiny fraction of current agricultural subsidies (49 billion USD per year in the United States in 2001, 93 billion USD in the European Union, 47 billion USD in Japan[15]) would go a long way towards funding the establishment of effective IP systems and labeling for agricultural GE products. In combination with larger productivity gains from GE crops and reduced IP costs through scale effects and technological innovation, such government support would enhance the competitive position of US GE crop farmers in segregated international markets. It would thus make segregation and IP more acceptable to US producers and reduce international trade tensions.

Governments could support product differentiation in a variety of ways. For example, they could fund additional storage capabilities— insufficient storage capabilities frequently act as bottlenecks in IP systems. Countries that are unwilling to adopt mandatory labeling (e.g., the United States) could facilitate voluntary labeling by setting tolerance levels and introducing certification and verification procedures for non-GE and GE products. They could provide detailed information on planting, yields, and prices of GE products and their conventional counterparts, thus enabling farmers to make more informed choices. They could, moreover, restructure farm support programs to take account of differences in production costs and prices of GE and non-GE crops.[16]

What form of labeling should countries adopt? Some economists advocate voluntary negative labeling as a more efficient alternative to mandatory positive labeling (see chapter 2).[17] Voluntary negative labeling means that producers may, subject to certain constraints and quality controls, voluntarily label their products as free of GE organisms. Positive mandatory labeling, which has prevailed in the European Union, Japan, and several other countries, means that products containing GE organisms must be labeled as such.

I submit that negative voluntary labeling alone will not help in solving problems of regulatory polarization, trade tensions, and negative market responses to agri-biotechnology. It would enable consumers to choose among GE and non-GE foods and would enable farmers to cultivate GE or non-GE crops. But it would impose labeling costs exclusively on producers and consumers of non-GE crops and is therefore unacceptable in countries whose population is generally critical of the technology. In addition, it would not help in increasing public confidence in the technology. Bullying or cajoling the European Union and other countries with mandatory positive labeling into converting to voluntary negative labeling is, from a political feasibility standpoint, a non-starter. Biotech adverse interest groups would be quick to interpret such attempts as a strategy by large foreign firms (the "gene giants") and their supporting governments to create a fait accompli ("contamination" of the food chain with GE organisms) and then try to impose on consumers the costs of obtaining "clean" (non-GE) products.

On more factual grounds, proposals for voluntary negative labeling subscribe to the assumption that, as long as no health or environmental risks have been demonstrated, labeling costs should be imposed on producers and consumers of non-GE products, and not on producers of GE products. As long as products do not differ in terms of risks, those who can fetch premiums for their products should pay for IP and labeling. Such premiums are currently being paid in some markets for non-GE products. Many agri-biotech proponents hope that non-GE products will thus be confined to niche markets. This assumption ignores the fact that agri-biotech adverse interest groups refuse to consider science as the sole yardstick for allocating IP and labeling costs. In fact, these groups consider it more appropriate to impose labeling costs primarily on those who they see as having caused consumer uncertainty and whose products do not offer consumer benefits.

In principle, this cost allocation problem could be solved through funding by biotech firms and governments for voluntary negative labeling systems.[18] But even if such funding was provided by industry and governments it would do little to address the aforementioned concerns.

Instead, international coordination designed to diffuse trade tensions over differing IP and labeling regulations could be founded on two observations: first, there is considerable uncertainty as to whether GE products or non-GE counterparts will pose greater health and environmental risks (or benefits) in the medium to long term; second and related, there is considerable uncertainty as to whether premiums for particular non-GE products or GE counterparts will be higher in the medium to long term.

Provided policy-makers accept these two observations, IP and labeling regulations that allocate the costs of labeling evenly and enhance consumer confidence in the technology are likely to be the most sensible options. A system relying on three categories of labels could meet these criteria: "contains no GE organisms" (with tolerance levels close to 0 percent); "may contain small amounts of GE organisms" (with tolerance levels lower than 1 percent); and "contains GE products for purpose xy." This system would probably result in three production chains: first, GE food and feed; second, conventional food and feed with small GE content (e.g., between 0 and 1 percent); third, organic/non-GE food and feed. The second label might turn out to be transitory if consumers opt for non-GE products or GE products with a clear consumer benefit rather than products with some GE content but no obvious consumer benefits.

IP and labeling policy along these lines would require substantial reforms, particularly in the United States, Canada, and other countries with lax agri-biotech regulations. These reforms would take several years to accomplish. In principle, countries with no IP and no mandatory labeling requirements could leave their domestic rules as they are and find a modus vivendi with trading partners that install stricter regulations. Government support for product differentiation among export-oriented producers would help in diffusing trade tensions.[19]

In the long term, however, this option suffers from at least three disadvantages. First, importing countries will demand full compliance with their own regulations. International standards in this area would thus be dictated by countries with stricter agri-biotech regulations. Second, ad hoc bilateral standard setting might prevail and distort and fragment global agricultural trade. Third, consumers in GE product exporting countries may increasingly ask why foreign consumers receive higher levels of protection against possible risks than domestic consumers. A 2001 USDA report, for example, notes that consumer survey data (which show public support for GE food in the United States) may not be a good predictor of where the market is heading.[20] Respondents may not have thought carefully about the issue or may not have answered truthfully. Data on the intensity of consumer preferences indicates that consumers with intensely negative views on agri-biotechnology outnumber those with intensely positive views. Moreover, firms' reactions to reputation problems or developments in foreign markets also play a role. In other words, consumer preferences in the United States may be less stable than existing surveys suggest.[21] They may well shift away from GE products and US producers may find it advantageous to prepare for this scenario at an early stage. Considering these uncertainties a more pro-active approach that focuses on international harmonization of IP and labeling could be useful.

It is crucial that labeling and IP systems are controlled by independent and impartial national and international authorities that are widely accepted as unbiased by private interests of biotech companies or biotech adverse environmental or consumer groups. Public trust in such authorities is key. As noted above, regulatory reforms in the European Union and other markets should aim at increasing public trust in regulatory authorities before ever more stringent, complex, and costly regulations are introduced, for example, regulations on tracing and labeling of products from animals fed on GE products.[22] Issuing regulations that end in implementation failures is, in many ways, worse than no regulation in terms of the effects on consumer acceptance of GE products. Successfully implemented labeling and IP systems in the European Union would also convince other countries to proceed along the same lines. Regulatory failures—whether one welcomes labeling and IP measures or not—are not in the interest of agri-biotech proponents because they destroy actual or potential markets for the technology.

As noted in the analysis of the European Union's food safety trilemma, increasing market differentiation, supported by IP and labeling rules, may raise questions about market concentration and anti-competitive practices. In the United States, for example, the food processing sector is already highly concentrated, with Cargill and ADM controlling a large part of the market.[23] So is the retail sector in Europe. Similar market concentration is observable in the agri-chemical and seed sectors. Some analysts expect that stricter regulation could lead to even higher concentration because of scale economies in IP and labeling as well as other factors.[24] For example: large food processors can more easily relocate production abroad to accommodate demand for non-GE products in these foreign markets. Smaller US-based processors and farmers servicing both the domestic and international market would be much harder hit. Such market concentration could also pose ever more severe problems for farmers in terms of higher input and lower output prices, and in terms of market risks being increasingly shifted to farmers. Government support for market-driven product differentiation must take account of such problems. As discussed above, centralization of regulatory authority can, to some extent, help in mitigating the effect of stricter regulation on market concentration. Another possibility would be to support on-farm storage facilities and movement of grains directly from farms to processors.

Finally, market-driven product differentiation can thrive only if the marketed products and related R&D and production processes are safe and GE products with obvious consumer benefits are forthcoming.

As regards food safety, countries cultivating GE crops and/or importing such products should implement strict risk assessment, risk management, and approval procedures. To facilitate international trade, the European Union and the United States should coordinate the accordant measures to the greatest extent possible and move towards joint standards. These standards could be multilateralized, for example, through CODEX, the WHO, the FAO, the OECD, or the UN Biodiversity Convention.

Measures for strengthening regulatory authorities (see above) should be designed to separate risk assessment (which must meet highest scientific and scholarly standards) and risk management (which involves socio-cultural, economic and environmental considerations in determining the level of acceptable risk). Pre-market product evaluation should be stringent and mandatory. New proteins or other compounds added to foods or feeds should, from a risk assessment and risk management perspective, be treated like other types of new substances added to food (e.g., food additives). The principle of "substantial equivalence" should not serve as a substitute for thorough risk assessment that focuses on unintended and possibly harmful changes in metabolites or other elements in GE products.[25] Environmental risks, for example, outcrossing, gene leakage, effects on pest resistance, must be thoroughly assessed before market approval is given. Incentive structures for scientists involved in risk assessment must be designed so as to maximize immunity from private industry and NGO influence. Approval decisions must be transparent and risk management must involve the principal stakeholders.

Risk assessment, risk management and approval procedures could, at least to some extent, be internationally harmonized. However, as long as scientific uncertainty persists, particularly with respect to environmental risks of GE organisms, differences across nations in the emphasis of the precautionary principle will almost unavoidably lead to differences in GE product approvals for food or feed, field testing, and cultivation. Global uniformity in GE product approvals or a global system of mutual recognition will also be difficult to achieve due to differences in local environmental, economic, and other conditions.

The best one can hope for are stricter and more uniformly applied risk assessment procedures. To the extent that these procedures lead to more similar scientific conclusions across countries as to the risks of specific GE products, the way in which the precautionary principle is applied in risk management may to some degree also converge internationally. At the very least, more transparent and internationally better coordinated risk assessment, risk management and approval procedures would reduce the scope for protectionist misuse of the precautionary principle. Thus they would also reduce the potential for trade tensions over regulatory differences. In combination with more powerful and science-oriented regulatory authorities stricter and more uniform risk assessment and risk management would also increase public trust in the technology.

As regards GE product characteristics, biotech firms, cultivators, and food processors and retailers should concentrate on GE food products that (unlike first generation GE foods) provide compelling consumer benefits, for example, much lower prices or greater health benefits. Social science studies of risk show that consumers are more willing to accept risks if they perceive substantial benefits in consuming the respective good. Mobile telephones, tobacco, and coffee are examples. R&D and marketing in richer countries of GE crops with agronomic traits (which involve less compelling consumer benefits) should focus on varieties that involve large environmental benefits (e.g., much lower pesticide and fertilizer use) and that do not cross-pollinate or outcross. Crops with no wild relatives and crops that propagate vegetatively are preferable in this respect. GE foods and ingredients that quickly spread throughout the food chain (e.g., GE soy, corn, wheat, rice) should be avoided, at least until robust IP systems and strong regulatory authorities and liability rules are in place. Such products are difficult and costly to segregate and trace and may thus undermine public confidence in IP systems and agri-biotech regulation more generally.

Cultivation of GE crops for non-food purposes, for example, for use in the chemical and paper industry, for producing renewable energy sources, or for the production of drugs, vaccines, or other medicinal products might be encouraged to the extent that environmental and public health benefits clearly outweigh the risks. Many analysts in fact believe that the market for such non-food GE products could, within the next few years, exceed the market for GE food products by a wide margin, with estimates of market size ranging from 100 to 500 billion USD by 2020.[26]

However, it would be a mistake to assume that the development and marketing of non-food GE products with apparent consumer benefits would, per se, eliminate opposition and open markets for the technology. Unless public trust in the food supply is restored through effective regulatory control mechanisms, including stronger regulatory authorities and IP, the marketing of non-food GE products could end in economic disaster for the firms concerned and perhaps even for entire agricultural sectors.

There are obvious linkages between non-food and food applications of biotechnology: most of the biotech drugs, vaccines, and industrial and research chemicals currently under development are produced through GE crops such as corn, tobacco, canola, potato, and tomato. It takes little imagination to recognize that opposition to currently marketed GE crops could quickly spill over to these new applications. The StarLink problem, the ProdiGene case as well as countless cases of detection of non-approved GE products in the European food supply suggest that the proponents of such GE products will in fact face a monumental task: they will have to convince the critics of biotechnology that non-food GE products, including some highly hazardous substances produced through GE corn or GE canola, will not find their way into the food supply. Imagine what would happen to the US corn industry if a potent drug produced with GE corn, for example, a vaccine against hepatitis B, cholera, or AIDS, or a contraceptive, was discovered in American breakfast cereals.

Support for Developing Countries

Proponents of agri-biotechnology have made mitigation of food security problems in developing countries one of their principal selling points. But the respective promises have thus far remained only little more than promises.[27] As pointed out above, this situation could become a legitimacy trap. Increased investment in R&D and marketing of GE products that provide compelling benefits for developing countries would help in avoiding such a trap. It would contribute significantly to increasing the legitimacy and public acceptance of the technology in poor and probably also rich countries.

In many developing countries superior yields are crucial to increasing food security, whereas in industrialized countries they are not.[28] Because of lower purchasing power in developing countries, food security problems in these nations are unlikely to be priorities in the R&D activity of the leading private sector firms in advanced industrialized countries.[29]

To fill this gap, governments, biotech firms, and international scientific associations should set up and fund an independent international organization that sponsors agri-biotech R&D in developing countries.[30] This organization should also conduct research into health and environmental issues associated with agricultural biotechnology in poorer countries.[31] The Consultative Group for International Agricultural Research, a network of 16 research centers around the world, could be the nucleus for such an institution. Moreover, existing intellectual property rights rules should be reconsidered so as to strike a better balance between property rights of biotech firms, which are mostly located in advanced industrialized countries, and the needs of poor farmers.[32] These measures would contribute to alleviating concerns, particularly in developing countries, about the "enclosure of the genetic commons" and about dominance of the food supply by "gene giants."

Most developing countries will require substantial financial and technical assistance from richer countries in establishing effective agri-biotech governance systems. In the absence of such assistance, developing countries envisaging production of both GE and non-GE crops are likely to be confronted with an awkward trade-off. Due to ineffective regulatory systems (e.g., in IP),[33] combined GE/non-GE production could lead to a breakdown of exports to markets governed by strict food safety regulations. Safeguarding export opportunities may thus force many developing countries to abstain or withdraw from GE crop production that might, domestically, be beneficial.

Avoiding regulatory failures in developing countries is also very much in the interest of pro-biotech circles in advanced industrialized countries. Regulatory failures in poorer nations could have global effects on the technology; either indirectly by reducing public confidence in the technology around the world; or directly in terms of affecting public health and the environment internationally via internationally traded GE products. Experience with the nuclear industry and international trade in hazardous recycling materials shows that one or a few regulatory failures anywhere in the world can inflict global harm on entire industries.

IF POLICY REFORMS WORK WELL

If the international community, and in particular the world's largest economies, can find a regulatory modus vivendi within the next few years, possibly along the lines suggested here, I expect perhaps five to ten more years of controversy and heterogeneous ad hoc responses by policy-makers. When the storm settles, we would find a variety of GE food, feed and non-food/feed products competing in the market with conventional and organic counterparts. These GE products would have compelling consumer and/or environmental benefits and would be labeled in an informative manner. All countries importing and/or exporting GE products would have established strong and politically independent regulatory agencies and liability rules. Approvals would be based on thorough risk assessment and risk management. Global agricultural markets would operate on the basis of market-driven product differentiation, involving robust IP and labeling systems. Effective international coordination would deal with still existing differences across countries in GE product approvals. Financial and technical support would be provided to developing countries, particularly for R&D, biosafety, and for establishing effective IP systems.

Neither the proponents nor the opponents of agricultural biotechnology are likely to greet such an outcome with enthusiasm. Many proponents will complain about stifling over-regulation driven by imaginary risks. Many opponents will claim that the governance system sketched here is too complex to effectively protect people against health and environmental risks and should be replaced by an outright ban of the technology.

I submit that, given the political, economic, and societal constraints examined in this book, the above scenario is the best outcome that moderate proponents and critics of the technology can hope for. It is naive and perhaps even dangerous for the technology's promoters to assume that bullying agri-biotech critical countries into more permissive regulation, pouring millions of dollars into pro-agri-biotech public relations campaigns and promising ever greater benefits and low risks of future GE products will resolve the current crisis. The same holds for efforts to establish ever stricter and more complex and costly regulations that are difficult to implement and increasingly divorced from scientific evidence of health and environmental risks.

Notes

PREFACE

1. For example, Rogers 1996; see also Gaskell and Bauer 2001:4-5.

CHAPTER 1: INTRODUCTION AND SUMMARY

1. rDNA technology was patented in 1973.
2. Agricultural biotechnology currently focuses on improving pest- and herbicide resistance of crops in an effort to increase yields and lower production costs. Such agronomic traits are obtained by transferring desirable genetic material from certain organisms (e.g., soil bacteria) into crop varieties. Hence the term "transgenic crops". The technology is described in more detail in chapter 2.
3. See Cantley (1995), Gaskell and Bauer (2001), Von Wartburg and Liew (1999), Durant et al. (1998), and Bauer and Gaskell (2002).
4. See, for example, Cadot et al. (2001) and Bijman and Joly (2001).
5. See, for example, www.isaaa.org, Carpenter and Gianessi (2001), and Philipps (2001).
6. McNeill (2000:32).
7. www.bccresearch.com; DZ Bank (2001); Union of Concerned Scientists, "Pharm and Industrial Crops", December 2002.
8. www.isaaa.org.
9. I use this simple distinction for reasons of convenience. A more complicated definition would, for example, have to identify some producers (e.g., farmers) as consumers/users of the technology and suppliers of GE food.
10. www.isaaa.org.
11. Throughout this book I use the term "benefits for farmers" in the sense of farm-level income, rather than in a more narrow agronomic sense (e.g., yields). As noted by Fernandez-Cornejo and McBride in a recent USDA report (Economic Research Service/USDA *Adoption of Bioengineered Crops / AER-810*, May 2002): "Because there are nonfarm concerns about the technology, an accurate read on benefits and costs to farmers is an important component of a more complete social welfare calculus."
12. The precautionary principle implies a "better safe than sorry" approach to regulation. Such policies are implemented when there might be a risk to public health or the environment but scientific knowledge of the respective risk is still incomplete.
13. Among the best analyses of that type are Meins (2002), Vogel (2001), Lynch and Vogel (2000), Gaskell and Bauer (2001), Joly and Marris (2001),

Lynch and Da Ros (2001), Lotz (2000), McNichol and Bensedrine (2001), and Echols (2001).

14. The former term refers to the vertical, the latter to the horizontal distribution of authority in political systems.

15. Protectionist piggy-backing in this context means that EU farmers actively seek regulation that restricts market access of (presumably more competitive) GE crops produced abroad.

16. Mutual recognition means that EU countries accept each others' national regulations and allow imports and sales of any good that has been lawfully produced in any other EU country.

17. This term was coined by David Vogel (1995).

18. *Economist*, January 29, 2000.

CHAPTER 2: CHALLENGES

1. Mendel's (1822–1884) most famous work is entitled "Experiments with Plant Hybrids". He is widely regarded as the "father" of modern genetics.

2. For a glossary of terms, see www.fao.org/biotech.

3. See, for example, Nelson (2001).

4. For example, Bouis (2002).

5. For example, www.toxicology.org; www.agbioworld.org; www.fao.org/biotech; *Scientific American* 284(4), 2000; Royal Society (2002).

6. ICSU (2003)

7. See www.freenetpages.co.uk/hp/a.pusztai/.

8. The controversy can be traced at www.agbioworld.org or by searching the internet with the keyword "Arpad Pusztai".

9. For example, *Fortune*, February 19, 2001; *New York Times*, October 14 and December 11, 2000; www.transgen.de; Segara (2001); www.foe.org/safe-food.

10. See Union of Concerned Scientists, "Pharm and Industrial Crops", 2002, www.ucs.org.

11. ICSU (2003).

12. See, for example, National Academy of Sciences (2002); Baskin (1999); www.eea.eu.int.

13. www.transgen.de; www.agbioworld.org; www.agbios.com.

14. Such "gene jumping" could also raise liability issues, for example, if adjacent organic (non-GE) crops were "contaminated" or if Bt resistance in organic crops increased (some organic farming uses Bt preparations in pest control).

15. Introgression in this context means the spread of genes typical of GE crops into related cultivated varieties or wild relatives.

16. Quist and Chapela (2001).

17. Reports on the issue, as it evolved, can be found on www.agbioworld.org and other dedicated websites.

18. See www.eea.eu.int.

19. See also Paarlberg (2000a,b, 2001a,b,c).

20. Urbanization implies that a declining number of farmers will have to feed a

growing urban population. Growing production of protein foods requires larger crop production because cattle, pork, and poultry are often fed on grains and other crops. Demand for protein foods tends to increase with economic development and urbanization.

21. See also Pinstrup-Andersen and Schioler (2000) and Persley and Lantin (2000).

22. See Bouis (2002) and Thomson (2002).

23. Union of Concerned Scientists, "Pharm and Industrial Crops", 2002, www.ucs.org.

24. For example, Altieri and Rossett (1999).

25. www.grain.org; www.biotech-info.net.

26. See Paarlberg (2001b).

27. With such crops, cultivators must purchase new seeds each year to get the best results. Biology thus helps in enforcing property rights.

28. The 1980 US Supreme Court ruling that allowed the patenting of living organisms altered by human interventions was a milestone in this context.

29. The so-called Technology Protection (or "terminator") system makes GE crops sterile, thus precluding seed-saving by farmers. Monsanto and other firms, facing fierce criticism by NGOs, have held back marketing of the technology since 1999. Note, however, that crop sterility could also have environmentally desirable effects in terms of preventing or limiting introgression, cross-pollination, and outcrossing. See www.transgen.de; www.agbioworld.org.

30. For example, Nelson et al. (1999), Foster (2002), Buonanno (2001), and www.corporatewatch.org.uk.

31. For example, Muttitt and Franke (2000) and www.rafi.org.

32. See the section below on the economics of green biotechnology. See also www.ers.usda; www.agbiotechnet.com.

33. Superior experience, financial means, economies of scale in R&D, authorization procedures, patenting, and marketing are said to be the main reasons why agricultural biotechnology has promoted industrial concentration. Useful analyses of this concentration process can be found in Joly (1998), Joly and Lemarié (1998), and EU (2000a).

34. DuPont and Monsanto in particular have acquired many seed companies. See EU (2000a) and www.rafi.org.

35. www.rafi.org; Foster (2002); EU (2000a).

36. The worst case for any farmer would consist of being burdened with oligopolistic overpricing of GE seeds and related crop protection chemicals and oligopolistic underpricing by processors and retailers, with no possibility of converting to non-GE crops due to a non-segregated (bulk commodity) crop handling system. Empirical studies suggest that, so far, this problem has not materialized to a significant extent, but that it remains a clear possibility because GE crops are generally grown under contract and require adjustments in growing and management. Moreover, systems of labeling and identity preservation are likely to promote vertical integration. See Alexander and Goodhue (1999) and Foster (2002).

37. Heffernan cited in EU (2000a:32).

38. For example, Falck-Zepada et al. (2000), Pray et al. (2001), and www.isaaa.org.

39. For example, Gaskell and Bauer (2001), Wright (2001), Harlander (1991), and Robinson (1999).

40. Whether or not such a product should be considered as non-vegetarian, non-organic, and containing swine ingredients is virtually impossible to define from a scientific perspective and would probably be a matter of consumer perception.

41. www.transgen.de; www.isaaa.org.

42. In principle, benefits of GE crops vis-à-vis conventional crops involve increased yields, lower production costs and easier management, reduced pesticide use, and higher profits. Insect resistant Bt corn varieties enable farmers to control the European corn borer, an insect pest that is hard to control through pesticides. Benefits include primarily increased yields and reduced insecticide use. Insect resistant Bt cotton varieties control the three most destructive pests (tobacco budworm, cotton bollworm, and pink bollworm). Benefits include reduced pesticide use and increased yields. Herbicide resistant Bt cotton allows farmers to use a broader spectrum of herbicides with smaller crop injury. Insect and virus resistant potato varieties are used to reduce insecticide input. The introduction of a highly effective conventional insecticide and problems of marketing GE potatoes have limited their adoption. Herbicide tolerant soybeans allow for more effective weed control at lower cost.

43. The number of studies on farm-level benefits of GE crops has grown rapidly since the late 1990s. The following assessment concentrates primarily on results reported in Carpenter and Gianessi (2001), EU (2000a), and USDA (1999a,b). See also www.isaaa.org; Nelson (2001); Fernandez-Cornejo et al. (1999); www.ers.usda.gov; www.rafi.org; Nelson et al. (1999); Traxler (www.a-g.auburn.edu/dept/aec/faculty/gtraxler.html). Updated and new assessments are regularly reported at www.agbioworld.org and other dedicated websites.

44. USDA, Economic Research Service/USDA *Adoption of Bioengineered Crops / AER-810,* May 2002.

45. I consider such "averages" more informative for the purpose of this study than the presentation of results that concentrate on particular years and limited geographic areas. Note that many studies proclaiming spectacular benefits or dismal performance of GE crops are based on single years and crop varieties, and small geographic areas, which does not permit generalizations.

46. For example, the evidence on whether GE canola and GE potatoes are more beneficial is inconclusive (see EU 2000a). Adoption rates suggest that GE canola in particular is attractive to some farmers, but we do not know whether it is on average more beneficial (in terms of actual returns) than non-GE canola. Results on a range of crops are regularly reported at www.agbioworld.org and other websites.

47. Assuming that GE crops lead to higher productivity, growing adoption of the technology will increase supply. Particularly as public concerns over the technology grow (which reduces demand for GE food), these supply and demand side developments will reduce prices and returns. This dynamic disadvantages late adopters.

48. Other problems in estimating benefits result from the fact that subsidies may have limited the price risk of adopting GE crops and may have contributed to

a dominant input orientation of farmers in a market where prices are generally low. Some analysts assume that this has promoted in particular the planting of GE soybeans (see Foster 2002; Nelson et al. 1999; EU 2000a). EU (2000a) contains a detailed discussion of methodological problems in assessing the benefits of GE crops.

49. A very detailed assessment by the European Union (EU 2000a) arrives at similar conclusions.

50. Some critics claim that agri-biotech firms have, through aggressive marketing strategies, misled US farmers.

51. The convenience effect describes the ease of insecticide or herbicide use and larger time windows for spraying, which increase flexibility. It may also relate to no-till practices or conservation tillage, which reduces labor, fuel and other costs, and reduces soil erosion. The biggest convenience effect appears to materialize with regard to GE soybeans.

52. See EU (2000a).

53. Studies by the USDA (1999a,b) and others observed that large farming operations accounted for most GE crop adoption. To jump to the conclusion that such farms benefited more from GE crops would, however, be premature. The USDA study also shows that GE crop adoption is associated with education levels of farmers, experience, location, use of production and marketing contracts, and other factors.

54. www.isaaa.org.

55. If yields of GE crops had been substantially higher, prices should have decreased.

56. Nutraceuticals are often referred to as the third generation of GE products. They are to produce immunity to a disease or increase the health value of food.

57. For example, EU (2000a).

58. The implications of agricultural biotechnology for national welfare and international competitiveness are even more difficult to assess than farm-level benefits. A study on New Zealand for example estimated that adopting GE crops would increase the national income by around 450 USD per capita and year, whereas ignoring or banning the technology could cost around 1350 USD per capita and year and result in a loss of 56,000 jobs. Pointing to a range of heroic assumption in the study, the critics have dismissed the results as no more than guesswork (see www.agbios.com, www.agbioworld.org). The same holds for the effects of differences in countries' adoption rates of the technology on international trade flows. Related to that, we know very little about whether and to what extent adopting agricultural biotechnology has bolstered the competitiveness of adopters in global agricultural markets. As long as we know rather little about the farm-level and national economics of the technology, the impact of variation in adoption rates on international trade flows is extremely difficult to assess. This difficulty is exacerbated by the fact that such trade flows are heavily shaped by agricultural policies, including subsidies and regulations that limit market access by foreign producers. I examine these issues in chapter 6. The analysis there suggests that it is far from clear that competitive advantages of GE crop producers (to the extent they exist) will translate into higher export earnings. The analysis of

actual trade flows shows that US GE corn and soy exports to Europe have declined, in part due to stricter regulation in the EU.

59. Segregation means that specific products are produced and marketed separately, and that this process is monitored. IP means that the source and nature of crops or raw materials is identified and preserved from production to consumption. IP ensures "traceability", that is, the ability of public authorities and producers to locate and withdraw problematic products at any time and at any point in the food or feed chain.

60. See Desquilbet and Bullock (2001) and USDA (2001).

61. The principal purpose of labeling is to reduce an information asymmetry between producers and consumers.

62. Because currently marketed GE products do not have superior quality traits, producers of such crops and foods would have no incentive to label them because they cannot fetch a premium. A voluntary labeling system would thus almost automatically shift the labeling costs to producers of non-GE products. Agri-biotech proponents hope that this would confine non-GE products to niche markets (perhaps identical with the current market for organic produce) and open the door for an expansion of GE crop production, particularly in developing countries where consumers may focus more on price than on quality. Current premiums for non-GE crops are still far below premiums for IP grains in the health food sector, suggesting that non-GE crops would in many countries be confined to a small niche market if voluntary negative labeling was introduced. Premiums for non-GE soybeans have varied substantially in the past few years (roughly between 1 and 10 percent of the farm-gate price), whereas IP costs for non-GE soy are estimated at around 4 percent (see EU 2000a). Because organic produce tends to fetch much higher premiums than conventionally produced non-GE produce, an IP system could drive more farmers into organic production.

63. Most other estimates have been sponsored by agri-biotech advocates and may thus tend to overestimate the costs of IP and labeling.

64. Among other things, IP costs are heavily contingent on the tolerance level for "GE contamination" of food and feed products. The higher the tolerance level the lower the IP costs. Existing tolerance levels in countries that have introduced labeling differ substantially (with low tolerance levels in the European Union and Switzerland and higher tolerance levels in Japan and Australia). Very low tolerance levels would increase production costs for GE-free products to levels that might make GE-free production unprofitable, thus reducing GE-free production to a niche market serving high income households. We should thus expect the agri-biotech industry and GE farmers to lobby for very low tolerance labeling of GE-free products if voluntary negative labeling is the issue. Other factors influencing IP costs include the propensity of GE crops for cross-pollination and volunteers, the volume of trade, the seasonality of crops, and the range of products derived from a GE crop (see EU 2000a:83).

65. In agri-biotech adverse countries, governments will probably be unwilling to resolve the problem for GE crop farmers by subsidizing labeling or IP systems.

66. The possibility of transferring labeling or IP costs to consumers depends also on the availability of substitutes for GE products, and on market structures. As to the latter, food processors and retailers usually possess more market power

than farmers. It is likely, therefore, that labeling or IP costs would be shifted predominantly to farmers in terms of lower prices.

67. Such a development would line up with ongoing reforms of the European Union's agricultural policy which emphasize reductions in oversupply (due to subsidies) and quality improvements in agricultural output. Experience with specialty crops (e.g., seed wheat production, which fetches a 10–20 percent premium) suggests that this prospect is not unrealistic (see EU 2000a). An alternative would be to design GE crops so that input costs decrease and yields increase so dramatically that production cost decreases overcompensate IP and labeling costs. Consumers might then buy GE products because they are much cheaper than conventional products. This cost advantage would have to be large enough to cancel out potential risks perceived by consumers. I suspect, however, that such a strategy will be less successful (from the agri-biotech proponent viewpoint) than a strategy focusing on superior quality.

68. The reader may consult internet platforms operated by agri-biotech proponents (e.g., www.isaaa.org, www.agbioworld.org) to cross-check my conclusion that proponents are generally enthusiastic about the commercial prospects of the technology. Their positive assessment is usually based on growing adoption of GE crops in the United States, Argentina, and (to a much smaller extent) in some other countries. It also relies on the reporting of positive results in field trials of new GE varieties (which in most cases are not yet commercialized).

CHAPTER 3: POLARIZATION

1. The early years of biotech regulation in the European Union are well described in Patterson (2000) and Cantley (1995). For overviews of EU agri-biotech regulation see MacKenzie and Francescon (2000), EU (2000b), and updates on www.transgen.de.

2. The principle of substantial equivalence assumes that conventional foods are, by virtue of long experience in consumption, largely safe—even without explicit scientific proof. Because foods consist of thousands of different substances scientific proof of safety is next to impossible. The principle of substantial equivalence simplifies testing. The extent to which a particular GE food is, in terms of composition (molecular structures), equivalent to its conventional counterpart determines the form and extent of risk-assessment to be carried out. Completely equivalent foods (e.g., refined oil from GE canola) must undergo no or less testing than non-equivalent foods (e.g., GE rice with higher beta-carotene content). Governments and scientists differ as to the extent and forms of testing required for different degrees of equivalence.

3. The precautionary principle implies a "better safe than sorry" approach to regulation. Such policies are implemented when there might be a risk to public health or the environment but scientific knowledge of the respective risk is still incomplete. For an analysis of differences between the European Union and United States in the application of the precautionary principle, see Wiener and Rogers (2002).

4. The European Council is the principal intergovernmental body of the European Union. It meets and decides on EU policies in different compositions (e.g., in meetings of ministers of agriculture or environment).

5. Other EU legislation relevant to agricultural biotechnology has, for example, focused on worker health and safety protection (90/679 and 93/88), and the contained use of GE organisms for commercial and research purposes (90/219). Medicinal applications of biotechnology are handled by the European Medicines Evaluation Agency. All documents on agri-biotech regulation in the European Union are available at www.europa.eu.int/eur-lex.

6. According to directive 90/220, which in the meantime has been revised, producers or importers of a GE product first have to notify the national authority of the EU country concerned and provide technical documentation and a full risk assessment. If the national authority approves the GE product, the request moves to the EU level, where the Commission and the other 14 member states are consulted. If there are no objections, the GE product is approved for cultivation and sale in the entire European Union. Only three varieties of GE carnation have been approved in this manner. If there is opposition by one or more EU member states (the most common case), the issue is dealt with by the EU Commission, the European Union's Regulatory Committee, and the Council. Based on the available scientific evidence, the Commission makes a proposal to the Regulatory Committee, which is composed of member state representatives. If the Committee does not endorse the request for approval (qualified majority vote) the issue moves to the European Council (i.e., EU countries' agriculture or environment ministers). The Council can adopt the Commission's proposal by qualified majority, but can reject the Commission's proposal only by unanimous vote. If the Council does not decide within three months the Commission decides. In essence, this means that the Commission should authorize approval requests submitted by EU member states if the request complies with EU regulation and is not unanimously rejected by the Council within the defined time-frame. In practice, EU countries overruled in this procedure have refused to accept GE crops in their countries—primarily by invoking the safety clause of Directive 90/220. Decision-making rules under the revised directive, adopted in 2001, are very similar.

7. Competent Authorities are government officials in EU member countries who are responsible for implementing EU regulations and representing their countries in EU negotiations and approval processes.

8. By April 1998, 16 agricultural GE products had been approved by the European Union, another 11 applications were pending, including four that had been approved by EU scientific committees but were rejected by member states.

9. The European Union's regulatory policy is continuously tracked and commented on at www.transgen.de.

10. See Chege (1998); www.transgen.de.

11. See, for example, Behrens (1997) and Chege (1998). The four "freedoms" (free movement of goods, services, capital, and people) are the cornerstones of the European Union's internal market.

12. www.efsa.eu.int.

13. See www.transgen.de.

14. These developments are tracked at www.transgen.de.

15. For comparison, the OECD's Bio Track database entries by country are: 71 percent for the United States, 9 percent for Canada, 5.3 percent for France, 2.4 percent for Italy, 2.1 percent for Australia, 1.9 percent for Germany, 1.2 percent for the United Kingdom, and 0.7 percent for Japan. See http://www1.oecd.org/ ehs/biobin.

16. Opposition to green biotechnology has also affected the patenting of new GE varieties under the European Union's 1998 directive on legal protection of biotech inventions.

17. The number of field trials in 1991–2002 in the other EU countries is: 3 in Austria, 126 in Belgium, 40 in Denmark, 20 in Finland, 122 in Germany, 19 in Greece, 5 in Ireland, 289 in Italy, 140 in the Netherlands, 1 in Norway, 12 in Portugal, 203 in Spain, 64 in Sweden, and 221 in the United Kingdom. See http:// biotech.jrc.it.

18. See www.isaaa.org and EU (2000a).

19. See, for example, www.foeeurope.org and www.greenpeace.org.

20. For example, Jasanoff (1995).

21. Earlier in 1984, the EPA had proposed to regulate biotechnology under the Federal Insecticide, Fungicide and Rodenticide Act and the Toxic Substances Control Act.

22. Holla (1995).

23. For example, www.bio.org and Jasanoff (1995).

24. National Research Council (1989). This report stated that "the product of genetic modification and selection constitutes the primary basis for decisions and not the process by which the product was obtained ." It confirmed conclusions of a 1987 report by the National Research Council.

25. Jasanoff (1995).

26. See Vogel (2001) and Young (2001).

27. The 2000 US Plant Protection Act equips APHIS with some new authorities in assessing and controlling environmental impacts of GE crops. It appears, however, that APHIS has not yet used these new authorities to establish greater control over green biotechnology.

28. For example, Moore (2000a,b).

29. These crops were chosen because they had undergone the most extensive field testing, and because none of these crops had wild relatives in the United States.

30. One indicator for this relaxation of approval practices is, for example, the number of field releases, which increased from 8 in 1987 to 1105 in 1998 (www.usda.govt).

31. www.nbiap.vt.edu/cfdocs/biopetitions1.cfm.

32. See Federal Register, May 29, 1992. In a 1992 policy statement, that is, its interpretation of the US Federal Food, Drug, and Cosmetic Act with regard to foods derived from new plant varieties, the FDA stated that it would require GE foods to meet the same rigorous standards as all other foods. It also announced that it would treat substances intentionally added to food through genetic engineering as food additives if they were significantly different in structure, function, or amount from substances currently in the food (*FDA Backgrounder* 1994, May 18, www.fda.govt).

33. The FLAVR SAVR^{TM} tomato is designed to remain on the vine longer before being picked (it softens more slowly). In 1994, Calgene, the producer of the tomato, engaged in consultations with the FDA's Center for Food Safety and Applied Nutrition (CFSAN). Based on an evaluation of the data provided by Calgene, the FDA determined that the tomato had not been significantly altered compared to other varieties of tomato. It was thus declared as safe as any other tomato commonly consumed (*FDA Backgrounder* 1994, May 18; Martineau 2001). The FLAVR SAVR^{TM} tomato has in the meantime been withdrawn from the market for commercial reasons.

34. The principle of "substantial equivalence" applied here implies that genes transferred from food and/or previously approved by the FDA are unproblematic. When novel gene sequences and their attendant proteins are introduced a fuller review is required.

35. See *FDA Backgrounder* 1994, May 18; Krimsky and Wrubel (1996). Technically, the FDA does not consider new genes and their protein products to be food additives. If regulated as food additives, such products would fall under section 409 of the Food, Drug and Cosmetic Act, which would force the FDA to use stricter pre-market approval processes.

36. For example, www.bio.org, Caswell (2000), Moore (2000a,b), and Meins (2002).

37. For example, higher than normal levels of lycopene, which can lower the risk of cancer or heart disease, would imply a change in composition. Higher levels of vitamin C would imply a change in nutritional value. The presence of a protein from peanuts in GE food might imply the presence of a peanut allergen, and thus a change in safety.

38. www.ificinfo.health.org.

39. www.bio.org. Examples include high laurate canola and high oleic acid soybeans. In those cases, the FDA confirmed the safety of these products but required labeling to inform consumers about the new ingredients.

40. For example, Jasanoff (1995).

41. For example, Council for Agricultural Science and Technology. The Proposed EPA Plant Pesticide Rule, October 1998.

42. *New York Times*, January 17, 2000.

43. www.thecampaign.org; www.purefood.org/ge/cong49label.cfm; www.foodsafetynow.org; www.agbios.com; www.agbioworld.org.

44. These bills were introduced by Dennis Kucinich (D-Ohio), Patrick Moynihan (D-New York), and Barbara Boxer (D-California). See www.thecampaign.org.

45. A compilation of past and ongoing legal action on agri-biotech issues is maintained by the Center for Food Safety (www.centerforfoodsafety.org). Most lawsuits have been launched against the FDA, EPA, and individual biotech companies.

46. See, for example, www.centerforfoodsafety.org; www.thecampaign.org.

47. www.agbioworld.org.

48. In November and December 1999, the FDA held public hearings on whether or not GE organisms should be defined as food additives, which would require mandatory labeling, and on whether or not stricter testing procedures

should be required to ensure consumer safety (FDA, Report on Consumer Focus Groups on Biotechnology, October 20, 2000). An influential study by the National Academy of Sciences, published in May 2000, supported in principle the FDA's product focus. However, it proposed three additional measures: long-term studies on risks posed by the consumption of GE foods containing substances other than those already on the market; the adoption of the EPA's 1994 proposal for regulation of pest resistant GE plants; and regulation of GE crops designed to resist viruses. The January 2001 FDA proposal reflects the proposals of the National Academy of Sciences rather than the results of the FDA's public hearings.

49. Food or feed developers have to notify the FDA at least 120 days before a GE food or feed is marketed. They also have to provide information demonstrating that the product is as safe as its conventional counterpart. This measure transforms the existing voluntary consultation procedure into a mandatory and more transparent one.

50. www.fda.gov. The FDA's proposal can be regarded as an attempt to cope with growing diversity in voluntary labeling practices that is driven by consumer demand. USDA stated that it would subject the Department's biotech approval process to independent scientific review, and that it would promote the standardization of tests for detecting small amounts of GE soy, corn, and other GE grains. The aim of this initiative is to support food-processing firms that wish to use GE free products or introduce voluntary GE labeling.

51. www.isaaa.org.

52. For example, www.ucsusa.org; www.greenpeace.org.

53. www.greenpeace.org; www.agbioworld.org; www.transgen.de.

54. This permissiveness is, for example, reflected in small budgets in the FDA and USDA for risk-assessments of GE products and the fact that the EPA has, in many ways, been side-lined.

55. For more details, see http://www1.oecd.org/ehs/biobin.

56. The low number of approved GE products in developing countries is difficult to interpret: it may reflect a situation where GE products already on the market have not yet been formally approved due to deficiencies of existing regulatory systems (or the absence thereof). In view of the experience in Europe, Japan, and Australia, it appears likely that the introduction of stricter approval processes in these countries (and thus perhaps also an increasing number of approved GE products) may drive these countries towards mandatory labeling.

57. See www.isaaa.org; www.agbioworld.org; www.greenpeace.org; www.transgen.de.

58. For example, www.isaaa.org, www.agbioworld.org, www.binas.uni-do.org, www.transgen.de.

59. Such tests and their results are, for example, reported in www.isaaa.org and www.agbioworld.org, albeit not on a systematic and comprehensive basis. Other sources include www.binas.unido.org and www.olis.oecd.org/biotrack.nsf. See also DaSilva (2001).

60. Although the ISAAA data are the most widely quoted data on GE crop production they should be regarded with caution because ISAAA is an industry lobbying group sponsored by the major agri-biotech firms (notably, Monsanto,

Syngenta, Aventis CropScience). For a critical comment on the ISAAA data see Greenpeace, International Genetic Engineering Campaign, Background Information, March 2002, www.greenpeace.org.

CHAPTER 4: INTEREST GROUP POLITICS

1. This chapter builds on collaborative work with Erika Meins (Bernauer and Meins 2002). See also Meins (2000, 2002).

2. Stigler (1971), Baron (1995, 2000), and Peltzman (1976).

3. Richards (1999).

4. In 2002, only three firms accounted for almost 50 percent of the global agrochemical market (Syngenta, Aventis, Monsanto). GE seeds, which made up around 10 percent of the world's commercial seed market, were produced almost exclusively by these firms. Four of the seven largest agrochemical firms in the world were from Europe (Syngenta, 22 percent world market share; Aventis, 13 percent; BASF, 11 percent; Bayer, 7 percent), and three from the United States (Monsanto, 13 percent; DuPont, 8 percent; Dow, 7 percent). Concentration was even more pronounced in the agri-biotech market: Monsanto's seed traits accounted for around 90 percent of the total world area planted to GE crops. See www.rafi.org; www.transgen.de; DZ Bank (2001).

5. Regulatory developments in the European Union and the United States are also puzzling for other reasons. Particularly in the 1960s and 1970s, US environmental, health, and safety regulations were extensively justified with the precautionary principle and were (and still are) very restrictive. Examples include regulations on mercury, lead, asbestos, or cyclamates. With regard to agricultural biotechnology, we observe the opposite tendency. Resembling the previous domestic political debates in the United States over environmental, health, and safety regulations, the European Union's agri-biotech regulation since the mid-1980s has been highly politicized and marked by substantial distrust of scientists, government, and industry (Vogel 2001; Lynch and Vogel 2000). The United States has, on average, adopted the strictest food labeling regulations in the world. Not so with regard to agricultural biotechnology. This absence of mandatory labeling is prima facie surprising. The European Union has, on average and compared to the United States, adopted less stringent food labeling legislation, but has enacted much stricter labeling standards for GE foods.

6. Many authors have exposed the empirical flaws and theoretical deficiencies of Stigler's producer dominance argument (e.g., Meier 1988; Gormley 1986). In the absence of a parsimonious alternative, most economists still subscribe to this model (see Baron 1995, 2000). Political scientists have mostly rejected Stigler's model and have offered more complex, more descriptive, and less generalizable alternatives (e.g., Gormley 1986; Héritier 1996, 2002; Majone 1996).

7. See in particular Olson (1965:48–65).

8. See also Frey and Kirchgässner (1994), Marwell and Oliver (1993).

9. Most authors argue that public outrage will grow with the extent to which a given risk is perceived to be involuntary, uncontrollable, or invisible, has a

delayed or catastrophic effect, is memorable, very uncertain, poorly understood, unfamiliar, unfairly distributed, and a technological hazard. Public outrage over risks with these properties tends to be even stronger in cases where less risky alternatives exist (see Slovic 1987, 2001; Groth 1994; Wohl 1998; Gaskell and Bauer 2001; Boholm 1998).

10. See Friedman (1991), Putnam (1993), and Friese (2000). For the theoretical background see Hall and Taylor (1996) and Kitschelt (1986).

11. "Rational choice" theories of politics assume that politicians behave opportunistically and strive for maximum voter support, and that bureaucrats strive for greater budgets and political support (see Frey and Kirchgässner 1994).

12. Several authors have proposed a further differentiation of this argument by distinguishing between regulations focusing on the quality of products and regulations focusing on production processes. They claim that product regulations are easier to instrumentalize for protectionist purposes than process regulations. Consequently, product regulations, on average, tend to be more stringent than process regulations and also vary more across countries. In many empirical cases, including agri-biotechnology, a straightforward distinction of product and process regulations is difficult. I thus stick with a simpler argument about protectionist benefits (see Murphy 1995; Scharpf 1996, 1998; Bernauer 2000).

13. See Stigler (1971) and Baron (2000).

14. See Foster (2002).

15. This type of research design is common in qualitative case study research that focuses on the empirical application of existing theories or on developing or refining new theories in close reference to important empirical cases (see Mitchell and Bernauer 1998).

16. In more academic terms, this explanatory framework contributes to theorizing on comparative biotechnology policy in four ways. First, it includes but goes beyond the most popular explanation, which views regulatory differences exclusively as the result of variation in public perceptions. Second, it connects more systematically to extant social science theories of regulation and is therefore more generalizable than explanations concentrating on "unique" factors, such as political culture and regulatory style. Third, it focuses on the analysis of causal hypotheses rather than description of policy networks. Fourth, it provides an explanation for empirical deviations from the conventional economic theory of regulation. For a larger list of potentially relevant explanations, see Gaskell and Bauer (2001:96–115).

17. See also Gaskell and Bauer (2001).

18. The most reliable indicator of consumer preferences would be differences in prices paid by well-informed consumers for GE and non-GE products. Such data is not available in reliable form. But sketchy evidence on premiums paid for non-GE products in the United States and the European Union is broadly consistent with available survey data (see USDA 2001).

19. See Gaskell et al. (2003).

20. See Gaskell and Bauer (2001:96–115). See also *Nature* 1997; 387: 821–836; *Nature Biotechnology* 2000; 18: 935–38, 939–42; www.pewagbiotech.org; www.angusreid.com; *Science* July 1998; 30: 714.

21. Hoban (1997a,b); *Science* July 1998; 30: 714; *Nature Biotechnology*

2000; 18: 935–38; Gaskell and Bauer (2001:52–79, 110–12); USDA/ERS, Economic issues in agricultural biotechnology, AIB-762.

22. BSE was first detected in British cattle in 1982, but the European Union accepted British assurances that there was no risk to humans. In the late 1980s, British authorities notified EU member states that their food safety might be at risk. In 1989–1990 a massive outbreak of BSE occurred and prompted the European Union to ban human consumption of BSE infected meat. Growing public concerns over food safety were again largely ignored by the British govern-ment and the European Union. The scandal finally broke when, in 1996, the British government announced the occurrence of ten cases of Creutzfeld-Jakob disease and related these cases to the consumption of BSE contaminated meat. See www.bse.org.uk.

23. See Gaskell and Bauer (2001).

24. Hoban (2000), for example, lists the following influences: "greater trust in government and scientists," "culture supports innovation and progress, and accepts risks and mistakes," "ongoing proactive education for industry, leaders, media, and consumers," "low impact and credibility of protest groups," "rela-tively balanced media coverage," "different views on farming and food," and "recognition of benefits from first products." Zechendorf (1998) concentrates on cultural, religious, geographic, and other influences. In a regression analysis, Gaskell et al. (2000:932) find that trust, age, gender, education, and knowledge each independently and significantly predict the probability of opposition to GE foods (see also Bredahl et al. (1998); Vogel (2001). Vogel (2001) in particular provides convincing evidence against cultural explanations of transatlantic differ-ences in consumer perceptions and regulation.

25. For example, many authors have proposed that public acceptance of biotechnology is a function of knowledge and awareness of the benefits of the technology (see Kamaldeen and Powell 2000). These explanations are difficult to support empirically. Empirical results thus far have been insignificant or contested.

26. See Kamaldeen and Powell (2000), Dittus and Hillers (1993), van Ravens-waay (1995), Slovic (1987, 2002), and Gaskell and Bauer (2001).

27. See Gaskell et al. (2003).

28. Eurobarometer (1999) data show that between 16 and 26 percent of the respondents trusted that consumer organizations, environmental organizations, and the medical profession were telling the truth about biotechnology. The percentage trusting universities, the government or the mass media ranged from 4 to 9 percent. See also *Nature* 1997; 387: 831–6; Eurobarometer (1996, 2001); Einsiedel (1997); Gaskell and Bauer (2001:52–79).

29. See Kamaldeen and Powell (2000), Hoban (1998), and Einsiedel (1997). While this argument is plausible, it is difficult to find empirical evidence directly supporting the underlying causal claim. In particular, it is virtually impossible to demonstrate with precision whether aversion to biotechnology causes low trust in regulators or vice versa.

30. See Vos (2000).

31. See Vos (2000) and Committee of Independent Experts (1999).

32. This new body strongly resembles the European Agency for the Evaluation

of Medicinal Products. The latter assists the Commission in the authorization of pharmaceuticals.

33. For example, Lok and Powell (2000).

34. See Hoban (1997a, b, 1998, 2000); Eurobarometer (1999, 2001); Vos (2000); Braun (2000).

35. See Joly and Lemarié (1998). Kalaitzandonakes and Marks (1999) found (by means of a content analysis) that unfavorable reporting on agri-biotechnology in the *Daily Telegraph* (UK) increased significantly due to the BSE crisis. They also showed that the coverage of agri-biotechnology in the *Daily Telegraph* increased from around 30 articles per year to almost 90 in 1998. In the same time period (1996–1998) the percentage of respondents strongly opposing GE foods increased from 29 to 40 percent.

36. See Young (2001).

37. Caswell (2000).

38. See Patterson (2000) and Gaskell and Bauer (2001).

39. The Commission first voted in favor of approval. The Competent Authorities in Belgium, Finland, France, Ireland, Spain, and Portugal agreed with the Commission, those in Austria, Sweden, Denmark, the United Kingdom voted against, and those of the other member states abstained. Because of this opposition, the issue was referred to the Environmental Council. Lack of unanimity there prevented the Council from amending the Commission's proposal. The issue thus went back to the Commission, which consulted three scientific committees and then authorized the two GE crops (Patterson 2000: 337–8).

40. See Young (1998) and Barling (1995).

41. For example, Egdell and Thomson (1999); www.greenpeace.org; www.foe.org; www.beuc.org.

42. See Kohler-Koch (1996), Webster (1998), Young (1998), and Young and Wallace (2000).

43. See, for example, Patterson (2000) and Vos (2000).

44. By the mid-1980s, France and the United Kingdom in particular had established systems of monitored self-regulation. The European Union's Directorate General for Science, Research, and Development advocated a product-oriented and strongly science-based approach, similar to the one adopted in the United States. In contrast, Directive 90/220 is clearly modeled after Denmark's Environment and Gene Technology Act, which was adopted in 1986 and is process-oriented (Patterson 2000: 321).

45. According to the Novel Foods Regulation, which entered into force in May 1997, labeling was mandatory only for products containing live GE organisms or GE-derived products that were not "equivalent" to conventional products. GE soy and corn were judged to be equivalent and thus no label was required by the Commission.

46. See Biliouri (1999), Barling (1995) and Young (1998).

47. For example, Barling (1995), Patterson (2000), Behrens (1997), and Chege (1998). In 1989 and 1990, for example, NGOs lobbied the European Parliament to eliminate the many GE products exempted in the Commission's draft for Directive 90/220. Forceful opposition by the EP's Committee on the Environment, Public Health, and Consumer Protection led to major revisions in

the draft. In the Directive eventually adopted, all products containing GE products had to meet the European Union's relevant product legislation and also process-based, environmental risk assessment standards (Patterson 2000). NGO lobbying also motivated the European Parliament, which had been divided in earlier readings of the Novel Foods Regulation, to pass a Biosafety Resolution with a large majority, requesting mandatory labeling of all foods containing GE soy, and to push for further regulation of GE products (Behrens 1997).

48. See Greenwood and Ronit (1995) and Patterson (2000). See also Bijman and Joly (2001) on the agri-biotech industry in Europe.

49. See also Assouline (1996).

50. Smaller biotech firms coordinated their efforts through the European Secretariat of National Bio-Industry Associations (ESNB). In September 1996, SAGB and ESNBA merged.

51. Scharpf (1985) in particular has provided a systematic explanation of this phenomenon, which he termed "Politikverflechtungsfalle" (policy integration trap).

52. Some analysts also point to patent laws as an explanatory factor. They claim that it has been easier to obtain patents on GE crops (or genetic events) in the United States than the European Union. Since the 1980 US Supreme Court decision authorizing the patenting of living organisms it has been comparatively easy to obtain such patents for the United States. In the European Union, such patents are governed largely by Directive 98/44/CE OJ L 213 of 30.7.1998. The patenting process in the European Union is said to be more complex than in the United States and to provide for a range of exceptions, notably for the human body, and also with regard to certain aspects of plant varieties and animal breeding. Farmers have also reserved the right to save GE seeds for own production. More complex patenting rules in the European Union might thus explain why most biotech firms in the European Union have not struggled very hard to prevent EU rules (they do not hold many patents and may thus not expect to easily obtain such patents in the future).

53. See DZ Bank (2001).

54. See, for example, www.greenpeace.org; www.foe.org; www.europabio.org.

55. See Caduff (2001). In 1999, the United States imposed retaliatory tariffs on several EU countries.

56. See Groth (1994), Wohl (1998), and Covello et al. (1991).

57. Monsanto, for example, invested more than two million USD in a campaign in the United Kingdom and France in 1997, only to find out that negative views of the technology increased from 44 to 51 percent in that time-period. See *Financial Times* October 23, 1997; *Wall Street Journal* May 11, 1999; *New York Times* January 25, 2001; *Business Week* June 12, 2000; Cadot et al. (2001a).

58. www.europabio.org.

59. See, for example, *Austin American-Statesman* January 27, 2003.

60. See Lynch and Vogel (2000) and Cadot et al. (2001b). This argument assumes that supply-expanding first generation GE crops lead to more concentration in the farm sector. Early adopters of the technology enjoy lower production costs. Later adopters face the risk of a supply-shift price effect (lower prices for

crops due to more supply) and higher production costs (due to outdated technology). This leads to larger farms and more bulk production based on the latest technology (in this case agri-biotechnology). The extent to which such effects or other causes are responsible for rapid adoption of GE crops in the United States remains disputed (see USDA 2001).

61. See www.acga.org; www.appsl.fao.org. For example, between 1996 and 1999, EU soybean imports rose from 14.3 million MT to 16.6 million MT. In that same time-period, the European Union's corn imports rose from 9.6 million MT to 11 million MT.

62. First generation GE crops have not produced consistently higher yields, but future generations might.

63. Vos (2000).

64. For example, *Financial Times* May 29, 2000; *ENDS Environment Daily* May 29, 2000; *New York Times* May 19, 2000.

65. See www.eurocommerce.be. See also Millstone (2000) who shows that only when mandatory labeling legislation was on the horizon did producers more systematically consult consumers, for example, through focus group discussions. When they found out that consumers, when offered a choice, would quite invariably purchase non-GE foods, they turned to non-GE supplies rather than labeled GE products. The policies of food manufacturers and retailers are tracked at www.greenpeace.org. See also Gaskell and Bauer (2001).

66. The controversy among different types of producers resulting from changing interests is reflected in Nettleton (1999).

67. See also Foster (2002).

68. See www.europa.eu.int/comm/competition/publications/studies/bpifrs/chap07.pdf; www.ers.usda.gov/briefing/foodmarketstructures; Dobson et al. (2000).

69. See also McNichol and Bensedrine (2001).

70. See Millstone (2000).

71. See www.ciaa.be; www.transgen.de; www.rafi.org.

72. See, for example, *Financial Times* January 8, 1998 and March 18, 1998; *Wall Street Journal* May 11, 1999; www.transgen.de.

73. A listing of individual food processors' and retailers' labeling policy can be found at: www.greenpeace.org/~geneng/reports/food/food004.htm.

74. See, for example, www.eurocommerce.be.

75. www.transgen.de; www.greenpeace.org.

76. See Millstone (2000).

77. See Millstone (2000).

78. Substantial premiums paid for non-GE soybeans demonstrate that world demand for non-GE soybeans exceeds supply. While large processors or retailers have found it easier to use their market power to purchase GE-free soybeans, smaller retailers in particular have often been found to sell GE soy contaminated products without labeling. The BSE crisis and the European Union's ban on animal protein feed have exacerbated these problems, because demand for soy feed has risen sharply. The ban on animal protein feed implies that around 1.3 million metric tons of animal protein needs to be replaced by the same amount of vegetarian protein. This is equivalent to 3.7 million tons of soybeans, or 6.2

million tons of sunflowers or 6.8 million tons of canola. Growing scarcity of non-GE soy may also have motivated processors and retailers to pressure farmers on the issue: because premiums for non-GE soy cut directly into processors' and retailers' profits, motivating farmers to increase the supply of (and reduce premiums for) non-GE soy is of direct interest to these producers. Once processors/retailers have switched to non-GE products, they can, particularly for reasons of reputation, not reverse their policy. See www.transgen.de; www.asa.org.

79. As of December 2002, 11 varieties of GM corn were approved in the United States, and only 4 in the European Union.

80. www.transgen.de; www.asa.org. See also chapter 6. In 2002 the European Union imported around 100,000 tons of non-GE soybeans, mostly grown under contract in the United States. Around 1.5 million tons of shredded non-GE soybeans were imported by the European Union in 2002, mostly from Brazil.

81. Since 2000, many large food processors and retailers in the European Union have moved even further against GE foods by restricting their meat supply to animals raised on non-GE feed.

82. www.transgen.de maintains a database of GE ingredients on the EU market.

83. In February 1975, a group of 140 scientists, primarily biologists, and a few lawyers, physicians, and journalists convened at the Asilomar conference center near Monterey, California, to discuss the safety of recombinant DNA research.

84. See Gaskell and Bauer (2001:98) and Krimsky and Wrubel (1996).

85. See Pollack and Shaffer (2001) and Young (2001).

86. See Moore (2000a,b) and Gaskell and Bauer (2001).

87. http://www.consumersunion.org/; Moore (2000a,b); www.fda.gov/oc/biotech/default.htm.

88. http://www.environmentaldefense.org/home.cfm; http://www.ucsusa.org/index.html; http://www.cspinet.org/; Moore (2000a,b). Similar positions have been adopted by other US consumer organizations, such as the Consumer's Choice Council and the Consumer Federation of America. See www.consumerscouncil.org and www.consumerfed.org.

89. For example, Jeremy Rifkin from the Foundation on Economic Trends.

90. For example, social scientists have not yet been able to determine whether public support for mandatory labeling has preceded or followed NGO campaigns for mandatory labeling.

91. Communication with the author, based at the University of Kiel, Germany.

92. See www.pewagbiotech.org; http://www.gmabrands.com/; Priest (2001); Hoban (1998, 2000); FDA (2000); www.ificinfo.health.org; *Nature Biotechnology* 2000; 18: 939–942; www.centerforfoodsafety.org; Gaskell and Bauer (2001:307–318).

93. Gaskell and Bauer (2001:52–79, 96-115).

94. For example, in a survey conducted by the Center for Science in the Public Interest (CSPI) in spring 2001, consumers were asked: "Would you buy fruits or vegetables that were labeled as being from crops which were" The responses were: 40 percent for "Sprayed with pesticides"; 43 percent for "Genetically engineered"; 37 percent for "Treated with plant hormones"; 44 percent for "Made from cross-bred

corn"; 26 percent for "None of the above"; and 8 percent for "Don't know". In the same survey, consumers were asked: "If you had a choice between two boxes of Wheaties, where the label on one box indicated that it contains genetically engineered ingredients and the label on the other box indicated that it does not contain genetically engineered ingredients, which would you choose, or would you not care?" The responses were: 8 percent would buy the product labeled "Contains genetically engineered ingredients", 52 percent the product labeled "Does not contain genetically engineered ingredients"; 38 percent would not care; 3 percent did not know. http://www.cspinet.org/new/poll_gefoods.html.

95. Consumers were asked: "If you could add one piece of information to food labels, such as on a box of Wheaties, which, if any, of the following would you add?" The responses were: 8 percent for "Contains imported wheat"; 17 percent for "Contains genetically engineered wheat; 31 percent for "Contains pesticides in minute amounts; 7 percent for "Contains lubricants from food processing machinery in minute amounts; 6 percent for "Or, would you add something else (specify)"; 16 percent for "No new information; and 15 percent for "Don't know". Moreover, consumers do not seem willing to pay much for labeling of agri-biotech products. They were asked: "Labeling about genetically engineered ingredients could increase the cost of food. Would you be willing to pay for such labeling if labeling increased the cost of your family's food by." The responses were: 7 percent for "Over $250 a year"; 5 percent for "$250 per year"; 16 percent for "$50 per year"; 17 percent for "$10 per year"; 44 percent for "Nothing"; and 11 percent for "Don't know". http://www.cspinet.org/new/poll_gefoods.html.

96. For example, *Nature Biotechnology* 2000; 18: 935–42.

97. Hoban (2000, 1998); Kalaitzandonakes and Marks (1999); www.ificinfo.health.org/; *Nature Biotechnology* 2000; 18 :935–42.

98. See Gaskell and Bauer (2001) and Bauer and Gaskell (2002).

99. Hoban (1994); Eurobarometer (1996, 1999); Enriquez and Goldberg (2000); Gaskell and Bauer (2001).

100. Hoban (2000); www.cspi.org.

101. See, for example, *Biodemocracy News* March 2001; 32; May 2000; 27 (www.organicconsumers.org); *Washington Post* November 26, 2000; *New York Times* July 19, 2000. Already in 1998, a coalition of NGOs filed a lawsuit against the FDA for failing to fulfill its regulatory duties. In March 2000, more than 50 consumer and environmental groups filed a legal petition with the FDA requesting pre-market and environmental testing as well as mandatory labeling. Both efforts were unsuccessful.

102. I will follow up on this point in chapter 5.

103. For a somewhat different view, see Young (2001).

104. See Gormley (1986), Holla (1995:414–15), and Moore (2000a,b).

105. See *Agribusiness Examiner* 2001, Supplement, Issue 1, January 15.

106. http://www.bio.org/. In addition, plant biotechnology companies are also represented by the American Seed Trade Association (ASTA).

107. See Moore (2000a,b); www.bio.org.

108. Input suppliers have also criticized voluntary "GE-free" labels because these could, in the eyes of some consumers, imply superior quality.

109. www.bio.org.

110. BIO members are listed at: http://www.bio.org/aboutbio/biomembers.asp.

111. For example, Moore (2000a,b).

112. www.bio.org; www.whybiotech.com.

113. Gormley (1986).

114. *New York Times* 2001, January 25.

115. For example, *Economist* November 18, 2000, November 14, 2000. In 2000, Burrill's index of medical biotech firms rose by more than 50 percent, whereas agri-biotech firms experienced a fall of more than 10 percent (*Economist* 2000, November 4; *Business Week* November 6, 2000).

116. In a USDA report, Fernandez-Cornejo and McBride show that the adoption of herbicide-tolerant soybeans does not correlate with farm size, but that adoption of GE corn does. USDA, Economic Research Service *Adoption of Bioengineered Crops / AER-810,* May 2002. See also Baker (1999); www.rafi.org; www.isaaa.org; Carpenter and Gianessi 2001.

117. www.afbf.org.

118. www.nffc.net/bio1.htm; www.nffc.org.

119. See Moore (2000a,b).

120. http://www.ers.usda.gov/.

121. See, for example, www.ncga.com.

122. www.grains.org.

123. ACGA, together with consumer and environmental organizations such as the Center for Food Safety, Consumers Union, Friends of the Earth, and the Institute for Agriculture and Trade Policy, has also signed the 1999 letter to the FDA by 49 Congressmen requesting mandatory labeling (http://www.acga.org/; www.thecampaign.org).

124. www.acga.org.

125. See Moore (2000a,b).

126. See http://apps.fao.org/ and http://www.ers.usda.gov/.

127. Future generations of GE foods might, for example, offer decreased allergenicity, lower fat content, and improved freshness and taste. Some biotech foods might also deliver medicines, for example, vaccines or compounds that help prevent cancer (www.bio.org).

128. www.gma.org; www.nfpa.org.

129. Moore (2000a,b); *Washington Post* August 15, 1999; www.sustain.org/biotech/news.

130. www.abf.org.

131. www.cspi.org.

132. See http://www.greenpeace.org/~geneng/.

133. *Wall Street Journal* July 30, 1999.

134. *New York Times* 2000, June 3.

135. *Fortune* February 19, 2001; www.cropchoice.com; www.innovasure.com; www.greenpeace.org.

136. For example, *BioDemocracy News* January 31, 2001.

137. See USDA (2001) and Corporate Watch (2000).

CHAPTER 5: REGULATORY FEDERALISM

1. For example, Rehbinder and Stewart (1985), Scharpf (1996, 1997), Murphy (1995), Vogel (1995), Oye and Maxwell (1996), Kelemen (2000, 2001), Bernauer (2000), Genschel (2000), Hix (1999), and Esty and Geradin (2001).

2. Scharpf (1996) provides a game theoretic explanation of why EU countries have a stronger incentive to harmonize product than process regulations. Related to that are explanations focusing on the race-to-the-bottom problem in federal political systems (see Revesz 1992). Harmonization of process regulation occurs primarily in cases of clear externalities, for example, transboundary pollution.

3. See Esty and Geradin (2001).

4. I assume that benefits from exports are higher than the costs of complying with stricter regulation.

5. See also Bauer and Gaskell (2002).

6. A February 2002 survey by the Pew Foundation, which contains a separate breakout for California, seems to support that assumption.
See http://pewagribiotech.org/.

7. For example, Kelemen (2000, 2001).

8. See McCormick (2001) and Bernauer and Ruloff (1999).

9. To keep the argument straightforward I rely on a somewhat simplified description of the European Union's "co-decision" procedure, which is required for the adoption of new regulation. Note also that in implementing regulation, authority is divided in complex ways between the Commission and EU member states (with no involvement of the European Parliament). For example, as noted in chapter 3, the decision-rules for GE product approvals equip the Commission with substantial authority. In practice, however, member states have, in this area, frequently overruled the Commission.

10. Unilateral bans on Bt corn in France and Austria, which were not based on systematic risk assessment but were justified under the safeguards clause of directive 90/220, could have been obvious targets of legal action. In another case, Italy banned imports of food containing EU approved GE corn varieties, claiming that these foods were not substantially equivalent. The European Union's Scientific Committee responded that the evidence provided by Italy did not justify the import ban. But the Commission and other EU member states did not press the case (e.g., through the ECJ).

11. The ability of the Commission and the ECJ to enforce verdicts is very limited. Only in a handful of cases have fines been imposed on European Union countries.

12. Predictions of voting behavior in the Parliament are more difficult than in the Council. However, if we assume that all MEPs (626) were present and voting and that all MEPs voted entirely in line with their government's position (these assumptions are quite adventurous), we can run a similar calculation as for the Council. Germany, Italy, Finland, and the Netherlands would command 233 votes in favor of a more facilitative policy. France, Greece, Austria, Sweden and Denmark (the most agri-biotech restricting countries) hold 171 votes. If we add the United Kingdom, the votes in favor of stricter agri-biotech rules increase to 258. 314 votes constitute a majority. If this calculation is anywhere near real-world conditions, neither group has a majority.

13. In the early- to mid-1980s, regulatory policy became somewhat more fragmented, but this trend was halted by the White House. See chapter 3.

14. The political science literature on European integration usually defines the European Union's political system as a system of "multi-level governance" (see Hix 1999).

15. More regulatory centralization in the United States than the European Union appears to exist in many other areas of environmental and consumer policy (e.g., Rose-Ackerman 1994).

16. See Oates (1997).

17. www.agbioworld.org.

18. See http://pewagbiotech.org.

19. See Moeller (2001); see also Rose-Ackerman (1994).

20. As noted above, the limits of EU countries' authority in agri-biotech regulation have not yet been tested in the ECJ. But that situation is more likely to reflect circumstances where EU countries with stronger than EU-wide restrictions would not back down if their regulations were invalidated.

21. Vogel (1995).

CHAPTER 6: INTERNATIONAL TRADE CONFLICT

1. For example, Bailey (2002), Philipps (2001), and Paarlberg (2000a,b); *International Trade Reporter* June 30, 1999; Patterson (2000). For a contrasting prediction, see Pollack and Shaffer (2000).

2. Nomination of Stuart Eizenstat To Be Deputy Treasury Secretary, Before Senate Committee on Finance, 106th Congress, 1999.

3. *New York Times* January 10, 2003. See also GAO (2001).

4. www.agbioworld.org.

5. See Park and Umbricht (2001), Hauser (2000), Milner (2002), Bush and Reinhardt (2000), and Young (2001).

6. WTO dispute settlement is defined here as coercive because decisions can be taken and implemented against the will of defendant countries (in our case the European Union).

7. Compensation involves an agreement, entered into voluntarily by two countries or groups of countries, under which one side compensates the other financially or by reducing trade restrictions in other than the disputed area.

8. This term was coined by Vogel (1995).

9. USDA, National Agricultural Statistical Service, Acreage Report, 2001; www.isaaa.org; www.whybiotech.com. One of the problems in assessing the trade effects of agri-biotech regulation is that there is no reliable data on the proportion of GE produce in total agricultural trade flows of the respective commodities. Data on trade flows of processed food products containing corn, soy, or other GE cereals is also not available.

10. The conclusions for corn and soy remain essentially the same if we look at quantities of crop exports, and not their value.

11. EU (2000a).

12. See Cadot et al. (2001).

13. While US soy exports to the European Union declined, the European Union's soy (and also corn) imports from Brazil and Argentina (and also total EU imports of these crops) surged (see Table 6.1). Around three-quarters of Argentina's soybean production is genetically modified. Brazil does not permit production of GE soy, but up to 20 percent of Brazilian soy exports may be contaminated with GE soy because of illegally imported GE seeds. EU soy imports from Brazil have remained persistently high (around 40 percent of the European Union's soy imports). This evidence suggests that prices have played a larger role than agri-biotech regulation in declining EU soy imports from the United States. See also EU (2000); www.ers.usda.gov/briefing/European Union/trade.htm; www.acga.org; www.appsl.fao.org; www.connectotel.com/gmfood.

14. US agricultural exports to the European Union in 2001 were 6.4 billion USD, those of the European Union to the United States 7.9 billion USD. The main products exported by the United States were soybeans, tobacco, and animal feed, those of the European Union wine and beer.

15. For a more complex analysis that arrives at similar results see Cadot et al. (2001).

16. For example, corn gluten used for animal feed, where the European Union is the most important market for US exports, is not yet subject to mandatory labeling.

17. See USDA (2001).

18. See USDA (2001).

19. See EU (2000a); www.isaaa.org.

20. Another option would be to market GE corn and GE soy that has a clearly superior quality. No such products are currently on the market.

21. For example, Reuters, *Business Brief* January 13, 2000.

22. The probability that US corn production will revert to non-GE varieties is rather small. Miranowski et al. (1999) have calculated that if the entire US food processing industry switched to non-GE corn, it would absorb only 8 percent of 1998 US corn production. The amount would increase to 20 percent if sweeteners and ethanol (corn by-products) production were to become non-GE. The upper limit of the market share for non-GE corn is estimated at 37 percent. We do not know what the situation is for soy.

23. EU (2000a).

24. Thirteen GE crop applications have been pending since 1998 (see EU 2000b).

25. *BioDemocracy News* January 31, 2001; www.transgen.de; www.agbio-world.org.

26. Hertel (1997) and McDougall et al. (1998).

27. Anderson and Nielsen (2000); see also Nielsen and Anderson (2000a,b).

28. In all three scenarios, the following countries have adopted GE corn and GE soybeans (i.e., they permit domestic production): North America, Mexico, Southern Cone region of Latin America, India, China, other East Asian countries except Japan and East Asian NICs, and South Africa. Western Europe, Japan, sub-Saharan Africa (except South Africa) and other countries do not adopt the technology.

29. See Anderson and Nielsen (2000a) for this and other assumptions in the model.

30. This preference shift is modeled as an exogenous 25 percent reduction in final consumer and intermediate demand for *all* imported coarse grains and oil seeds. It is assumed that there is a problem with imperfect information on whether imported corn and soybeans are GE crops or not. This scenario assumes perfect and credible (in the eyes of consumers) enforcement of the European ban on domestic GE crop production. Such enforcement and signaling is assumed to be cost free. Consumers opting against GE food will thus buy domestic produce.

31. See Caduff (2002).

32. See the analysis of export revenues in the previous section.

33. Estimating national welfare effects is in any event useful, irrespective of whether such effects explain the likelihood of trade wars. At the very least it allows for a judgment on whether or not escalating a trade dispute over agri-biotech regulation would, from the viewpoint of the United States as a whole, be economically beneficial.

34. See Milner (2002).

35. For example, Berger and Dore (1996), Bernauer (2000), and OECD (1994, 1999). Some analysts claim that internationally negotiated reductions of tariffs and quotas have motivated countries to establish ever more (and less visible) domestic regulations that shield domestic producers from international competition. Governments have an incentive to introduce such regulation because it is harder to identify and challenge by foreign producers, their governments, as well as domestic consumers (for whom protectionist regulation means higher prices).

36. Policies for coping with regulatory diversity in international trade are discussed in Kahler (1996), Nivola (1997), Sykes (1995), and OECD (1994, 1999).

37. See Moss (2002) for a superb analysis of justifications for government regulation in theory and practice in a range of policy areas.

38. See Caduff (2002).

39. See also Buckingham and Phillips (2001).

40. See Young (2001). In principle, the WTO's SPS and TBT agreements could provide avenues for de facto international harmonization of agri-biotech regulation. These agreements do not involve efforts at formal harmonization, but they encourage such harmonization in other fora (notably the CODEX Alimentarius Commission, the Office International des Epizooties, and the FAO's International Plant Protection Convention). In the agri-biotech case, primarily the CODEX standards are relevant. Moreover, the SPS and TBT agreements apply international standards in dispute settlement. These two agreements are discussed further below. In reality the effect of the SPS and TBT agreements on national health, environment and safety regulations has been weak (see Victor 2000). Other international efforts to harmonize biotech standards include the work of the FAO's International Undertaking on Plant Genetic Resources, which in the early 1990s produced a draft code of conduct for biotechnology, the 1992 OECD safety considerations for biotechnology, the OECD work on harmonization of regulatory oversight in biotechnology (see www.biotrack.org), the FAO's work on fisheries and timber, and UNEP's international technical guidelines for safety in biotechnology. Efforts to establish a working group on biotechnology in the WTO have been unsuccessful.

41. For an in depth analysis of the CODEX standard setting process, which has produced more than 3000 standards, see Victor (1998). See also www.fao.org.

42. For example, Micklitz (2000).

43. See Victor (2000).

44. Regular updates on CODEX work in this area can be found at www.codexalimentarius.net; www.ictsd.org; www.fao.org.

45. Such concerns may be of an ethical, religious or dietary nature, or may derive from consumer demands for "the right to know."

46. See Millstone et al. (1999).

47. See www.biodiv.org and www.iisd.ca./linkages/. For detailed analyses of the Protocol, see Falkner (2000, 2002) and Bail et al. (2002).

48. The relevant clause states: "lack of scientific certainty due to insufficient relevant scientific information and knowledge shall not prevent that Party from taking a decision, as appropriate, with regard to the import of the living modified organism in question."

49. Anderson and Nielsen (2000) take the former, Falkner (2000) the latter position.

50. See Vogel (1995) and Bernauer and Meins (2002).

51. See www.thecampaign.org; www.centerforfoodsafety.org; www.biotech-info.net.

52. These law proposals, submitted in 14 US states, include requests for mandatory labeling, treatment of GE products as food additives (which would require more extensive risk assessment), mandatory pre-market approval by the FDA, and more research and transparency (see www.thecampaign.org; Young 2001).

53. See www.ncga.com, www.asa.com; www.bio.org, and Young (2001).

54. The WTO per se does not have the authority to impose and enforce fines or other punitive measures.

55. For analyses of the basic rules and dispute settlement procedures of GATT/WTO, see www.wto.org, Victor (2000), and Bernauer and Ruloff (1999).

56. See www.icts.org; www.wto.org.

57. See Anderson and Nielsen (2000).

58. Sanitary measures are those that protect human and animal health. Phytosanitary measures are those that protect plant health. The provisions of these agreements are described in www.wto.org, OECD (1999:52–7), and Victor (2000).

59. See, for example, www.ictsd.org.

60. Keller and Heckman (2000).

61. The country introducing stricter standards should be able to demonstrate that alternative measures would have been less effective and/or costlier.

62. These exemptions to the SPS Agreement and the principles designed to discipline their use are defined in Article 5.

63. See www.ictsd.org. The TBT and SPS Agreements also established a notification procedure for national measures. This procedure is meant to produce more transparency and enable countries to address potentially trade-restricting measures at an early stage.

64. A more detailed description of the SPS agreement can be found in Victor (1998, 2000).

65. See Gaskell and Bauer (2001).

66. See Stillwell and Van Dyke (1999), Appleton (2000), Christoferou (2000), and Cors (2001).

67. See Victor (2000) for an analysis of the three cases.

68. Victor (2000:3) concludes: "The 'rational relationship' test is probably leading to more use of risk assessment and greater attention to risk management, which may lead to more diversity in SPS measures and levels but no systematic trend 'up' or 'down'."

69. As noted above, CODEX and the Biosafety Protocol are unlikely to establish clear-cut standards for GE crops in the foreseeable future. And even if they did so, agri-biotech adverse countries would remain largely free to deviate from these standards. The above discussion of CODEX and the Biosafety Protocol has also shown that, if international standards were established, they would probably emphasize the precautionary principle and the need for risk assessment. As Falkner (2000) notes, the Cartagena Protocol has actually strengthened the nation state as the principal source of environmental governance. The European Union would find it rather easy to justify its regulations in such terms.

70. It is interesting to note in this context that the much feared transfer of decision-making authority to international organizations captured by industrial interests has in practice not materialized.

71. See also Victor (2000). Paradoxically, pressure on countries to play the WTO mandated "risk assessment game" may result in more regulatory diversity of SPS levels and policies as countries use more extensive risk assessment to tailor SPS measures more closely to local conditions.

72. See also OECD (1999) (notably p. 29).

73. See Kelemen (2001) and Garrett and Smith (1999).

74. For analyses of WTO dispute settlement in environmental and consumer health cases, see Kelemen (2001), Victor (2000), Bernauer and Ruloff (1999), and Bernauer et al. (2000).

75. Large and vertically integrated food processors and retailers in mass product markets (such as the current GE food market) could, in principle, benefit from increasing product differentiation and labeling at the expense of smaller producers—large producers can control their entire supply chain more effectively and at lower cost. In practice, large European processors and retailers are unlikely to embark on a strategy of re-establishing markets for GE foods. In addition to NGO, farmer, and consumer opposition, they would also encounter opposition from smaller processors and retailers. Under these circumstances, large processors and retailers would, among themselves, face an important collective action problem. Each firm would want to wait for the others to move first and bear the costs of re-establishing the GE food market and follow as a free-rider once the market has been re-opened.

76. See www.ictsd.org.

77. A transatlantic agri-biotech dispute could also hamper other WTO efforts, such as those on intellectual property. As noted in the introduction, patent regulations are another major area of conflict in the trade–biotech arena.

78. For more details, see Caduff (2002), Vogel (1995), and Victor (2000).

79. See also Millstone (2000). Some analysts view the growth hormones case as an exception, where the limits of the dispute settlement system designed in the Uruguay Round (with the festering growth hormones case in mind) were fully tested. In their view, this case clearly demonstrated the limits of the system and countries are unlikely to try again in comparable cases.

80. For a more generic analysis of why the European Union finds it particularly hard to change domestic rules in response to negative WTO verdicts, see Alasdair Young, *The Incidental Fortress: The Single European Market and World Trade*, manuscript.

81. See Hudec et al. (1993) and Bush and Reinhardt (2000).

82. See Pollack and Shaffer (2000) and Levidow (2001).

83. See www.nftc.org; http://agriculture.house.gov/hearings/1081.pdf.

84. www.ers.usda.gov/publications/tb1903/tb1903.pdf.

85. See www.nftc.org; http://agriculture.house.gov/hearings/1081.pdf.

CHAPTER 7: COPING WITH DIVERSITY

1. For a contrasting view, see Krueger (2001).

2. For example, Gaskell and Bauer (2001).

3. Statement at the Annual Meeting of the American Association for the Advancement of Science, 18 February, 2001.

4. See www.biotech-info.net. I am grateful to Philipp Aerni for directing my attention to this point.

5. www.biotech-info.net.

6. For a similar conclusion, see Victor and Runge (2002). They suggest that the current agri-biotech crisis can be resolved and investment in the technology sustained if the European Union and the United States avoid a "hot" trade war over this issue, if public funding for agri-biotech R&D that benefits developing countries is increased, and if intellectual property rights are reformed for the benefit of poor farmers. I fully agree with these proposals but argue in this chapter that the first proposal can only be a short-term measure. To sustain public and private investment in the technology in the long run, more comprehensive regulatory reforms must be implemented. See also Paarlberg (2001b) and EU–US Biotechnology Consultative Forum (2000).

7. One example is the Global Food Safety Initiative by retailers. See www.globalfoodsafety.com.

8. Gaskell et al. (2003).

9. See also Buonanno et al. (2001).

10. I am grateful to Ellen Voss for directing my attention to this issue.

11. For example, Huffman et al. (2001). Much less is known about the effects on consumer choices of different sources of information and of GE foods with consumer benefits.

12. For example, USDA (2001).

13. Taylor and Tick 2003.

14. For an analysis of reasons why markets may fail to adjust to domestic or foreign demand for product differentiation, see USDA (2001).

15. These figures are Producer Subsidy Equivalents calculated by the OECD (www.oecd.org).

16. For a superb analysis of this issue, see USDA (2001).

17. For example, Runge and Jackson (1999).

18. See Runge and Jackson (1999).

19. Jackson (2002) argues that, from an economic efficiency perspective, internationally harmonized labeling standards are likely to perform worse than heterogeneous standards. Based on an economic simulation model that takes into account quite realistic assumptions about costs of segregation and consumer preferences for non-GE products she claims that benefits of increased consumer information compensate for trade inefficiencies introduced by heterogeneous labeling standards.

20. USDA (2001).

21. Note that this argument questions the claim by many analysts that, because export markets for US producers are relatively minor compared to domestic markets, market-differentiation in the United States is driven much more by domestic consumer preferences than by pressure from foreign markets.

22. See also Huffman and Tegene (2000).

23. Corporate Watch (2000).

24. For example, Buonanno et al. (2001), Foster (2002), and Bijman and Joly (2001).

25. See Millstone et al. (1999).

26. See Union of Concerned Scientists, "Pharm and Industrial Crops", 2002, www.ucs.org.

27. For an overview of forthcoming and potential new GE products, see Philipps (2001).

28. In advanced industrialized countries higher yields would contribute to lowering consumer prices but would exacerbate existing problems with farm support programs. Unlike many developing countries, most advanced industrialized countries suffer from oversupply rather than undersupply problems.

29. See, for example, Persley and Lantin (2000) and Paarlberg (2001a).

30. See Paarlberg (2000a,b) and Leisinger (2000).

31. For similar proposals, see Paarlberg (2001a).

32. See also Victor and Runge (2002).

33. Because large parts of the food supply in developing countries are usually traded through informal markets or are not traded at all (subsistence agriculture) mixed GE/non-GE production and IP may not be technically and/or economically feasible in some cases. Foreign support should then focus on IP programs for export-oriented parts of agriculture.

References

Aerni, Philipp. 2002. *Public Attitudes Towards Agricultural Biotechnology in South Africa.* Cambridge, MA: Harvard University, Center for International Development, manuscript.

Alexander, Corinne, and Rachael E. Goodhue. 1999. *Production System Competition and the Pricing of Innovations: An Application to Biotechnology and Seed Corn.* Paper prepared for the 1999 AAEA annual meeting, Nashville, TN.

Altieri, Miguel A., and Peter Rossett. 1999. Ten Reasons Why Biotechnology Will not Ensure Food Security, Protect the Environment and Reduce Poverty in the Developing World. *AgBioForum* 2/3: 155–62.

Anderson, Kym, and Chantal Pohl Nielsen. 2000. *GMOs, Food Safety and the Environment: What Role for Trade Policy and the WTO?* Adelaide: University of Adelaide, Center for International Economic Studies, Policy Discussion Paper 0034.

Appleton, Arthur. 2000. The Labeling of GMO Products Pursuant to International Trade Rules. *NYU Environmental Law Journal* 8/3: 566–78.

Assouline, Gérald. 1996. European Industry Strategies in Biotechnology. *Biotechnology and Development Monitor* 26: 10–12.

Bail, Christoph, Robert Falkner and Helen Marquard, eds. 2002. *The Cartagena Protocol on Biosafety: Reconciling Trade in Biotechnology With Environment and Development.* London: Royal Institute of International Affairs.

Bailey, Ronald. 2002. *The Looming Trade War Over Plant Biotechnology.* Washington, DC: Cato Institute, Trade Policy Analysis Paper 18.

Baker, Ken. 1999. Encouraging Innovation in European Agricultural Biotechnology. *Agro-Food-Industry Hi-Tech* September/October: 29–32.

Barling, David. 1995. The European Community and the Legislating of the Application and Products of Genetic Modification Technology. *Environmental Politics* 4/3: 467–74.

Baron, David. 1995. The Economics and Politics of Regulation: Perspectives, Agenda and Approaches. In Banks, J. S., and E. A. Hanushek, eds. *Modern Political Economy.* Cambridge: Cambridge University Press: 10–62.

_____. 2000. *Business and its Environment.* Upper Saddle River, NJ: Prentice Hall.

Baskin, Yvonne. 1999. Into the Wild. *Natural History* October: 34–7.

Bauer, Martin W., and George Gaskell, eds. 2002. *Biotechnology: The Making of a Global Controversy.* Cambridge: Cambridge University Press.

Behrens, Maria. 1997. *Genfood: Einführung und Verbreitung, Konflikte und Gestaltungsmöglichkeiten.* Berlin: Sigma.

Berger, Suzanne, and Ronald Dore, eds. 1996. *National Diversity and Global Capitalism.* Ithaca, NY: Cornell University Press.

Bernauer, Thomas. 2000. *Staaten im Weltmarkt: Zur Handlungsfähigkeit von Staaten trotz wirtschaftlicher Globalisierung.* Opladen: Leske & Budrich.

Bernauer, Thomas, and Erika Meins. 2002. Technological Revolution Meets Policy and the Market: Explaining Cross-National Differences in Agricultural Biotechnology Regulation. *European Journal of Political Research* in press.

Bernauer, Thomas, and Dieter Ruloff, eds. 1999. *Handel und Umwelt: Zur Frage der Kompatibilität internationaler Regime*. Wiesbaden: Westdeutscher Verlag.

Bernauer, Thomas, Kenneth A. Oye, and David G. Victor. 2000. Regulatory Diversity: Can the World Trading System Cope. *Swiss Political Science Review* 6/3: 96–108.

Bijman, Jos, and Pierre-Benoît Joly. 2001. Innovation Challenges for the European Agbiotech Industry. *AgBioForum* 4/1: 4–13.

Biliouri, Daphne. 1999. Environmental NGOs in Brussels: How Powerful are Their Lobbying Activities? *Environmental Politics* 8/2: 173–82.

Boholm, Asa. 1998. Comparative Studies of Risk Perception: A Review of Twenty Years of Research. *Journal of Risk Research* 1/2: 135–64.

Borlaug, Norman E. 2001. *Feeding the World in the 21st Century: The Role of Agricultural Science and Technology*. Speech given at Tuskegee University, April.

Bouis, Howarth E. 2002. The Role of Biotechnology for Food Consumers in Developing Countries. In Qaim, M., A. Krattiger, and J. von Braun, eds., *Agricultural Biotechnology in Developing Countries: Towards Optimizing the Benefits for the Poor*. Dordrecht: Kluwer, in press.

Braun, R. August. 1999. The Public Perception of Biotechnology in Europe: Between Acceptance and Hysteria. *Biolink* (Communication on Biotechnology, Worb, Switzerland).

Bredahl, Lone, Klaus G. Grunert and Lynn Frewer. 1998. Consumer Attitudes and Decision-Making with Regard to Genetically Engineered Food Products. *Journal of Consumer Policy* 21/3: 251–77.

Buckingham, Donald E., and Peter W. B. Phillips. 2001. Issues and Options for the Multilateral Regulation of GM Foods. *Estey Journal of International Law and Trade Policy* 2/1: 178–89.

Buonanno, Laurie, Sharon Zablotney, and Richard Keefer. 2001. *Politics versus Science in the Making of a New Regulatory Regime for Food in Europe*. European Integration Online Papers 5/12, www.eiop.or.at/eiop/.

Busch, Marc L., and Eric Reinhardt. 2000. *Testing International Trade Law: Empirical Studies of GATT/WTO Dispute Settlement*. Atlanta, GA: Emory University, Department of Political Science, manuscript.

Cadot, Olivier, Landis Gabel and Daniel Traça. 2001a. *Monsanto and Genetically Modified Organisms*. Fontainebleau: INSEAD.

Cadot, Olivier, Akiko Suwa-Eisenmann and Daniel Traça. 2001b. *Trade-Related Issues in the Regulation of Genetically Modified Organisms*. Paper prepared for the INSEAD workshop on European and American Perspectives on Regulating Genetically Engineered Food, Fontainebleau, June 7–8.

Caduff, Ladina. 2002. *Regulating the Use of Growth Hormones in Meat Production in the European Union and the United States*. Zurich: ETH Zurich, Center for International Studies, manuscript.

Cantley, Mark. 1995. The Regulation of Modern Biotechnology: A Historical and

European Perspective. A Case Study in How Societies Cope with New Knowledge in the Last Quarter of the Twentieth Century. In Rehm, H. J., et al., eds. *Biotechnology: Legal, Economic and Ethical Dimensions*. Volume 12. Weinheim: VCH Verlagsgesellschaft: 505–681.

Carpenter, Janet E., and Leonard P. Gianessi. 2001. *Agricultural Biotechnology: Updated Benefit Estimates*. Washington, DC: National Center for Food and Agricultural Policy, www.ncfap.org.

Caswell, Julie A. 2000. Labeling Policy for GMO's: To Each his Own? *AgBioForum* 3/1: 305–09, http://www.agbioforum.org.

Chege, Nyaguthii. 1998. Compulsory Labeling of Food Produced from Genetically Modified Soya Beans and Maize. *Columbia Journal of European Law* 4/ Winter–Spring: 179–81.

Christoforou, Theofanis. 2000. Settlement of Science-Based Trade Disputes in the WTO. *NYU Environmental Law Journal* 8/3: 622–48.

Committee of Independent Experts. 1999. *First Report on Allegations Regarding Fraud, Mismanagement and Nepotism in the European Commission*. Brussels: European Union, March 15.

Corporate Watch. 2000. *Control Freaks – the GMO Exporters*. Oxford: CorporateWatch, GE briefing series, www.corporatewatch.org.

Cors, Thomas. 2001. Biosafety and International Trade: Conflict or Convergence? *International Journal of Global Environmental Issues* 1/1:87–103.

Covello, Vincent T., Peter M. Sandman and Paul Slovic. 1991. Guidelines for Communicating Information about Chemical Risks Effectively and Responsibly. In Mayo, Deborah G., and Rachelle D. Hollander, eds. *Acceptable Evidence: Science and Values in Risk Management*. New York: Oxford University Press: 95–118.

DaSilva, Edgar J. 2001. GMOs and Development. *Electronic Journal of Biotechnology* 4/2.

De Greef, Willy. 2000. Regulatory Conflicts and Trade. *NYU Environmental Law Journal* 8/3: 579–84.

Desquilbert, Marion, and David S. Bullock. 2001. *Market Impacts of Segregation and Non GMO Identity Preservation*. Paper prepared for the INSEAD workshop on European and American Perspectives on Regulating Genetically Engineered Food, Fontainebleau, June 7–8.

Dittus, K. L., and Hillers, Virginia N. 1993. Consumer Trust and Behaviour Related to Pesticides. *Food Technology* 477: 87–9.

Dobson, Paul and Michael Waterson. 2000. Retailer Power: Recent Developments and Policy Implications. *Economic Policy* 28/April: 135–64.

Durant, John, Martin W. Bauer, and George Gaskell, eds. 1998. *Biotechnology in the Public Sphere: A European Sourcebook*. London: Science Museum.

DZ Bank. 2001. *In Focus: Green Biotechnology*. Frankfurt: DZ Bank.

Echols, Marsha A. 1998. Food Safety Regulation in the European Union and the United States: Different Cultures, Different Laws. *Columbia Journal of European Law* 4: 525–43.

———. 2001. *Food Safety and the WTO: The Interplay of Culture, Science, and Technology*. Dordrecht: Kluwer.

Egdell, Janet M., and Kenneth J. Thomson. 1999. The Influence of UK NGOs on the Common Agricultural Policy. *Journal of Common Market Studies* 37/1: 121–31.

Einsiedel, Edna F. 1997. *Biotechnology and the Canadian Public: Report on a 1997 National Survey and some International Comparisons*. Edmonton: University of Calgary.

Enriquez, Juan, and Ray Goldberg. 2000. Transforming Life, Transforming Business: The Life Science Revolution. *Harvard Business Review* March–April: 102–12.

Esty, Daniel C., and Damien Geradin, eds. 2001. *Regulatory Competition and Economic Integration: Comparative Perspectives*. Oxford: Oxford University Press.

EU (European Union). 2000a. *Economic Impacts of Genetically Modified Crops on the Agri-Food Sector. A First Review*. Brussels: European Union, EU Working Document Rev.2, Directorate-General for Agriculture.

————. 2000b. *Questions and Answers on the Regulation of GMOs in the EU*. Brussels: EU, Memo/00/277.

Eurobarometer. 1996, 1999, 2001. Brussels: European Union, http://europa.eu.int/comm/public_opinion.

EU-US Biotechnology Consultative Forum. 2000. *Final Report*. December.

Falck-Zepada, José Benjamin, Greg Traxler, and Robert G. Nelson. 2000. Rent Creation and Distribution From Biotechnology Innovations: The Case of BT Cotton and Herbicide Tolerant Soybeans in 1997. *Agribusiness* February.

Falkner, Robert. 2000. Regulating Biotech Trade: The Cartagena Protocol on Biosafety. *International Affairs* 76/2: 299–314.

————. 2002. International Trade Conflicts over Agricultural Biotechnology. In Russell, Alan, and John Vogler, eds. *The International Politics of Biotechnology: Investigating Global Futures*. Manchester: Manchester University Press: 142–56.

Fernandez-Cornejo, Jorge, Cassandra Klotz-Ingram, and Sharon Jans. 1999. *Farm-level Effects of Adopting Genetically Engineered Crops in the US*. Paper presented at the international conference Transitions in Agritech: Economics of Strategy and Policy. Washington, DC, June 24–25.

FDA (Food and Drug Administration). 2000. *Report on Consumer Focus Groups on Biotechnology*. Washington, DC: FDA.

Foster, James L. 2002. *Globalization, New Technology and the Competitive Use of Regulation: Environmental Regulation and the Global Food Market*. Cambridge, MA: MIT, Center for International Studies, manuscript.

Frey, Bruno S., and Gebhard Kirchgässner. 1994. *Demokratische Wirtschaftspolitik: Theorie und Anwendung*. München: Vahlen.

Friedman, Monroe. 1991. Consumer Boycotts: A Conceptual Framework and Research Agenda. *Journal of Social Issues* 47/1:149–68.

Friese, Susanne. 2000. Consumer Boycotts: Effecting Change Through the Marketplace and the Media. *Journal of Consumer Policy* 23/4: 493–7.

GAO (General Accounting Office). 2001. *International Trade: Concerns over Biotechnology Challenge US Agricultural Exports*. Washington, DC: GAO, June, GAO-01-727.

Garrett, Geoffrey, and Smith McCall. 1999. *The Politics of WTO Dispute Settle-*

ment. Paper presented at the annual meeting of the American Political Science Association, Atlanta, GA.

Gaskell, George, and Martin W. Bauer, eds. 2001. *Biotechnology 1996–2000: The Years of Controversy*. London: Science Museum.

Gaskell, George, Nick Allum, Martin Bauer et al. 2000. Biotechnology and the European Public. *Nature Biotechnology* 18/9: 935–8.

Gaskell, George, Nick Allum, Sally Stares et al. 2003. Europeans and Biotechnology in 2002. Eurobarometer 58.0. (2nd Edition: March 21st 2003) A report to the EC Directorate General for Research from the project 'Life Sciences in European Society' QLG7-CT-1999-00286.

Genschel, Philipp. 2000. Die Grenzen der Problemlösungsfähigkeit der EU. In Grande, Edgar and Markus Jachtenfuchs, eds. *Wie problemlösungsfähig ist die EU? Regieren in europäischen Mehrebenensystemen*. Baden-Baden: Nomos: 191–207.

Gormley, William T. 1986. Regulatory Issue Networks in a Federal System. *Polity* 18: 595–620.

Greenwood, Justin, and Karsten Ronit. 1995. European Bioindustry. In Greenwood, Justin, ed. *European Casebook on Business Alliances*. Hemel: Prentice Hall: 128–42.

Groth, Edward. 1994. *Consumer Perceptions of and Responses to Potentially Hazardous Technologies*. In ICGFI. Document No. 18. Vienna: ICGFI: 4123–24.

Hall, Peter A., and Rosemary C. Taylor. 1996. Political Science and the Three New Institutionalisms. *Political Studies* XLIV: 936–57.

Harlander, Susan. 1991. Social, Moral, and Ethical Issues in Food Biotechnology. *Food Technology* 45/5: 152–61.

Hauser, Heinz. 2000. Die WTO Streitschlichtung aus einer Law and Economics Perspektive. In Berg, Hartmut, ed. *Theorie der Wirtschaftspolitik*. Berlin: Duncker und Humblod: 79–111.

Héritier, Adrienne. 1996. *Ringing the Changes in Europe*. Berlin: Walter de Gruyter.

Héritier, Adrienne, and Mark Thatcher, eds. 2002. Regulation and the State. Special issue of *Journal of European Public Policy* in press.

Hertel, Thomas W., ed. 1997. *Global Trade Analysis: Modeling and Applications*. Cambridge: Cambridge University Press.

Hix, Simon. 1999. *The Political System of the European Union*. Basingstoke: Macmillan Press.

Hoban, Thomas J. 1997a. Consumer Acceptance of Biotechnology: An International Perspective. *Nature Biotechnology* 15/March: 232–4.

———. 1997b. Trends in Consumer Attitudes about Biotechnology. *Journal of Food Distribution Research* 27/1: 1–10.

———. 1998. Trends in Consumer Attitudes about Agricultural Biotechnology. *AgBioForum* 1/1: 3–7.

———. 2002. *American Consumers' Awareness and Acceptance of Biotechnology*. National Agricultural Biotechnology Council (www.cals.cornell.edu/extension/nabc/).

Holla, Roger. 1995. Safety Issues in Genetic Engineering: Regulation in the

United States and the European Communities. In Fransman, Martin, et al. *The Biotechnology Revolution?* Oxford: Blackwell: 414–5.

Hudec, Robert E., Daniel L. M. Kennedy, and Mark Sgarbossa. 1993. A Statistical Profile of GATT Dispute Settlement Cases, 1948–1989. *Minnesota Journal of Global Trade* 2: 1–100.

Huffman, Wallace E., and Ababayehu Tegene. 2000. *Public Acceptance of and Benefits from Agricultural Biotechnology: A Key Role for Verifiable Information.* Paper presented at the 4th conference of the ICABR, Ravello, Italy, August 24–28.

Huffman, Wallace E., Jason F. Shogren, Matthew Rousu et al. 2001. *The Value to Consumers of GM Food Labels in a Market With Asymmetric Information: Evidence from Experimental Auctions.* Paper presented at the 5th Conference of the ICABR, Ravello, Italy, June 15–18.

ICSU. 2003. *New Genetics, Food and Agriculture: Scientific Discoveries–Societal Dilemmas.* Paris: International Council for Science (www.icsu.org).

Jackson, Lee Ann. 2002. *Is Regulatory Harmonization Efficient? The Case of Agricultural Biotechnology Labeling.* Adelaide: Adelaide University, Australia, Center for International Economic Studies, Discussion Paper No. 206.

Jasanoff, Sheila. 1995. Product, Process, or Programme: Three Cultures and the Regulation of Biotechnology. In Bauer, Martin, ed. *Resistance to New Technology.* Cambridge: Cambridge University Press: 311–31.

Joly, Pierre-Benoit. 1998. Firmes: La Naissance d'un cartel? *Courrier de la Planete* 46/July–August: 30–32.

Joly, Pierre-Benoit, and Claire Marris. 2001. *Agenda Setting and Controversies: Comparative Approach to the Case of GMOs in France and the US.* Paper prepared for the INSEAD workshop on European and American Perspectives on Regulating Genetically Engineered Food, Fontainebleau, June 7–8.

Joly, Pierre-Benoit, and Stéphane Lemarié. 1998. Industry Consolidation, Public Attitude and the Future of Plant Biotechnology in Europe. *AgBioForum* 1/2: 85–90.

Kahler, Miles. 1996. Trade and Domestic Differences. In Berger, Suzanne, and Ronald Dore, eds. *National Diversity and Global Capitalism.* Ithaca, NY: Cornell University Press: 298–332.

Kalaitzandonakes, Nicholas, and Leonie A. Marks. 1999. *Public Opinion of AgBiotech in the US and UK: A Content Analysis Approach.* AAEA National Meetings.

Kamaldeen, Sophia, and Douglas A. Powell. 2000. *Public Perceptions of Biotechnology. Food Safety Network Technical Report.* Guelph: University of Guelph, Department of Plant Agriculture.

Kelemen, R. Daniel. 2000. Regulatory Federalism: EU Environmental Regulation in Comparative Perspective. *Journal of Public Policy* 20/2: 133–67.

———. 2001. The Limits of Judicial Power: Trade-Environmental Disputes in the GATT/WTO and the EU. *Comparative Political Studies* 34/6: 622–50.

Keller and Heckman LLP. 2000. *Comments on Non-Tariff Trade Barriers for Processed Foods and Beverages: Mandatory Bioengineered Food Labeling Requirements.* Investigation No. 332-421, submitted to the US International Trade Commission.

Kitschelt, Herbert P. 1986. Political Opportunity Structures and Political Protest: Anti-Nuclear Movements in Four Democracies. *British Journal of Political Science* 16/1: 57–85.

Kohler-Koch, Beate. 1996. Die Gestaltungsmacht organisierter Interessen. In Jachtenfuchs, Markus, and Beate Kohler-Koch, eds. *Europäische Integration.* Opladen. Leske&Budrich: 193–222.

Krimsky, Sheldon, and Roger P. Wrubel. 1996. *Agricultural Biotechnology and the Environment: Science, Policy, and Social Issues.* Urbana, IL: University of Illinois Press.

Krueger, Roger W. 2001. The Public Debate on Agrobiotechnology: A Biotech Company's Perspective. *AgBioForum* 4/3: 209–20.

Leisinger, Klaus M. 2000. *The Political Economy of Agricultural Biotechnology for the Developing World.* Basel: Novartis Foundation, manuscript.

Levidow, Les. 2001. *Regulating Science in Transatlantic Trade Conflicts Over GM Crops.* Paper prepared for the INSEAD workshop on European and American Perspectives on Regulating Genetically Engineered Food, Fontainebleau, June 7–8.

Lok, Corie, and Douglas Powell. 2000. *The Belgian Dioxin Crisis of the Summer 1999: A Case Study in Crisis Communications and Management.* Guelph: University of Guelph, Department of Plant Agriculture, Technical Report, www.plant.uoguelph.ca/safefood.

Lotz, Helmut. 2000. *Free Trade and Frankenfood: National Identity and International Conflict.* Paper prepared for the annual meeting of the International Studies Association, Los Angeles, March.

Lynch, Diahanna, and Jérôme Da Ros. 2001. *Science and Public Participation in Regulating Genetically Engineered Food.* Paper prepared for the INSEAD workshop on European and American Perspectives on Regulating Genetically Engineered Food, Fontainebleau, June 7–8.

Lynch, Diahanna, and David Vogel. 2000. *Apples and Oranges: Comparing the Regulation of Genetically Modified Food in Europe and the United States.* Paper prepared for the Annual Meeting of the American Political Science Association, August 31–September 3.

MacKenzie, Ruth, and Silvia Francescon. 2000. The Regulation of Genetically Modified Food in the European Union: An Overview. *NYU Environmental Law Journal* 8/3: 530–55.

Majone, Giandomenico. 1996. *Regulating Europe.* London: Routledge.

Martineau, Belinda. 2001. Food Fight: The short, unhappy life of the Flavr Savr Tomato. *The Sciences* Spring: 24–9.

McCormick, John. 2001. *Environmental Policy in the European Union.* Houndsmills: Palgrave.

McDougal, Robert A., Aziz Elbehri and Truong P. Truong, eds. 1998. *Global Trade, Assistance, and Protection: The GTAP 4 Data Base.* West Lafayette: Purdue University, Center for Global Trade Analysis.

McNeill, John. 2000. *Something New Under the Sun: An Environmental History of the Twentieth Century.* London: Penguin Books.

McNichol, J., and J. Bensedrine. 2001. *National Institutional Contexts and the Construction of Multilateral Governance Systems: US-EU Struggles Over*

Labeling Rules for GM-Food. Paper prepared for the INSEAD workshop on European and American Perspectives on Regulating Genetically Engineered Food, Fontainebleau, June 7–8.

Meier, Kenneth J. 1988. The Political Economy of Regulation: The Case of Insurance Regulation. Albany, NY: University of New York Press.

Meins, Erika. 2000. Up or Down? Explaining the Stringency of Consumer Protection. *Swiss Political Science Review* 6/2: 94–9.

———. 2002. *Politics and Public Outrage: Explaining Transatlantic and Intra-European Diversity of Regulation of Food Irradiation and Genetically Modified Foods*. Zurich: ETH Zurich, Center for International Studies, dissertation.

Micklitz, Hans. W. 2000. International Regulation on Health, Safety, and the Environment. *Journal of Consumer Policy* 23/1: 3–24.

Millstone, Erik. 2000. Analysing Biotechnology's Traumas. *New Genetics and Society* 19/2: 117–32.

Millstone, Erik, Eric Brunner, and Sue Mayer. 1999. Beyond 'Substantial Equivalence'. *Nature* 401: 525–26.

Milner, Helen V. 2002. International Trade. In Carlsnaes, Walter, Thomas Risse and Beth Simmons. *Handbook of International Relations*. London: Sage: 448–61.

Miranowski, John A., Giancarlo Moschini, Bruce Babcock et al. 1999. *Economic Perspectives on GMO Market Segregation*. Ames, IA: Iowa State University, manuscript.

Mitchell, Ronald, and Thomas Bernauer. 1998. Empirical Research on International Environmental Policy: Designing Qualitative Case-Studies. *Journal of Environment and Development* 7/1: 4–31.

Moeller, David R. 2001. *State GMO Restrictions and the Dormant Commerce Clause*. Farmers' Legal Action Group, Inc.

Moore, Elizabeth. 2000a. *Food Safety, Labeling and the Role of Science*. Paper presented at the ECPR workshop on The Politics of Food, Copenhagen, April 14–19.

———. 2000b. *Science, Internationalization, and Policy Networks: Regulating Genetically-Engineered Food Crops in Canada and the United States, 1973–1998*. Toronto: University of Toronto, Department of Political Science, dissertation.

Moss, David. 2002. *When All Else Fails: Government as the Ultimate Risk Manager*. Cambridge, MA: Harvard University Press.

Murphy, Dale D. 1995. *Open Economics and Regulations: Convergence and Competition among Jurisdictions*. Cambridge, MA: MIT, Department of Political Science, dissertation.

Muttitt, Greg, and Dirk Franke. 2000. *Control Freaks – the GMO Exporters*. Oxford: Corporate Watch.

National Academy of Sciences. 2002. *Environmental Effects of Transgenic Plants*. Washington, DC: National Academy Press.

National Research Council. 1989. *Field Testing Genetically Modified Organisms*. Washington, DC: National Academy Press.

Nelson, Gerald C., ed. 2001. *Genetically Modified Organisms in Agriculture*. London: Academic Press.

Nelson, Gerald C., Timothy Josling, David Bullock et al. 1999. *The Economics and Politics of Genetically Modified Organisms in Agriculture: Implications for the WTO 2000*. Urbana-Champaign, IL: University of Illinois, College of Agricultural, Consumer and Environmental Sciences.

Nettleton, Joyce A. 1999. *Food Industry Retreats from Science*. Chicago, IL: Institute of Food Technologists, September 9.

Nielsen, Chantal Pohl, and Kym Anderson. 2000a. *Global Market Effects of Alternative European Responses to GMOs*. Adelaide: University of Adelaide, Center for International Economic Studies, Policy Discussion Paper 0032 (published in 2001 in *Weltwirtschaftliches Archiv/Review of World Economics* (137) 2: 320–46).

Nielsen, Chantal Pohl, and Kym Anderson. 2000b. *Global Market Effects of Adopting Transgenic Rice and Cotton*. Adelaide: University of Adelaide, Center for International Economic Studies, manuscript.

Nielsen, Chantal Pohl, Sherman Robinson and Karen Tierfelder. 2002. *Trade in Genetically Modified Food: A Survey of Empirical Studies*. Available at www.ifpri.org.

Nivola, Pietro S., ed. 1997. *Comparative Disadvantages? Social Regulations and the Global Economy*. Washington, DC: Brookings Institution Press.

Oates, Wallace E. 1997. *Environmental Federalism in the United States*. College Park, MD: University of Maryland, manuscript.

OECD. 1994. *Regulatory Cooperation for an Interdependent World*. Paris: OECD, Public Management Studies.

———. 1999. *Food Safety and Quality: Trade Considerations*. Paris: OECD.

Olson, Mancur. 1965. *The Logic of Collective Action*. Cambridge, MA: Harvard University Press.

Oye, Kenneth, and James Maxwell. 1995. Self-Interest and Environmental Management. In Keohane, Robert, and Elinor Ostrom, eds. *Local Commons and Global Interdependence*. London: Sage: 191–222.

Paarlberg, Robert L. 2000a. Genetically Modified Crops in Developing Countries: Promise or Peril? *Environment* 42/1: 19–27.

———. 2000b. The Global Food Fight. *Foreign Affairs* 79/3: 24–38.

———. 2001a. The Politics of Precaution: Genetically Modified Crops in Developing Countries. *Food Policy Statement* 35/October.

———. 2001b. *Shrinking International Markets for GM Crops?* Paper presented at the USDA Agricultural Outlook Forum 2001, Arlington, VA, Feburary 22–23.

———. 2001c. *The Politics of Precaution: Genetically Modified Crops in Developing Countries*. Baltimore, MD: Johns Hopkins University Press.

———. 2003. *Reinvigorating Genetically Modified Crops*. Issues in Science and Technology, US National Academy of Sciences, Spring.

Park, Young Duk, and George C. Umbricht. 2001. WTO Dispute Settlement 1995–2000: A Statistical Analysis. *Journal of International Economic Law* 4/1: 213–30.

Patterson, Lee Ann. 2000. Biotechnology Policy: Regulating Risks and Risking Regulation. In Wallace, Helen, and William Wallace, eds. *Policy-Making in the European Union*. Oxford: Oxford University Press: 317–43.

Peltzman, Sam. 1976. Towards a More General Theory of Regulation. *Journal of Law and Economics* August: 211–40.

Persley, Gabrielle J., and Manuel Lantin, eds. 2000. *Agricultural Biotechnology and the Poor*. Washington, DC: Consultative Group on International Agricultural Research, Proceedings of an International Conference, October 21–22.

Philipps, Michael J. 2001. *The Future of Agricultural Biotechnology*. Lecture at the College of Agriculture and Environmental Science, University of Georgia, October 1, www.bio.org.

Pinstrup-Andersen, Per, and Ebbe Schiøler. 2000. *Seeds of Contention*. Baltimore, MD: Johns Hopkins University Press.

Pollack, Mark A., and Gregory C. Shaffer. 2000. Biotechnology: The Next Transatlantic Trade War? *The Washington Quarterly* 23/4: 41–54.

———. 2001. The Challenge of Reconciling Regulatory Differences: Food Safety and Genetically Modified Organisms in the Transatlantic Relationship. In Pollack, Mark A., and Gregory C. Shaffer, eds. *Transatlantic Governance in the Global Economy*. Lanham, MD: Rowman and Littlefield: 153–78.

Pray, Carl E., Danmeng Ma, Jikun Huang et al. 2001. Impact of Bt Cotton in China. *World Development* 29/5: in press.

Priest, Susanna. 2001. *A Grain of Truth: The Media, the Public, and Biotechnology*. Lanham, MD: Rowman & Littlefield.

Putnam, Todd. 1993. Boycotts are Busting Out all Over. *Business and Society Review* 85: 47–51.

Quist, D. and Chapela, I.H. 2001. Transgenic DNA Introgressed into Traditional Maize Landraces in Oaxaca, Mexico. *Nature* 414: 541–3.

Rehbinder, Eckard, and Richard Stewart. 1985. *Environmental Protection Policy*. Berlin: de Gruyter.

Revesz, Richard L. 1992. Rehabilitating Interstate Competition: Rethinking the Race-to-the-Bottom Rationale for Federal Environmental Regulation. *New York University Law Review* 67: 1210–54.

Richards, John E. 1999. Toward a Positive Theory of International Institutions: Regulating International Aviation Markets. *International Organization* 53/1: 1–37.

Robinson, Jonathan. 1999. Ethics and Transgenic Crops: A Review. *Electronic Journal of Biotechnology* 2/2.

Rogers, Everett M. 1996. *Diffusion of Innovation*. 4th edition, New York: Free Press.

Rose-Ackerman, Susan. 1994. Environmental Policy and Federal Structure: A Comparison of the United States and Germany. *Vanderbuilt Law Review* 47: 1587–622.

Royal Society. 2002. *Genetically Modified Plants for Food Use and Human Health – An Update*. London: Royal Society.

Runge, C. Ford, and Lee Ann Jackson. 1999. *Labeling, Trade and Genetically Modified Organisms (GMOs): A Proposed Solution*. University of Minnesota, Center for International Food and Agricultural Policy, Working Paper WP99-4.

Scharpf, Fritz W. 1985. Die 'Politikverflechtungsfalle': Europäische Integration und deutscher Föderalismus im Vergleich. *Politische Vierteljahresschrift* 26/4: 323–52.

_____. 1996. Politische Optionen im vollendeten Binnenmarkt. In Jachten-fuchs, Markus, and Beate Kohler-Koch, eds. *Europäische Integration*. Opla-den: Leske & Budrich: 109–40.

_____. 1997. Introduction: The Problem-Solving Capacity of Multi-Level Governance. *Journal of European Public Policy* 4/4: 520–38.

_____. 1998. Globalization: The Limitations of State Capacity. *Swiss Political Science Review* 4/1: 92–8.

Segarra, Alejandro, and Jean M. Rawson. 2001. *StarLink TM Corn Controversy: Background*. Washington, DC: CRS Report for Congress.

Slovic, Paul. 1987. Perception of Risk. *Science* 236/17: 280–5.

_____, ed. 2001. *The Perception of Risk*. London: Earthscan.

Stigler, George. 1971. The Theory of Economic Regulation. *The Bell Journal of Economics and Management Science*, Spring: 114–41.

Stillwell, Matthew, and Brennan Van Dyke. 1999. *An Activist's Handbook on Genetically Modified Organisms and the WTO*. Washington, DC: Center for International Environmental Law.

Sykes, Alan O. 1995. *Product Standards for Internationally Integrated Markets*. Washington, DC: Brookings Institution.

Taylor, Michael, and Jody Tick. 2003. Post-Market Oversight of Biotech Foods: Is the System Prepared. Washington DC: Resources for the Future (www.pe-wagbiotech.org).

Thomson, Jennifer A. 2002. *Genes for Africa: Genetically Modified Crops in the Developing World*. Cape Town: University of Cape Town Press.

USDA. 1999a. *Value-Enhanced Crops: Technology's Next Stage*. Washington, DC: USDA, Economic Research Service, Agricultural Outlook, March.

_____. 1999b. *Impacts of Adopting Genetically Engineered Crops in the US: Preliminary Results*. Washington, DC: USDA, Economic Research Service.

_____. 2001. *Biotech Corn and Soybeans: Changing Markets and the Govern-ment's Role*. Washington, DC: USDA, Economic Research Service.

Van Ravenswaay, Eileen O. 1995. *Public Perceptions of Agrichemicals*. Ames, IA: Council for Agricultural Science and Technology Task Force.

Victor, David G. 1998. *Effective Multilateral Regulation of Industrial Activity: Institutions for Policing and Adjusting Binding and Nonbinding Legal Commitments*. Cambridge, MA: MIT, Department of Political Science, disser-tation.

_____. 2000. *WTO's Efforts to Manage Differences in National Sanitary and Phytosanitary Politics*. Berkeley, CA: University of California, Center for German and European Studies, Working Paper, May.

Victor, David G., and C. Ford Runge. 2002. Farming the Genetic Frontier. *Foreign Affairs* 81/May–June: 107–18.

Vogel, David. 1995. *Trading Up: Consumer and Environmental Regulation in a Global Economy*. Cambridge, MA: Harvard University Press.

_____. 2001. *The Regulation of GMOs in Europe and the United States: A Case-Study of Contemporary European Regulatory Politics*. Berkeley, CA: University of California, manuscript.

Von Wartburg, Walter P., and Julian Liew. 1999. *Gene Technology and Social Acceptance*. Lanham, MD: University Press of America.

Vos, Ellen. 2000. EU Food Safety Regulation in the Aftermath of the BSE Crisis. *Journal of Consumer Policy* 23: 227–55.

Webster, Ruth. 1998. Environmental Collective Action. In Greenwood, Justin, and Mark Aspinwall, eds. *Collective Action in the European Union*. London: Routledge: 176–95.

Wiener, Jonathan B., and Michael D. Rogers. 2002. Comparing Precaution in the US and Europe. *Journal of Risk Research* in press.

Wohl, Jennifer B. 1998. Consumers' Decision-Making and Risk Perceptions Regarding Foods Produced with Biotechnology. *Journal of Consumer Policy* 21: 387–404.

Wright, Susan. 2001. *Legitimating Genetic Engineering*. Sandpoint, IO: AgBio-Tech InfoNet.

Young, Alasdair R. 1998. European Consumer Groups. In Greenwood, Justin, and Mark Aspinwall, eds., *Collective Action in the European Union*. London, Routledge: 149–75.

———. 2001. *Trading Up or Trading Blows? US Politics and Transatlantic Trade in Genetically Modified Food*. European University Institute, Robert Schuman Center, Working Paper.

Young, Alasdair R., and H. Wallace. 2000. *Regulatory Politics in the Enlarging European Union: Weighing Civic and Producer Interests*. Manchester: Manchester University Press.

Zechendorf, Bernhard. 1998. Agricultural Biotechnology: Why Do Europeans Have Difficulty Accepting it? *AgBioForum* 1/1: 8–13.

Index

ACGA *see* American Corn Growers Association
additives 89
adjustments, markets 123, 145–8
advocates 7, 66–101
AFBF *see* American Farm Bureau Federation
Africa 116, 134–5, 164
agency networks, EU 175
agricultural biotechnology, overview 1–43
aid 116, 164
allergens 25, 57
American Corn Growers Association (ACGA) 96–7
American Farm Bureau Federation (AFBF) 96
American Soybean Association (ASA) 96–7
animal feed 129–30
approvals: EU 45–52; harmonization 142–3; moratorium 45–6, 50, 108, 131; non-EU/US countries 61–3; risk assessments 181–2; US 54–9; worldwide table 62
ASA *see* American Soybean Association
assessments, risk 155, 160–1, 180–1
authorities 76–80, 90, 92–3, 174–5
autonomy 109, 113
awareness 92

Bacillus thuringiensis (Bt) 23
beef production 160–1
benefits: consumers 4–5, 20–1, 181–2; GE crops 37–8; strict regulations 70–1
BIO *see* Biotechnology Industry Organization
biopharming 5–6, 26–7
Biosafety Protocol, Cartagena 144–5, 154
biotechnology, overview 1–43; white 5–6, 26–7; green 1–43
Biotechnology Industry Organization (BIO) 94–5
BioTrack program 63–4
'boardroom' policy making 94–5
bottom-up approaches 66–72
BSE crisis 76–7

Bt *see Bacillus thuringiensis*
bulk commodities 145

campaigns 81–2
CAP *see* Common Agricultural Policy
Cartagena Biosafety Protocol 28, 144–5, 154
centralization: decentralization 73; EU 174–5; US 12–13, 90, 94, 111–14
cereal demand table 29
coalition, US producers 94
CODEX Alimentarius Commission 142–3, 154–5, 160–1
CODEX Food Labeling Committee 143–4
coercive measures 17, 123–4, 148–65, 171–2
collective action capacity 66–7, 68–72
commercial crops 52–4, 59–61, 63–5
Commission, EU 79, 110
Common Agricultural Policy (CAP) 86
compensation 122–3, 140–1
concern: *see also* environmental issues: ethical, 33–4, 153, 156; health 24–5, 144–5; religious 34, 153, 156; safety 26, 50–1, 172–4
conflicts *see* trade conflicts
Consultative Group for International Agricultural Research 183
consumers: benefits 4–5, 20–1, 181–2; collective action capacity 68–72; demand 6–7; EU 73–80, 92, 106; labeling 34, 39–40; surveys 74–8; US 90–4, 99, 179
contamination, seeds 85
Coordinated Framework for the Regulation of Biotechnology 55–6
corn: ACGA 96–7; EU 84, 89; export revenues 125–9; GTAP 132–3; Mexico 28; NCGA 96; StarLink 25, 93, 99, 131
costs *see also* losses: IP 40–1, 128–9; labeling 40–1, 128–9; regulatory polarization 124–31, 136; testing methods 88–9; US 141

decentralization 173
developing countries: field tests 64; food
    supplies 28–30; free trade agree-
    ments 164; new organization 21;
    R&D 21, 117; regulatory polariza-
    tion 8–9; revenue losses 18–19; small
    farmers 43; support 182–4; trade
    conflicts 134–5
Directive 90/220 45–6, 50, 79, 81
Directive 2001/18/EC 47, 50–1
dispute procedures 120, 123–4, 148–65
DNA 22–3
downstream producers 86–90, 98–9, 146–
    7
draft proposals, EU 50–2

ECJ see European Court of Justice
economic issues 34–42, 71, 131–6
EFSA see European Food Safety Authority
Egypt 151, 159
environmental issues: Cartagena Biosafety
    Protocol 144–5; collective action
    capacity 68–72; EPA 8, 54–9, 93,
    112, 146; EU 73–80; NGOs 78, 99;
    risks 27–8; US 90–4
enzymes 89
EP see European Parliament
EPA see United States Environmental
    Protection Agency
escalation, conflicts 16–17, 119–24, 133–
    4, 161–7
ethical concerns 33–4, 153, 156
Eurobarometer surveys 74–7, 175
European Court of Justice (ECJ) 109–10
European Food Safety Authority (EFSA)
    50–1, 77, 175
European Parliament (EP) 80, 110
European Union (EU): agency networks
    175; approvals 45–52; Cartagena
    Biosafety Protocol 144–5; centrali-
    zation 173–5; coercive measures
    148–65; Commission 79, 110;
    consumers 16, 73–80, 92; countries
    11–13, 106–11, 131; Directive 90/
    220 45–6, 50, 79, 81; Directive
    2001/18/EC 47, 50–1; draft propo-
    sals 50–2; federalism 106–11; food
    safety 172–5; harmonization 80,
    141–4; interest groups 66–7, 72–90;
    market issues 52–4; mutual recogni-
    tion 137–40; non-GE crops 36;

policies 13, 107, 179–80; precau-
    tionary principle 8, 43, 145, 156,
    181; process/product-orientated
    approaches 80–1; protectionism 122;
    public trust 174–5; regulatory
    polarization 1–2, 7–8, 10, 44–54;
    soybean imports table 130; spillover
    effect 131; trade flows 126; trade
    wars 161–7; 'trading up' 146–8; trust
    76–8, 174–5; Western Europe 132–
    6; WTO dispute procedures 148–65
export revenues 125–31
export subsidies, US 163

farmers: developing countries 43; EU 83–
    6; profits 34–8; US 7, 95–8
FDA see United States Food and Drug
    Administration
federalism 11–13, 102–15
feed 129–30
field trials 52–4, 59–61, 63–5
financial compensation 122
food issues: aid 116, 164; biotechnology
    crises 42–3; developing countries 28–
    30; processors 86–90, 98–9; safety
    concerns 172–5; security issues 183;
    US 60
free trade agreements 164

GATT see General Agreement on Tariffs
    and Trade
GE see genetically engineered products
General Agreement on Tariffs and Trade
    (GATT) 150
genetically engineered products (GE),
    overview 1–43
genomics 22–3, 170–1
Global Trade Analysis Project model
    (GTAP) 131–6
GMA see Grocery Manufacturers of
    America
Golden Rice 29–31
green biotechnology see agricultural
    biotechnology
green revolutions 3–4
Greenpeace 78, 99
Grocery Manufacturers of America
    (GMA) 98
growth hormones 160–1
GTAP see Global Trade Analysis Project
    model

harmonization: EU regulations 80, 141–4; IP 142–4, 179; labeling 142–4, 179; negotiations 123; non-coercive measures 141–4; product-orientated approaches 103–6; upward harmonization 104–5
health issues 24–5, 144–5
heterogeneity, regulations 110–11
hormones, growth 160–1

identity preservation (IP) 39–42, 52, 128–9, 175–80
industry: biotechnology 2, 18, 21; farming 7, 34–8, 43, 83–6, 95–8; food processors 86–90, 98–9; input suppliers 94–5; Monsanto 32, 94–5, 164; multinational frims 30–3, 42, 82, 173; pharmaceuticals 26; producers 66–7, 70–2, 80–90, 94–100; retailers 86–90, 98; small to medium size firms 82
imports 84, 89, 130
industrial concentration 30–3
industrialized agriculture 32
input suppliers, US 94–5
interdependencies 36–7
interest groups 7, 10–11, 66–101
international issues 14–17, 103, 118–67, 179
interstate commerce clause 112
investments 18, 21, 117
IP see identity preservation
Iraq war 165

Japan 40–1, 159

labeling: allergens 57; CODEX Food Labeling Committee 143–4; consumers 34, 39–40; costs 39–42, 128–9; EU 45–52, 88; harmonization 142–4; multinational firms 82; mutual recognition 137–40; non-EU/US countries 61–3; product differentiation 175–9; TBT Agreement 152–4; US 54–9; worldwide table 62
laxity, regulations 111–14
legal issues 20, 148–65
legitimacy trap 19, 170, 183
liability laws 20
Logic of Collective Action 68

losses see also costs: developing countries 18–19; US 16, 121–2, 124–33, 134; Western Europe 132–3

market issues: adjustments 123, 145–8; concentration 86–7, 180; EU 52–4; mutual recognition 138; niche markets 173; product differentiation 175–82; regulatory polarization 15; 'trading up' 145–8; US 59–61; world markets 6, 15
media coverage 107–8
Mendel, Gregor 3
Mexican corn 28
Miami group 145
models, GTAP 131–6
monarch butterfly 27, 58, 90
Monsanto 32, 94–5, 164
moratorium, approvals 45–6, 50, 108, 111, 131
multilevel regulatory systems 70
multinational firms 30–3, 42, 82, 173
mutual recognition 122, 137–40

National Corn Growers Association (NCGA) 96–7
national economic welfare 131–6
National Family Farm Coalition (NFFC) 96
National Food Processors Association (NFPA) 98
NCGA see National Corn Growers Association
Nestlé 87–8
NFFC see National Family Farm Coalition
NFPA see National Food Processors Association
NGOs see non-governmental organizations
niche markets 173
non-coercive measures 16–17, 122–3, 136–48
non-EU/US countries 61–5, 116
non-food products 63, 182
non-genetically engineered crops 36
non-governmental organizations (NGOs) 66–73; campaigns 81–2; EU 77–80; Greenpeace 78, 99; public outrage 11; R&D 18; surveys 75; trust 77–8; US 90–4; WTO dispute procedures 158

Novel Foods Regulation 1997 45–7, 51, 79
nutraceuticals 43

OECD *see* Organisation for Economic Co-
    operation and Development
opponents 11, 66–101; *see also* non-
    governmental organizations:
    European Union
Organisation for Economic Co-operation
    and Development (OECD) 63–4
outcrossing 27–8

panels, GATT 150–1
Pareto criterion 138
patents 30–3
pharmaceutical products 26
polarization *see* regulatory polarization
policies: 'boardroom' policy making 94–5;
    conflict resolution 122; EU 13, 107;
    reforms 3, 19–21, 174–84; US 14
political issues 66–101, 157–9, 162–5
potatoes 25, 29, 31
precautionary principle 8, 43, 145, 156,
    181
process-orientated approaches: EPA 58;
    EU firms 80–1; federalism 102–3;
    regulations 44–5, 55
processors *see* food processors
Prodigene Incorporated 26–7, 93
producers: collective action capacity 70–2;
    interest groups 66–7, 80–90; US 94–
    100
product differentiation 20, 128, 172, 175–
    82
product-orientated approaches: EU firms
    80; FDA 58; federalism 102–6;
    regulations 44–5, 55
production issues 52–4, 59–61, 134
profits 34–40, 42
proponents 7, 66–101; *see also* multina-
    tional firms: United States
protectionism: benefits 70–1; EU 122;
    federalism 102–3; strict regulations
    82–4; WTO 156
public opinion 75, 91–2, 107
public outrage 11, 69–73
public sector support 1–3
pull/push effects 71–2

R&D *see* research and development
'ratcheting-up' 12, 108–11

reforms, policies 174–84
regulatory polarization 1–2, 7–15, 44–65;
    bottom-up approaches 67–72; costs
    124–31, 136; R&D 117; top-down
    approaches 102–6; trade conflicts
    15; world markets 15
religious concerns 34, 153, 156
research and development (R&D) 18, 21,
    117, 183
retailers 86–90, 98
risks: assessments 155, 160–1, 180–1;
    environment issues 27–8; health risks
    24–5; management 180–1; science-
    based arguments 19

safety issues 26, 50–1, 172–4
sanctions 120, 148, 163
Sanitary and Phytosanitary Measures
    Agreement (SPS) 152–6, 160–1
scenarios; escalation 165–6; GTAP
    132–3
science-based arguments 19, 152–5, 167
security issues 183
segregation, grains 127
small to medium size firms 80
soybeans 84, 89, 96–7, 125–33
spillover effect 131
SPS *see* Sanitary and Phytosanitary
    Measures Agreement
stakes, agricultural biotechnology 5–6
StarLink corn 25, 93, 99, 131
states, US 108, 111–14
sub-Saharan Africa 134–5
subsidies 115, 133, 163, 177
substantial equivalence 143, 154, 181
suppliers 94–5, 129
support, developing countries 2–3, 182–4
surveys 74–8, 91–2, 175
sweet potatoes 29, 31

Technical Barriers to Trade Agreement
    (TBT) 152–4, 160–1
testing methods 88–9, 143
Thailand 151
tomato puree 24
top-down approaches 67, 102–6
traceability 39–42, 52, 128–9, 175–80
trade conflicts: developing countries 134–
    5; escalation 16–18, 133–4; interna-
    tional conflicts 118–67; production
    134; regulatory polarization 15;

wars 121, 123–4, 133–4, 161–7;
  WTO 15–17
trading issues: EU/US flows 126; free trade
  agreements 164; international regulations 103; international trade 15–
  17, 118–67; sanctions 120, 148;
  'trading up' 123, 145–8
trust: EU 76–8, 174–5; US 92–3; WTO 162

Unilever 87
United States Department of Agriculture
  (USDA) 8, 54–9, 93, 112, 146–7
United States Environmental Protection
  Agency (EPA) 8, 54–9, 93, 112,
  146
United States Food and Drug Administration (FDA) 8, 54–9, 93, 95, 112, 146,
  174
United States (US): approvals 54–9;
  Cartagena Biosafety Protocol 144–5;
  centralization 12–13, 90, 94, 111–
  14; coercive measures 17, 123–4,
  148–65; consumers 90–4, 99, 179;
  Coordinated Framework for the
  Regulation of Biotechnology 55–6;
  environmental issues 90–4; escalation 16–17, 119–24, 133–4, 161–7;
  federalism 111–14; harmonization
  141–4; interest groups 66–7, 72–3,
  90–100; labeling 54–9; losses 16,

121–2, 124–33, 134; multinational
  firms 31; mutual recognition 138–
  40; NGOs 82, 90–4; policies 14;
  producer interests 94–100; regulatory polarization 1–2, 10, 44–61;
  StarLink corn 131; states 108, 111–
  14; trade flows 126; trade wars 161–
  7; 'trading up' 145–8; trust 92–3;
  WTO dispute procedures 120, 123–
  4, 148–65
upward harmonization 104–5
USDA see United States Department of
  Agriculture

vertical integration 32
vitamins 89
voluntary policies see non-coercive
  measures
voting, EU bodies 109

welfare, GTAP 131–6
Western Europe 132–6
world markets 6, 15
World Trade Organization (WTO): coercive measures 171–2; dispute procedures 120, 123–4, 148–65; SPS
  Agreement 152–6; TBT Agreement
  152–4; trade conflicts 15–17, 161–5;
  trust 162
WTO see World Trade Organization